Fake News vs Media Studies

D1351988

"Building on a wealth of professional and academic expertise, McDougall invites us into lively conversations with diverse thinkers to convince us that serious critical engagement with the media matters more than ever – and that it can be fun!"
—Sonia Livingstone OBE, *Professor of Social Psychology, London School of Economics, UK*

"In an age of fake news, how can Media Studies respond? McDougall puts the case for making Media Studies compulsory in schools by super charging the subject - ensuring it is critical, contemporary and creative and enabling it to be politically relevant and socially imperative. Full of practical advice and illuminating interviews, this is an important intervention at a crucial moment in time - all teachers of Media Studies take note: read this book and get ready."
—Natalie Fenton, *Professor of Media and Communications, Goldsmiths, University of London, UK*

"Reading this book is like watching a media literacy hologram exhibit in a modern agora where impressive experts are speaking from their own perspective and Julian is waiting for you at the exit with the word cloud EDUCATION in his hands... He is bringing us back to the origins of media studies..."
—Igor Kanižaj, *University of Zagreb, Croatia*

"In a time of increasing paranoia about the future of our media industries and infrastructures, Julian McDougall has emerged with a compelling and rich inquiry into why Media Studies matters now, perhaps more than ever before. This book – rigorous, witty, and dynamic – offers a series of keen insights, first person stories, research and examples from the field to provide a comprehensive portrait of a discipline that is re-emerging as a force for democracy, civility and social change when needed most."
—Paul Mihailidis, *Professor of Civic Media and Journalism, Emerson College, USA*

"This book is a timely and important contribution to debates about the role of media education in an era of 'Fake News'. McDougall lets us hear from key figures in the field as he makes a convincing case for media literacy to be a compulsory component in young people's formal education. An essential read."
—Dave Harte, *Birmingham City University, UK*

Julian McDougall

Fake News
vs
Media Studies

Travels in a False Binary

Julian McDougall
Centre for Excellence in Media Practice
Bournemouth University
Poole, UK

ISBN 978-3-030-27219-7   ISBN 978-3-030-27220-3   (eBook)
https://doi.org/10.1007/978-3-030-27220-3

This Palgrave Macmillan imprint is published by the registered company Springer Nature Switzerland AG
The registered company address is: Gewerbestrasse 11, 6330 Cham, Switzerland

Foreword

At one point during the TED Talk about the complicity of social media in the death of democracy by Carol Cadwalladr, I thought to myself: *Who is listening?* Obviously, the audience in their top-dollar seats, somewhere deep in Silicon Valley were listening. The wider sense of the problem of who was listening stayed with me while she continued her talk. It was there through the truth about the fake propositions and posts that drove voters and elections to the seismic shocks of 2016 in the United Kingdom and the United States. It was there through the applause. After 15 minutes, who was listening? There are almost two million views at the time of writing, but the most important people listening, it turns out, were not those with the power to determine what happens next. Well, except one of them: the founder of Twitter, who the following week was at the White House. The others all stayed away.

To recap: Carol Cadwalladr reported on two years' worth of careful, detailed, dogged investigation, amongst other things, into the pernicious influence on social media of particular right-wing interest groups in the UK EU referendum, a dry run, as it turns out, for the election of Trump in America. She paced the stage, adopting the TED tropes of walking and talking and presenting slides; this meticulous and courageous journalist inviting the haters into the room with her assertion that social media had broken democracy.

What does this TED Talk have to do with this book? This book is also an important piece of work that challenges orthodoxies and doctrines: namely, those around media education, media studies, and media literacy. Those derided tropes and Mickey Mouse areas of learning which, it turns out, are not so useless after all, except in the literal sense of concerning themselves with educating about power, institutions, representation, identity, audience, and politics. We are where we are, in this benighted era of fake news, because few are given the opportunity, as an educational right, to understand what fake news really means or does not mean.

Fake news. These very words contain an existential threat to the term itself. For isn't everything fake, in some way, isn't everything broadcast or shared to a hungry populace owned and distributed? What does it mean to think of there being true news and fake news? Trump, for one, understands the importance of owning the terms first. He understands the non-ironic use of it to describe his opponents and detractors, when, at least at the time of writing, his Twitter finger is still active on the trigger.

This is an important book because it walks the reader through the maze. Written with fierce intelligence from long experience of working in media education, it invites the reader to pause for thought over a series of carefully constructed chapters. It is idealistic and realistic while also absolutist and relativist at the same time. It takes readers into a world in which so much of what we decide is real about the world is a construct, which is relatively straightforward to, well, *de*-construct. In whose interest is it to have a world in which digital media is the dominant mode of communication and to have children grow up without access to any form of compulsory education about it?

The argument is not couched in such simple terms. This is the luxury of writing the preface. I have not had to go to the lengths of the author, with his careful and reflexive account of the research poured into the work. For this is the truth. This is no fake, soapboxing account of the situation we find ourselves in. It is grounded in years of experience, hundreds of hours of conversations on the subject with what we are required to call stakeholders, even as the options in which they hold stakes are likely, if this work is not heeded, to give only a small return.

So, we have a text based on research, whose scope of reference is very wide. The casual reader of this might be forgiven for thinking that this is pure polemic, or even a cynical and hopeless piece of work, adrift in the ocean of false witness, datafication and media manipulation. Actually, however, it is a hopeful book—not so much that it offers a solution as it offers a programme for change, a way of looking again at media, of looking again at education.

The spoiler alert in this preface is the fact that this book offers a way of framing digital media and education for years to come. If you want a way through the morass of debate on news, media, and fakery—and if you are weary and fearful of what happens next—there is a way through the false binary. There is a better way.

London, UK   John Potter

Acknowledgements

For Bass to Bream and Roy's Diamond.

Thanks to all the people who gave up their time for interviews, to participate in workshops and/or to send me stuff.

I'm obliged, especially, to the US Embassy in London; Natalie Fenton, David Buckingham, John Potter and the Media Education Association; Alice Lee and Hong Kong Baptist University, Anna Kolchina and the National Research University Higher School of Economics in Moscow; Paul Mihailidis, Monica Bulger, Mel Crawford, Karen Fowler-Watt, Stephen Jukes, Roman Gerodimos, Akshay Kulkarni; Maya Parchment, Josh Wilde, Gayatri Nanda, Claire Pollard, the English and Media Centre and the Goldsmiths PGCE group; Antonio Lopez, Igor Kanižaj, Jane Secker, the European Commission and NESET II.

Contents

List of Figures

Toolkit

These case studies and suggested activities are direct teaching/study links between the topic being explored within the chapters and the Media Studies curriculum.

Apps

These are 'onward journey' applications of key ideas from the interviews and workshops, offering links to resources, materials or examples that participants shared with me.

App	Chapter	Resource/Material	Link
1	Introduction	*Fact-Check EU*	https://factcheckeu. info/en/article/ le-président-de-lue-est-il-élu
2	Introduction	What is a Critical Perspective?	https://rl.talis.com/3/gold/ lists/6C7BE40C-36CB-1849- A541-6446670BEA5C. html?lang=en-US
3	Contexts	*Duped by the Internet?*	https://www.buzzfeed.com/ tag/fake-news-quiz
4	Contexts	*Media in Action*	http://mediainaction.eu/pt/ class-activity-nutritional-la-bels-for-news/
5	Contexts	BBC: *The Fake News Challenge to Politics*	https://www.bbc.co.uk/ programmes/w3csvvdy
6	Contexts	UNESCO: *Fight Fake News*	https://en.unesco.org/ fightfakenews

(continued)

App	Chapter	Resource/Material	Link
7	Democracy	Fergal Keane: *From Where I Stand*	https://www.cemp.ac.uk/ summit/2018/
8	Democracy	European Union: *InVID*	https://www.invid-project.eu/
9	Democracy	The Civic Media Project	http://civicmediaproject.org/ works/civic-mediaproject/ citizenjournalismandcivicin- clusionaccessdorset
10	Democracy	*Get Bad News* *MD Lab*	https://getbadnews. com/#intro https://mdlab.lau.edu.lb/
11	Internet	*Trust, Truth, Technology*	http://www.lse.ac.uk/ media-and-communica- tions/truth-trust-and-tech- nology-commission/ The-report
12	Internet	Dave Harte: Fake News and Digital Journalism	http://daveharte.com/ fake-news/
13	Internet	Evolving Media	https://blog.lboro.ac.uk/ news/art/time-travelling-to- the-civil-rights-era/
14	'All News is Fake News': Discuss	BBC ireporter	https://www.bbc.co.uk/ news/resources/idt- 8760dd58-84f9-4c98- ade2-590562670096
15	'All News is Fake News': Discuss	*The Guardian*: Newswise	https://www.theguardian. com/newswise
16	'All News is Fake News': Discuss	Glasgow Media Group Jeremy Deller on Orgreave	http://www.glasgowmedia- group.org/media-kit http://www.jeremydeller. org/TheBattleOfOrgreave/ TheBattleOfOrgreave_ Video.php
17	Post-truth	Mind over Media	https://propaganda.mediaed- ucationlab.com/node/1
18	Post-truth	Yan Phu: Video Essay on 七警	https://vimeo.com/219175314

(continued)

App	Chapter	Resource/Material	Link
19	Post-truth	*Malware for Humans* Douglas Rushkoff: *Team Human* Paul Mason: *Clear, Bright Future* Sarah Jones: *Towards the Unknown*	https://www.byline.com/column/67/article/2412 https://teamhuman.fm/ https://www.paulmason.org/clear-bright-future-a-radi-cal-defence-of-the-human-being/#more-145 https://www.youtube.com/watch?time_contin-ue=4&v=R36DujXd7Pg
20	Fake News vs Media Studies	CEMP: *Media Literacy vs Fake News: The Toolkit*	http://mlfn.cemp.ac.uk/

1

Introduction

This book is about Media Studies.

To clarify terms, at the outset, Media *Studies* is a subject in schools that leads to qualifications. It develops media *literacy* and is part of the broader project of media *education*.

It's written for teachers, students, academics, librarians, journalists and researchers with an interest in Media Studies or concerns about fake news or both.

It explains how Media Studies can help us with our anxieties about fake news and misinformation.

But it's also for parents, politicians, policymakers and everyone else who wants to think seriously about the role of media in our society and the role of education in response to the ever-changing media landscape.

For all its intended audiences, the book makes an argument for the teaching of Media Studies in schools and it makes a new case for changing the status of the subject for students from optional to compulsory.

> Centralized gatekeepers, human fact checkers and algorithmic verification can only do so much to combat the spread of false information. In the end, for us to truly combat disinformation in the digital world, we need

© The Author(s) 2019
J. McDougall, *Fake News vs Media Studies*,
https://doi.org/10.1007/978-3-030-27220-3_1

to teach the public how to think critically about information and where it comes from. (Leetaru 2019: 2)

Seriously. We need to talk about Media Studies.

A paradox has emerged, and we need to face up to it. In educational, political, media and policy discourse, concerns about Fake News and misinformation are widespread. A plethora of events, conferences, articles, documentaries, initiatives, policies, projects, toolkits and online resources pose the question—what can we do about this pressing societal challenge before it becomes a crisis, if it hasn't already, with the potential to be as threatening to our democracies as climate change is to our environment? But the answer is right there, right now, in most of our schools, but only for the minority of young people who choose Media Studies as an option. For a number of reasons, all of the influential stakeholders in young people's education are ignoring it or looking for answers elsewhere.

By Media Studies, I am referring to the optional subject currently only taken by a minority of students in UK schools.

I am arguing that it should be compulsory.

But that doesn't mean the current Media Studies curriculum, exactly as it is, in the form of the specifications Media teachers are forced to use, in order to get them through the exam. Lots of the ideas, teaching strategies and resources I draw on in this book wouldn't directly map to the GCSE and A Level qualifications as they are currently. I am referring to the school subject, as framed by the key learning areas published as its subject content (DfE 2016).

Again, to be clear, media literacy refers to the goal and desired learning outcomes of Media Studies. Media literacy features prominently here because I draw on international perspectives, and outside of the United Kingdom, media literacy is used rather than Media Studies. I also refer to examples from Media Studies in universities. Again, this is because those ways of working inform the subject in schools, just as the school history curriculum responds to the work of historians in higher education. To re-state then, the book draws together viewpoints and examples from a wide community to support, and exemplify, the argument that teaching Media Studies to all young people in schools is the best response to the problem of fake news.

A decade ago, I was interviewed on the Radio 4 *Today Programme* about this old debate—the academic credibility of Media Studies. The conversation commenced with the command to Defend Your Discipline!!. I did pretty well, I think, but the same argument kept coming back at me: the presenter relentlessly comparing the kinds of learning I was giving as examples with more important aspects of Maths and Physics and, of course, the works of Shakespeare. This book won't spend any more time than this on those arguments. It's not going to be defensive, responding to either the BBC class snobbery nor the Physics v Media Studies economic binary (for a detailed deconstruction of the latter, see Cramp and McDougall 2018). That work has been done and the framing of the derision—bound up in ideas about academic substance, a self-preserving media establishment and resistance to bringing popular culture and digital/social media into schools—is well rehearsed by now.

Instead of wasting time on the haters, then, this book will go back to the energy generated by the *Manifesto for Media Education* (CEMP 2011) which the research centre I lead crowd-sourced at the start of the decade, around the same time as my grilling on *Today*. It will make the case that we need to prepare all young people to engage as positive citizens in our society in the era of fake news and misinformation. Media Studies is *already* doing this work, but only for the minority who choose it:

> My Year 13s this year have been exploring the role that the media play in shaping the identity of minority groups. Case studies that have been explored include; the negative representation of Muslims in light of the ISIS moral panic, how transgender people have utilised new media to develop more pluralistic identities, and how governments reinforce heterosexual ideologies through manipulative representation. Students have used theorists and concepts like Baudrillard's post-modernism and Butler's Gender Trouble to further examine these case studies. Within this module, we have delved into sociology, cultural studies, politics, psychology, philosophy, history and more. Try telling these students that Media Studies is a 'doss option'. (Gardiner 2018: 7)

The 2011 manifesto was an open access collection of prominent media educators' visions for Media Studies, in the same spirit as this book but with a broader scope. A discourse analysis of the outcomes of that project arrives at four dominant themes—the central role of the media in the continuing transformation of societies and the need for a philosophical dimension in Media Studies; the importance of media education for the critique of power and of technology; the individual's role in developing creative thinking and making and the need for teachers to embrace participative pedagogies so that learning design includes problem-solving, experiential learning, collaborative learning, scenarios, simulations, models and interdisciplinary learning. Given we asked for manifesto-type contributions, many of them were ambitious and at the end of the decade, we'd be stretched to claim the discipline had warranted the claim for it to be *a disruptive catalyst transporting learning into the third millennium*, if we're honest.

The hypothesis at hand for this new manifesto is this. Fake news and misinformation may be old wine in new bottles or a brand new problem, an inevitable symptom of imploding capitalism and austerity politics or an in-built destabilising strategy as foreseen by William Rees-Mogg at the end of the last century who "predicted that digital technology would make the world hugely more competitive, unequal and unstable. Societies would splinter. Taxes would be evaded. Governments would gradually wither away. Welfare states would simply become unfinanceable. In such a harsh world, only the most talented, self-reliant, technologically adept person, the 'sovereign individual' would survive." (Beckett 2018: 32). But, however we analyse the moral panic over fake news, it exists and has the nervous attention of the media, politicians and educators (see Shafer 2016).

Enter Media Studies.

Or rather, the teaching workforce are already there, trained and doing the job. The curriculum is 'on the shelf', with accredited examinations and a route to higher education. The exams taken in schools don't currently focus on fake news, so this is not a textbook or a teacher's guide for those current specifications. But the broader Media Studies subject knowledge set out by the Department for Education *does* require an overarching critical understanding of media in society. The argument this book is making is that a more media literate citizenry, a population who has received a Media Studies education at school, will already be more resilient to fake news or misinformation. And if this campaign, this new manifesto *were* successful—meaning that every young person studied the media in schools, as a mandatory citizen entitlement, complying with UNESCO's declaration that, "As access to information and participation are core principles of today's society, MIL (Media and Information Literacy) must be regarded as an enabler of human rights" (2016: 6), then we would have large cohorts of media undergraduates ready and waiting to develop into teachers to do the work.

It's a no brainer.

Methodology

The argument is presented as a set of recommendations from research, specifically the validation of this hypothesis—that Media Studies is the best weapon to arm young people with resilience in the fight against Fake News—through an ethnography of Media Studies and journalism in 2018–2019. This ethnography is conducted through three workshops and a set of interviews with media teachers, journalists, some people who are in both categories and some intersection stakeholders, such as librarians and historians. The interviews took approximately 45 minutes and were held in a variety of locations—classrooms, offices, coffee shops, pubs, conference rooms, through Skype/Hangout, by email; one participant made a film, another a blog post in response to the questions.

In each case, the interviews were semi-structured, but circulating around the core line of enquiry—tell me how Media Studies can help with this problem of Fake News. After each interview, participants sent me an example, to write about and analyse, as part of the ethnography, as a case or a text—in some cases, this was a teaching resource or lesson plan, in others an article or a visual media text. The outcomes of each interview fed into the next as a deliberately partly nomothetic and relational variable. I would share statements from the previous respondent and ask, "What do you think, what's your reaction to that, do you agree, do you have similar experiences or ideas to share?"

The workshops were conducted at the Media Education Summit in Hong Kong (media educators); the English and Media Centre in London (trainee media teachers); the National Research University Higher School of Economics (media educators), Moscow and Olympic Park, London (media educators, students, journalists and library professionals).

The result is this book, in which my own analysis of fake news and Media Studies' efficacy for a societal response is interwoven with and generated from the twenty-five interviews and four workshops; linked to twenty 'onward journey' applications (Apps)—teaching strategies/ educational resources I collected from this immersion in my community of practice and illustrated by ten *Toolkit #* examples of how the existing Media Studies curriculum relates to the issues covered in each chapter.

The participants were recruited through personal networks and events. This was purposive, reputational case sampling. There was also an element of negative case sampling, since I knew that most of the interviewees would resist the binary in the title of the book, and seek to complicate matters. Three aligned projects also feed into this book, an international Media Education Summit, which I convene as part of my role at CEMP; a funded research study for the US Embassy on critical media literacy and resilience to misinformation and a co-edited special issue of the journal *Cultura y Educación* on digital literacy, fake news and education. These associated activities provided an element of snow-ball sampling, as both the inputs from the participant groups at the workshops (librarians, media educators, students and journalists) and the articles published in the journal are used here as an extra dataset, and those additional contributions were generated through the existing 'relational network' (Bliss et al. 1983).

Over a decade or so, I've been very privileged to be put on a plane to talk about this stuff at conferences and symposia all over the world, as well as co-hosting our Media Education Summit in the United Kingdom, Europe, America and Asia. My travels in the binary have taken me all over the United Kingdom and to Rome; Beirut; Boston, MA; Riga; Sarajevo; Johannesburg; Paris; Brussels; Warsaw; Zagreb; Tbilisi;

Fairfield; Prague; Vancouver; Segovia; Belfast; Lisbon; Cork; Jersey; Stockholm; Christchurch, NZ; Salzburg; Helsinki; Moscow and Dundalk. This networking fed into the sampling and gave me an in when approaching participants. But it also means I have some confidence in the argument this book is making as I am deeply embedded in the community of practice I'm speaking to and for here (Fig. 1.1).

The ethnographic approach here is partly a way of thinking, trying to offer a 'thick description' (Geertz 1973) of the intersection between media education and journalism right now by talking to lots of people in those spaces, asking the fields what is going on, trying to see it from the participants' points of view. It's also partly a physical journey—my travels, to meetings, events, working on projects across borders and time zones. So, whilst I am rightly anxious about another white, middle-aged man putting all this on paper on behalf of everyone else (I quote Benjamin Zephania on this, later) and pompous though it may sound, these physical travels mirror an intellectual journey. Thus, the book is written in such a style as to try to capture that. The primary focus is to start a campaign to make Media Studies a mandatory school subject

Fig. 1.1 The Media Education Summit: community of practice (*Source* Hong Kong Baptist University)

in the United Kingdom. But media literacy education is a global entitlement, and my travels across the international community of practice and back show that.

Here is the dataset, consisting of interviewees and those workshop participants who gave informed consent to be named. The total sample, including the interviews, named participants in the group discussions and those who either stated a request for anonymity or didn't complete a consent form, is 88.

Name	Organisation(s) where disclosed	Role
James Blake		Media Educator
Sarah Bluck	City and Islington College	Student
Maria José Brites	Universidade Lusófona do Porto	Media Educator
Ryan Broderick	BuzzFeed	Journalist
David Buckingham	Loughborough University/ Leverhulme/Media Education Association	Media Educator
Monica Bulger	Data and Society Research Institute	Media Educator
Flora Carmichael	BBC	Journalist
Premrvedi Chanpuangsen	St Joseph's High School	Student
Michelle Cannon	UCL Institute of Education	Media Educator
Steve Connolly	University of Bedfordshire	Media Educator
Mel Crawford	Peters	Library Professional
Nick Crowson	University of Birmingham	Historian
Natalie Fenton	Goldsmiths University/Media Reform Coalition	Media Educator
Catherine Freeland	St Catherine's School	Student
Karen Fowler-Watt	Bournemouth University	Media Educator
Divina Frau-Meigs	Nouvelle Sorbonne	Media Educator
Jenny Grahame	English and Media Centre	Media Educator
Haris Hafeez		Student
Dave Harte	Birmingham City University	Media Educator
Ummi Hoque	City and Islington College	Student
Richard Horavik		Media Educator
Sarah Jones	Birmingham City University	Media Educator
Stephen Jukes	Bournemouth University	Media Educator
Igor Kanižaj*	University of Zagreb	Media Educator
Akshay Kulkarni	Bournemouth University	Student
Marcelo Kunova	Journalism.co.uk	Journalist
Fergal Keane	BBC	Journalist
Sandra Laville	The Guardian	Journalist
Sonia Livingstone	London School of Economics	Media Educator

Name	Organisation(s) where disclosed	Role
Jackie Long	Channel 4	Journalist
Antonio Lopez	John Cabot University	Media Educator
Richard Mayers	The Priory School	Media Educator
Rebecca Morris	Camden and Islington College	Media Educator
Jad Melki*	Lebanese American University	Media Educator
Paul Mihailidis*	Emerson College/Salzburg Media Academy	Media Educator
Gayatri Nanda	Bournemouth University	Student
Sarah Newstead	Principal Examiner, OCR Media Studies	Media Educator
PGCE Media Studies cohort	Goldsmiths University/English and Media Centre	Media Educators
Rose Pacatte		Media Educator
Maya Parchment	Bournemouth University	Student
Shradda Patel	Alperton Community School	Student
Sarah Pavey	SP4IL	Consultant/Library Professional
Claire Pollard	English and Media Centre	Media Educator
Julie Posetti	Reuters Institute for the Study of Journalism, Oxford University	Journalist
John Potter	UCL Institute of Education	Media Educator
Simon Quy	Media Education Association	Media Educator
Raul Reis	Emerson College	Media Educator
Jane Secker	City University/CILIP Information Literacy Group	Library Professional
Alison Tarrant	School Library Association	Library Professional
Darryl Toerien	Oakham School/CILIP Information Literacy Group	Library Professional
Sister Nancy Uselmann	Pauline Center for Media Studies, Los Angeles	Media Educator
Helen Walker	Queen Mary's Grammar School	Library Professional
Sarah Webster	St Joseph's High School	Media Educator
Joshua Wilde	Bournemouth University	Student
Iain Williamson	South Island School, Hong Kong	Media Educator

Because this research adopts ethnographic principles (trying to see my own community of practice, media education, and that of professional journalism from the perspectives of the people I interviewed), the book includes personal narratives from the teachers and journalists interviewed, and extracts from transcriptions are longer and more free range than might otherwise be the case. To more tightly edit the interviews down and frame them with my commentary would be against the spirit of such an ethnography. Using this approach also means I am making no claims to have captured a robust, scientific evidence of what media teachers and journalists are currently doing and thinking. This is an account of what two main participant groups (teachers and journalists), with two supplementary clusters (students and librarians) and overlaps between their roles, are saying about the subject of the research, at this moment in time. Media Studies sets up a kind of 'third space' between the first space (the private domain, home, the 'lifeworld') and the second space of formal, public education. So it's important to account for how this works, and what this means, for the media teachers in particular, but also for journalists, as there is increasing work about the importance of empathy and the personal reflections of 'mainstream media' workers, bound up in bigger things at stake in the preservation of professional journalism in the era of fake news.

The interest in the personal journeys of the participants was influenced by Renee Hobbs' edited collection *Exploring the Roots of Digital and Media Literacy through Personal Narrative* (2016). For Hobbs' project, key media education practitioners identified intellectual 'grandparents' and reflected on their influence on both their personal history and intellectual development.

A conundrum for Hobbs is evident in the white, Eurocentric field represented by the choices of her authors, as Lopez observes in his review:

> The fact is, media studies and media education historically have been mostly a white male, Euro-American endeavor, something that needs to be addressed by the field in general. While it's true that for the most part, this is our historical heritage, we can also stretch our legs a little and find inspiration in the works of postcolonial theorists, queer theorists, and black academics. (Lopez 2016: 142)

Primarily, the method was formative in developing this project—the focus on the way that a field emerges as a horizontal discourse (Bernstein 1996) and the fusing of the public-facing educator and the personal narrative, I wanted to take such a line of enquiry into this book:

> Beyond forging connections of the past to the present, exploring the history of the field can deepen intellectual curiosity and understanding for those who work in media literacy education, ignite interest in others, and drive investigation into understanding the relationships of the facets and fundamentals of media literacy from past to present and into the future. Just as our individual experiences shape and define our personal identities, a community's past and present shape how the field sees itself today and shapes a vision for the future. (Bordac 2014: 1)

Another disclaimer. My sample is purposive and reputational, as described, but it is only representative of an echo chamber as the snowball effect is network framed and I have made no attempt to talk to educators or journalists with affiliations to the alt-right. Whilst many of my interviewees offered the resistant 'sense checking' I needed on both the concept of fake news and the idea of the binary presented by my hypothesis, I knew it was highly unlikely that any would be enthusiastic about the other, much more powerful, network that joins Steve Bannon to Russia Today to Nigel Farage and via YouTube to Alex Jones.

This, then, it could well be argued, is the 'liberal elite' talking to itself.

Each chapter looks at a specific strand or subgenre of the societal challenge at hand, that of equipping citizens with the ability to be critically literate in the new media landscape and to be resilient to the potential dangers of fake news and misinformation. After establishing the academic context in which Media Studies is presented as an answer, the lens is cast on challenges to democracy; the precise difference the internet has made, is making and will make to what we are talking about when we talk about media; the specific question of fake news and the idea that we are living in a post-truth era. Each chapter begins with a presentation of what we know about the issue at the time of writing and then moves on to the interviews with media teachers and journalists. Next, the examples, texts or cases offered by the participants from both fields are discussed, before each chapter concludes with specific examples of how Media Studies offers a response to the challenge, how this is already happening and why everyone in school should be benefiting from it: Media Studies for the many, not the few.

The final chapter brings the findings from the ethnography together with another dataset, from dialogic research with media teachers, journalists, digital media creatives, librarians and actual young people, captured at a series of workshops and feeding into the production of a media literacy resilience toolkit. To bolster the case this book is making, the specific ways in which Media Studies offers this kind of resilience, to fake news and mediation more broadly, will be foregrounded.

The Situation: *You're Fake News!*

At the time of writing this book, it was difficult to keep up with the constant incoming onslaught of new books, reports, projects, resources and events on the topic of fake news, misinformation and conspiracy, the state of journalism, the future of democracy and the need for more, less or different regulation. For a year, every time a new resource, article, event or project on fake news entered my Twitter feed or arrived by email, or found its way to me via radio or television, I would add it to a huge document called Fake News Stuff, then read through it, draw out key themes in an old-school notebook, and work out where it would fit into these chapters and which interviews it should appear alongside. But it got ridiculous; I was working on at least a handful of new items on most days. The cutoff date for accepting new items was December 4, 2018, with a few more examples added in the final edit.

Each chapter sets out a context for media studies as an educational space for working these things through with the people who will have to deal with it in the future, and the book attempts to include as much of this hyperactivity as possible up to the point of submitting the manuscript. A kind of discourse map is drawn out, chapter by chapter, with Media Studies located as a navigation tool, notwithstanding its own discursive framing.

An orthodox narrative is emerging, presented by professional journalists (see Subedar 2018), that 'Fake News' as a specific new development first came to attention during the 2016 US presidential election, in the form of inaccurate posts with significant viral dissemination on social media, most commonly Facebook. Following a BuzzFeed investigation that brought to light an unusual geographical clustering for the originators of these posts, the Macedonian town of Veles became famous as a kind of fake news factory, but the unexpected consequences of this came out of President Trump's enthusiastic adoption of the term to describe negative mainstream news reporting of his actions and policies:

> At a fractious press conference President-elect Trump refused to take a question from CNN reporter Jim Acosta. "I'm not going to give you a question," Trump said. "You are fake news." Since then, "fake news" has been a topic of mainstream obsession and debate, although what is meant by the term varies hugely. Some insist on the original definition - fake stories of the type pumped out by those Macedonian teenagers. Others lump in politically motivated conspiracy theories. But people have also used "fake news" to describe honest mistakes, opinion, spin, propaganda or - like President Trump - news outlets or reporting that they simply don't like. Not only that, but often stuck under the banner of "fake news" is satire or parody, which on the surface appears harmless, but could still fool people - with potentially negative consequences. (Subedar 2018: 2)

The issues we are dealing with here are contested, to say the least, and this book's title intends to signpost this as a false binary—the versus is frivolous and at once validating and mocking the idea that education can be the space where these huge ramifications of global capitalism are resolved. Binaries, or the broader notion of polarisation are, of course, a factor in the apparent crisis of democracy and a symptom of austerity politics. But, as in the BBC version above, the status of fake news is always configured according to the discourse which speaks it. Take these three examples, all published while I was writing this book, to exemplify:

Print press organisations and broadcasters are in the process of intensifying their efforts to enforce certain trust enhancing practices. This includes cooperating with civil society organisations and academia to formulate and implement skill and age-specific media and information literacy approaches, continue investing in quality journalisms and equip newsrooms with professional automatic content verification tools for audiovisual and text-based reports spread online; ensuring the highest levels of compliance with ethical and professional standards to sustain a pluralistic and trustworthy news media ecosystem. (European Commission 2018: 41)

If journalism is a force of immense influence - and I think it is, and should be - then it surely deserves scrutiny. Investigative journalism is very slow, expensive, and sometimes yields very little direct return. No management consultant on earth would conclude that it represents a sensible investment of time or resources: a newsroom run strictly on metrics could never justify it. If journalism is, in some sense, a public service, then an editor has to understand the ethos of public service – something which is of value to a society without necessarily making a direct financial return. This means thinking of this kind of journalism in the same way you might think of a police, ambulance or fire service. You would, as a citizen, expect such services to be run efficiently, but you would not expect them to have to justify themselves on grounds of profit. But now, journalism is facing an existential economic threat in the form of a tumultuous recalibration of our place in the world. And on both sides of an increasingly scratchy debate about media, politics, and democracy, there is a hesitancy about whether there is any longer a common idea of what journalism is and why it matters. (Rusbridger 2018: 360)

The source of 'fake news' is not only the trollism, or the likes of Fox News, or Donald Trump, but a journalism self-appointed with a false respectability, a 'liberal' journalism that claims to challenge corporate state power but in reality courts and protects it. (Edwards and Cromwell 2018: xii)

The first extract is from a high-level policy forum, setting out a high-level strategy for solving a problem, across the 28 (again, at the time of writing) member states of the European Union. It locates mainstream, professional media as the safeguarding establishment, working to get their own houses in order to maintain and sustain their own trustworthy services for a public at risk from the alternative. There is some implication of fault, clearly the need to enforce trust enhancement arises from a lack of trust. The second account, from a *Guardian* editor, is an insider narrative that places this breakdown of trust in an economic context—the internet creates conditions of possibility for free news, journalism responds with a financial strategy rather than making the case for itself as a public service; the rest is already history. The third takes a hammer to this existential crisis discourse by putting Rusbridger and his profession at the heart of the problem itself.

Most of my interview respondents challenged the term fake news pretty early in the discussions, so it's important to recognise that not only are we thinking about a false binary, but we might also be dealing with a fake idea. But if we can agree on a working definition of the thing, we might end up deciding it isn't a thing, which for the purposes of this project, would mean that fake news would be distinct by its explicit and deliberate intention to mislead or distort. It is often—but not always—political and it is sometimes used as a kind of attack, for example by one nation on another, to destabilise. It certainly isn't new, but there are new aspects to its contemporary manifestations, such as 'algo-journalism' and 'empathic media' (see Bakir and McStay 2017). As several of the participants in this study quickly reminded me, it should also be understood as economic, from clickbait attention generation for advertising and/or the financial trading of data, most famously through Facebook. Related to this, of central importance to how Media Studies responds to this is the question of whether search engines and social media platforms are defined as media providers (i.e., of content) or purely technology companies providing services for other parties to share content—in this sense the regulatory definitions determine not only the political and legal response to fake news but also the academic response.

David Buckingham sums up the spirit of what we're trying to achieve in this book and foregrounds the challenges ahead in his blog (2017), with my annotations in italics:

> Most media literacy educators are likely to respond to this with a degree of weariness. Duh! Isn't that what we've been trying to do for decades

– despite the fact that we have been consistently marginalized within the mainstream curriculum? (*yes, that's the point, this book will attempt to make this case, positively, 'once and for all'*)

Yet there is a broader problem here. Media literacy is often invoked in a spirit of 'solutionism'. When media regulation seems impossible, media literacy is often seen as the acceptable answer – and indeed a magical panacea – for all media-related social and psychological ills. Are you worried about violence, sexualisation, obesity, drugs, consumerism? Media literacy is the answer! Let the teachers deal with it! (*true, hence the interviews and contextual framing attempt a more nuanced, deeper investigation and are, as such, my travels on exactly this 'false binary'*)

Fake news is a symptom of much broader tendencies in the worlds of politics and media. People (and not just children) may be inclined to believe it for quite complex reasons. And we can't stop them believing it just by encouraging them to check the facts, or think rationally about the issues. (*granted, but the argument here is going to be that we should resist the solutionist binary, for sure, but make sure that we do put Media Studies forward as the place to foster critical thinking about news, even if we don't assume that will magically transform into action*)

The False Binary vs Neither/Other

My first interview was with Natalie Fenton, professor of Media and Communications at Goldsmiths University of London. This was an exploratory discussion with the purpose of establishing the framework for the others and is thus presented as a standalone in this introduction. It had the status of a pilot study. Natalie was chosen for this stage as her work spans *all* the subfields of this arena, academically, politically, as an activist, a writer, Media Studies subject advocate and teacher. She describes her research as *concerned to address one of the most complex and vital issues of our age—the role the media play in the formation of identities and democracies and why and how people seek to change the world for socially progressive ends.* At Goldsmiths, she is co-Director of the Centre for the Study of Global Media and Democracy and the Leverhulme Media Research Centre. Her research is also linked to her activism as Chair of the Media Reform Coalition and former vice chair of the *Hacked Off* campaign, the prominent campaign for a more accountable journalism, partly in response to the phone hacking scandal and the subsequent Leveson inquiry. She's also an ideal person to kick off this project because her writing about mediated subjects and public spaces offers helpful clarity amidst the claims and counter-claims for civic engagement in the online age:

> Despite the potential for participatory democracy, our digital existence is enmeshed in global capitalism. The emancipatory potential of the internet is at the same time subsumed under capital. The paradox is that, while it creates and embeds forms of capitalism, it also raises the prospect of new forms of post-capitalism. It is neither all of one nor all of the other. (2016: 101)

Tired from a full day of meetings, Fenton was reflective when we met about the 'head space' afforded by the desirable view of London from her office in the Professor Stuart Hall Building of Goldsmiths in East London. More than anyone else, she's across the intersection this book addresses, having been heavily involved in curriculum reform for A Level Media Studies in the United Kingdom, a prominent figure in the Media, Communications and Cultural Studies Subject Association, and working at one of a tiny number of UK universities to offer a teacher training course for Media Studies. The first in her family to go to University, she graduated from Bristol Polytechnic in Humanities, one of the first courses to include the study of media, *"because I didn't get the right A level grades so I went into clearing"*, so her established status as a leading professor in the field tells a story in itself. She remembers her academic apprenticeship in the 1980s of Thatcherism, through the Miners' Strike (pertinent in our discussion as we are both from the same part of Nottingham, and to Media Studies, as we return to the reporting of the strike later) and Poll Tax riots, new political movements and rainbow coalitions:

> In terms of formative approaches to Media Studies, that helps explain my position, I've always said you can't understand the world without the media nor the media without the world. They take the piss out of

me here because they say I never talk about the media. I do spend long periods of time with my gaze turned away from the media, because I'm seeking to understand what's going on out there, and then the role of the media in that context. I'm always putting the social, the political and the economic (contexts) first. And I've always been a political activist. For me, it's delusory to pretend that the production of knowledge somehow comes from a neutral perspective.

The Department of Media, Communications and Cultural Studies at Goldsmiths is an impressive convergence of research (ranked top of the league in the United Kingdom by the Research Excellence Framework) and teaching with a focus on asking the hard questions about the future of media and society. This is striking, especially in a discipline where we are often expected to privilege industry training and engagement with 'the creative industries' as they are, rather than how they could be different. Further, using this space to visibly connect political activism to research and to teaching young people who come to a course with a wide variety of ambitions, expectations and degrees of critical awareness, can't be easy to protect, I suggest.

> There's a complete blurring now. The outwardly political work I do with Media Reform Coalition and what I've done with Hacked Off, I've learned more about power and the media from that than from thirty years of academic research. So I've come to see it as much more of a type of participatory action research.

Fenton is animated in response to my question about the tensions I assumed exist between the politics and the vocational neoliberal framing of Media Studies:

> Why would I pretend (to students) that I don't have a vision for how we can live together better in this world? I'm in this field because I thought it was one place where you can have a political voice. They don't have to agree with me, I don't claim to have the truth and I expect some push-back and students are invited to challenge me. I think that my teaching is the most important and also the most political thing that I do, but I can't do it well without the other things. What the students really love is when

I am engaged in a struggle with power and I can tell them that story, they can hear it and they can feel it and they see what that power is like up close and that's got to be the best way of teaching, to bring them into your experiences in that way.

In *Digital, Political, Radical* (2016) Fenton theorises this kind of 'praxis' in ways which are clear and present for Media Studies, whereby 'a new politics marked by the characteristics of speed and space, horizontality and diversity and connectivity and participation' (p. 23) not only asserts the importance of political context for understanding media but also the digital mediation of politics. She agrees with me that it's a positive analysis, but says the opposite is often the response. My sense of hope from the book is to do with the possibilities for Media Studies as a form of what she calls 'counter power' (p. 174). I have heard her talk about the subject as 'redistributive' and it's this strand of her thinking that I'm latching onto to kick off this book: " *The challenge of the field of media studies is to actively put politics back into the picture ... by addressing and analysing the actual politics as well as its mediation.*" (p. 179).

Back to our discussion, on the specific question, Fake News vs Media Studies:

For me fake news is the obvious endpoint of decades of a heavily commodified product (news). My anxiety is that if it seen as an educational project coming down solely to the need for better 'media literacy' then that loses sight of a broader political citizenship that seeks to understand how our worlds have been created in particular political and economic configurations and then how our media fit into that, which is, of course, vital. So I want young people to be able to critique and analyse media but as part of a critique of advanced global capitalism. To focus on a kind of techno-fix to fake news as though just teaching the kids that if they can identity fake news, all will be fine, is a useful distraction; but it may well result in letting legacy media, which has got us to this problem in the first place, off the hook, as they claim that they, and only they, can show us what the truth is. Meanwhile we miss doing meaningful analysis of the news media as hugely concentrated oligopolies with no or very little desire for democratic intent; no or very little care whatsoever for the human consequences of what they put out and certainly no sense in which they are enhancing political participation in any way, shape or form. So Media Studies has a job to do in teaching young people about how media is part and parcel of a system of the global dominance of capital.

Summary and Links to Next Chapter

Three themes stand out from my exchange with Natalie Fenton, to be developed in the first chapter, in which we'll set out the contextual landscape for thinking about news media, education and democracy in 2019:

1. Setting out the project of reclaiming the critical dimension of Media Studies and its politics but also its place in an understanding of politics;
2. Asserting the role of mainstream media in the crisis we are addressing and thus resisting any opposition between 'real' and 'fake' and/or reducing the educational response to fact-checking, remembering that the point of the subject is to deconstruct the selection and construction of *all* media, including news; and
3. Being mindful of the problem of 'just media studies', whereby we teach our students merely to understand without any agency or desire for change, maintaining the idea that media are produced *for* them and *to* them and not *by* them.

Onward Journeys (Applications)

Each chapter of this book will conclude with examples for Media teachers and students to work with, discuss or reflect on. They have been suggested by the people I interviewed. Some are from their own pedagogy, some from research, others are media examples to use as case studies.

For the purposes of exemplifying, by way of introduction, our false binary, let's compare a more reactive microresource with the more critical and holistic Media Studies approach this book will be advocating.

App 1 *Fact-Check EU* is an interactive site that enables users to post questions or statements relating to the European Union or view previous questions and answers under categories such as economics, law, politics and business. Writing this from the United Kingdom, it seems fair to say it would have been useful in 2016. The questions are fact-checked by a network of 'verified signatories' with moderation by journalism experts. The network's published objective is to *create a direct link with our readers and restore some trust in the media by being transparent about our choices and replying to our audience's questions directly, regardless of their partisan preferences.*

Fact-checking is the most common model for an educational response to fake news, outside of Media Studies. This EU resource is a more direct approach, with users being directly 'taught' facts. Another mode is where students are taught to fact-check themselves. But fact-checking 'as a thing' raises the question of the kind of resilience to misinformation this is fostering, in the absence of any deeper understanding of the political and economic motivations for 'fake news' or the extent to which 'all news is fake news'.

Follow up: https://factcheckeu.info/en/article/le-président-de-lue-est-il-élu.

App 2 I asked Natalie Fenton for something from her teaching, as opposed to her published research or campaigning for reform, as I'm interested in how this translates into Media Studies pedagogy. She provided the information her Goldsmiths students receive for an early module, on power and critique:

SESSION 1: What is a Critical Perspective on Political Communications? (Natalie Fenton)

What does it mean to have a critical perspective? At its most basic this simply means questioning the validity of arguments and ideas; approaching each and every idea with a desire to interrogate its premise and challenge assumptions therein. A critical perspective seeks therefore to understand the creation of meaning from a variety of perspectives, using each to draw the other into question. In this manner, a critical perspective will always seek to engage with a debate from many different angles and interpretations from those concerned with individuals, institutions, organisations, technology, politics, economics etc. To ask, not just 'what' but 'why' and offers an explanatory framework. The intention is that 'being critical' deepens and enriches our own understandings and enables us to make considered judgements which we can then act upon in order to bring about social transformation. Critical theory ultimately seeks human emancipation and is consequently normative. In terms of political communications this means that we don't just look to the institutions of mainstream media and establishment politics to understand it but also to civil society and radical media, to people as both audiences and producers as well as states and corporations in a bid to develop an analysis of the present and a new politics of the future.

The module outline includes session descriptions, key questions, readings and a menu of essay choices covering critical theory of political communications, the contradictions of media power, the 'turn to affect', democracy and digital activism, structure and agency, the datafication of society, social media, power and elites, the role of the media in media in defining, representing, normalizing or challenging inequality and the most agentive, perhaps: *Write your own media manifesto for the twenty first century for a country of your choice and explain why the changes you propose are necessary?*

The questions are primers for preparations for the sessions. Each session is a three-hour workshop where Natalie uses different formats and approaches to tackle different issues – from project work to dynamic debating to interventionist approaches trying to influence media coverage, to planning and delivering media activism. The teaching team takes an active approach to decolonising the curriculum and addressing issues of gender by asking students from around the world to bring work from scholars in their country that the academics may not be aware of. Fake News is not directly addressed in this module, although the focus on communication, politics and is likely to take students into that territory. Applying these frames of reference to our focus in this book, the question that arises out of writing your own media manifesto would be its preservation of the notion of the national boundary and whether such a view of media governance could hold. Students at Goldsmiths are required to address areas of media policy-making where national contexts are insufficient in global contexts, a challenge which is presented throughout the course.

The reflexivity demanded of the media student here, to negotiate *what* critical is about and then getting into *ways of being* critical, accordingly, and then addressing media from such an approach, rather than the other way around, is striking and resonates very clearly with Fenton's 'way of doing' Media Studies – power first, media second (my paraphrasing) or in her words "the media analyst's subject of study is not the media per se but media power". The module starts with the question of what it is to be critical and ends with *Being Political and the Politics of Being*.

Follow up: (reading list for this module): https://rl.talis.com/3/gold/lists/6C7BE40C-36CB-1849-A541-6446670BEA5C.html?lang=en-US.

*in these cases, I had both face-to-face discussions whilst visiting the participants and follow-up Skype interviews. Where these conversations appear, I have situated them in their physical locations rather than distinguished between real and virtual.

References

Bakir, V., & McStay, A. (2017). Fake News and the Economy of Emotions: Problems, Causes, Solutions. *Digital Journalism, 6*(2), 154–175.

Beckett, A. (2018, November 10). Mystic Mogg. *The Guardian.*

Bernstein, B. (1996). *Pedagogy, Symbolic Control and Identity: Theory, Research, Critique.* London: Taylor & Francis.

Bliss, J., Monk, M., & Ogborn, J. (1983). *Qualitative Data Analysis for Educational Research.* London: Croom Helm.

Bordac, S. (2014). Introduction to Media Literacy History. *Journal of Media Literacy Education, 6*(2), 1–2.

Buckingham, D. (2017). *The Strangulation of Media Studies.* https://davidbuckingham.net/2017/07/16/the-strangulation-of-media-studies/.

Centre for Excellence in Media Practice. (2011). *Manifesto for Media Education.* Bournemouth: Centre for Excellence in Media Practice: http://www.manifestoformediaeducation.co.uk/.

Cramp, A., & McDougall, J. (2018). *Doing Theory on Education: Using Popular Culture to Explore Key Debates.* London: Routledge.

Department for Education. (2016). *Subject Criteria for Media Studies.* London: Department for Education (DfE).

Edwards, D., & Cromwell, D. (2018). *Propaganda Blitz: How the Corporate Media Distort Reality.* London: Pluto Press.

European Commission. (2018). *A Multi-Dimensional Approach to Disinformation: Report of the Independent High Level Group on Fake News and Online Disinformation.* Luxembourg: Publications Office of the European Union.

Fenton, N. (2016). *Digital, Political, Radical.* London: Polity.

Gardiner, S. (2018). Media Studies: Why the Bad Press? *Media Magazine, 65,* 6–7.

Geertz, C. (1973). Thick Description: Toward an Interpretive Theory of Culture. In C. Geertz (Ed.), *The Interpretation of Cultures: Selected Essays.* New York: Basic Books.

Hobbs, R. (Ed.). (2016). *Exploring the Roots of Digital and Media Literacy Through Personal Narrative*. Philadelphia: Temple University Press.

Leetaru, K. (2019). *Combatting Fake News Requires Provenance and Information Literacy*. Forbes. https://www.forbes.com/sites/kalevleetaru/2019/03/16/combatting-fake-news-requires-provenance-and-information-literacy/#52ce8101debb. Accessed 10 April 2019.

Lopez, A. (2016). Review of Exploring the Roots of Digital and Media Literacy Through Personal Narrative. In R. Hobbs (Ed.), *Media Education Research Journal, 7*(2), 142–144.

Rusbridger, A. (2018). *Breaking News: The Remaking of Journalism and Why It Matters Now*. London: Canongate.

Shafer, J. (2016). The Cure for Fake News Is Worse Than the Disease. *Politico*. https://www.politico.com/magazine/story/2016/11/the-cure-for-fake-news-is-worse-than-the-disease-214477.

Subedar, A. (2018, November 27). The Godfather of Fake News. *BBC News*. https://www.bbc.co.uk/news/resources/idt-sh/the_godfather_of_fake_news.

UNESCO. (2016). *Riga Recommendations on Media and Information Literacy*. http://www.unesco.org/new/fileadmin/MULTIMEDIA/HQ/CI/CI/pdf/Events/riga_recommendations_on_media_and_information_literacy.pdf.

2

Contexts

A good place to start is the Data and Society Research Institute's 2018 report, given that it helpfully observes that *Media literacy has become a center of gravity for countering "fake news"* (Bulger and Davison 2018: 3).

The report goes on to argue that media education needs to *develop a coherent understanding of the media environment, improve cross-disciplinary collaboration, leverage the current media crisis to consolidate stakeholders and develop curricula for addressing action in addition to interpretation* (2018: 4). Clearly this book is a product of the leverage described and is concerned with such dialogue between the discipline of Media Studies and the journalism profession (Fig. 2.1).

The media environment, though, is very complex, and so this chapter is about navigating our way through the intersecting contexts that impact any educational response to fake news or misinformation.

> Autonomous technologies, run-away markets, and weaponized media seem to have overturned civil society, paralyzing our ability to think constructively, connect meaningfully, or act purposefully. It feels as if civilization itself were on the brink, and that we lack the collective willpower and coordination necessary to address issues of vital importance to the very survival of our species. It doesn't have to be this way. (Rushkoff 2019: 3)

© The Author(s) 2019
J. McDougall, *Fake News vs Media Studies*,
https://doi.org/10.1007/978-3-030-27220-3_2

Fig. 2.1 Media literacy, centre of gravity (*Source* Minuteworks)

Indeed; and Media Studies can help, surely? It can be a big part of 'Team Human'.

To restate the core argument of this book, or the hypothesis the project is testing, how robust is the conceptual framework of Media Studies for preparing young people for the current information disorder? If it is sufficiently robust, then are the plethora of new projects, toolkits and resources being generated by UNESCO, the media industries, journalists, regulators and civic society *for* educators just reinventing the wheel or even distracting from more effective approaches that media teachers are already utilising with their students?

This book is an attempt to draw breath, certainly, by working with the established overarching framework for Media Studies, cutting across all specifications, levels, age groups and degrees of specialism, applied to the current moral panic over fake news. This framework, then, is our first key context for what follows.

Context: Media Literacy

International research has led to the dissemination of a number of frameworks for 'media literacy', most notably provided by UNESCO and the European Union (EU), with the following shared key competences:

- *Access*: the ability to find and use media skilfully and to share suitable and valuable information with others (including browsing, searching, filtering and managing data, information and digital content).
- *Analysis and evaluation*: the capacity to comprehend messages and use critical thinking and understanding to analyse their quality, veracity, credibility and point of view, while considering their potential effects or consequences.
- *Creation*: the capacity to create media content and confidently express oneself with an awareness of purpose, audience and composition techniques.
- *Reflection*: the capacity to apply social responsibility and ethical principles to one's own identity, communication and conduct, to develop an awareness of and to manage one's media life.
- *Action/agency*: the capacity to act and engage in citizenship through media, to become political agents in a democratic society.

A recent review of media literacy education across the EU (McDougall et al. 2018) reported "an urgent but ongoing need for media literacy educators and stakeholders to document their best practice in the form of empirical classroom research, and to address enduring disconnects between theory and practice, conceptual frameworks and pedagogic practice, and educational/political policy and classroom practices." (p. 63). Best practice was found to involve moving away from competence models and protectionist approaches to embrace the complexity of 'dynamic literacies' through pedagogy that combine and/or cross boundaries between spaces and roles—the classroom and the extended 'third space', teachers and students working in partnership to co-create learning, and professional development in hybrid combinations of physical and virtual networks. The policy recommendations from this report included:

Policymakers should invest in further research into good 'sense-making' practices in teaching media literacy to build resilience to misinformation and conspiracy theories (such as inoculation approaches).

Research findings should be used to resolve the debate around media literacy and students' belief systems, and facilitate far-reaching dissemination of these best practices for consistent adoption by media educators.

Policymakers should support the inclusion of an assessment of students' media literacy competences in the next round of the OECD PISA test. (McDougall et al. 2018: 65–66)

Context: Media Studies

Curriculum specifications—the concept formally known as a syllabus—change over time and are themselves a site of much tension. The recent reforms to A Level Media Studies have been described by David Buckingham as nothing less than a 'strangulation' of the subject:

> The new specifications require a superficial grasp of a large quantity of material, and very little in-depth engagement. The marginalization of practical work undermines a key opportunity for creativity, and for exploring and generating new theoretical insights. None of this provides anything like effective preparation for university courses, which is one of the primary functions of A-levels. Media Studies has been strangled, although it continues to draw breath. Committed, creative media teachers will still engage and challenge their students – although now they will be doing so *despite* the framework of assessment, rather than being enabled and supported by it. (2017a: 1)

In the United Kingdom, the stipulated subject content for Media Studies (the only directly institutionalised, assessed version of media literacy education currently in existence in mainstream education) is published by the Department for Education (2016). This stipulated knowledge and understanding includes media language, media representation, media industries and audiences. A set of skills is prescribed that students must develop for each of these, as follows:

> Analyse critically and compare how media products, including products outside the commercial mainstream, construct and communicate meanings through the interaction of media language and audience response

> Use and reflect critically upon a range of complex theories of media studies and use specialist subject specific terminology appropriately in a developed way

Debate critically key questions relating to the social, cultural, political and economic role of the media through sustained discursive writing

Apply knowledge and understanding of media language, representation, media industries and audiences to a cross-media production

Apply knowledge and understanding of the digitally convergent nature of contemporary media

Use media language across media forms to express and communicate meaning to an intended audience. (DfE 2016: 11)

TOOLKIT#1 The Key Concepts: Media Studies vs Media

Applying this framework to the project of facilitating, through education, greater resilience to fake news, we can identify news articles or social media posts as either media products or products outside the commercial mainstream. There are a range of complex theories at teachers' and students' disposal for thinking critically about fake news and the nature of the media and the social, cultural, political and economic contexts for traditional media's sustainability under challenge from fake news is a fundamental critical debate. Producing a cross-media production involves experiential learning about convergence, mobile media and new media dynamics, all of which are part of the ecosystem in which fake news has emerged. Finally, there is no doubt that fake news operates across media forms and uses media language with a specific modality. The sum of these parts, then, would be a cohort of media students who have the tools of critical media literacy for resilience to fake news at their disposal.

Media students study media forms and genre, the latter bridging the former. News will be understood in the intersection between these—i.e., social media is a form, news is a genre, social media news is a subgenre. The blurring of these kinds of boundaries is always part of the equation. Media institutions or industries is another key area. Again, the impact of convergence on these organisations and the complexity of understanding whether a global platform like Facebook is a media organisation or part of an industry of any kind that can be pinned down is a complex area of study. The theoretical framework that is applied to media texts within these forms and genres and produced by these institutions within various industries is made up of media language (including theories of narrative); media representation and media audiences. The study of audience is often done in two parts—the identification of a 'target audience' for students' own production work, accounting for creative decisions made with the audience in mind, using a range of theoretical ideas about identity and pleasure combined with sociodemographic and other forms of audience profiling; and also the more complex work of applying reception theory and postmodern ideas about audiences to texts and debates, considering the extent to which mediation of identity is a 'window on the world', neutral representation of how people are or an ideological reinforcement of, or challenge to, powerful discourses about 'the order of things' in the social world.

Media representation is at the heart of the subject, and the entire conceptual framework hinges on the development of a critical media literacy, with which students can read media as representing things, places, people and ideas in particular ways, and how these representations are accepted, negotiated, opposed, challenged or subverted by audiences. Specific theories that are taught to students for this work include Stuart Hall's theories of representation and power relations, David Gauntlett's analysis of how identity is constructed through representation and Judith Butler's concept of gender as performance; theories of otherness; feminist approaches articulated by writers such as bell hooks and Lisbet Van Zoonen and issues of ethnicity and post colonialism in the work of theorists such as Paul Gilroy. These people are named in the current specifications for Media Studies as a canon of theorists.

Media Studies asks quantitative and environmental questions about who is making use of what media and then qualitative questions about how they interpret media and its function in their lives, with change a constant factor for students working on these topics; this constant flux makes the study of broader societal issues of access, power and democracy— who owns and controls media and what kinds of power do they exercise—more *dynamic*. Media Studies' focus on media texts and a range of approaches to textual reception that enable the media student to deconstruct the ways in which meaning is made in and between texts, which is never in isolation from these macro societal, political and philosophical ideas and concerns. This work is all informed by studies of media audiences with particular regard to demographics such as local or national culture, gender, sexuality, age, social class and ability/disability.

Audience, though, is much harder to understand than it used to be. Writing towards the end of the long debate about the difference the web 2.0 has made to Media Studies and whether we need a Media Studies 2.0, or a way to teach the subject 'after the media' (see Bennett et al. 2011) but just *before* the explosion in public debate about disinformation and the abuse of data, Will Merrin challenged long-standing conceptions of audience in Media Studies.

"If we all become media producers, we need to know how that production may be used against us. This, for us, is what defines the new 'usersphere', where the user differs from the audience, therefore, in being personally responsible (Merrin 2014: 161)".

So, if it wasn't already, it's hopefully obvious by now that, to make all these complex connections, a student of media needs a lot of synoptic skill—to critique, synthesise, put ideas in dialogue and form an academic view on what it all means for the human race.

Before we move on, there's an important disclaimer to re-state here. As another chapter discusses in detail, for Media Studies, in a sense, all news is fake news. The subject should resist any notion that our job is to teach students the difference between fake news and the real thing. Instead, critical media literacy will facilitate healthy cynicism about and resilience to *all* media and in this sense, if we go with the false binary up to a point, then *Fake news vs Media Studies* is just the latest instalment.

In the US context, Paul Mihailidis (2018) observes a more optimistic 'state of the art' for a more activist, civic form of media literacy:

> Between and beyond explorations of national politicians, refugee crises, the dark web, and fake news, there exists a groundswell of innovative and dynamic small-scale and hyper-local initiatives that have leveraged technologies to impact positive social change in the world. (Mihailidis 2018: x)

For Mihailidis, the goal is to *…re-imagine media literacies as guided by a set of value constructs that support being in the world with others, and that advocates for social reform, change, and justice. Civic media literacies shift the focus of media literacy from individual competencies to those of the community, a form of media literacy that is activist in orientation and related directly to participation* (2018: xi).

However, this would require a more intense 'reflexive activism' to understand the positive *uses* of media literacy as akin to a 'repertoire of contention':

A repertoire of contention is the collection of strategies and tactics a given contextually rooted social movement both knows how to do and is able to do, given the context and available resources; and chooses to deploy. (Feigenbaum and McCurdy 2018: 1890)

So we can see that media literacy isn't understood here merely as educational resilience building but instead that there is a competing, less visible and more agentive/dynamic use of media literacy by young people that can be potentially harnessed by education, or even that such education can learn from these forms of engagement:

Social media have become increasingly central to civic mobilisation and protest movements around the world. Emotions, symbols, self-presentation and visual communication are emerging as key components of networked individualism and connective action by affective publics challenging established political norms. These emerging repertoires have the potential to reignite civic engagement. Our analysis reveals the creation of a loose "me too" collective: an emotionally charged hybrid of self-presentation and participation in a shared moment of historic significance, which otherwise lacked particular norms, political agendas or hierarchies....an imagined community that combined co-presence in physical space with virtual solidarity. As in other cases of post-systemic grassroots engagement, individuals came together for a short period of time and expressed the need for change. (Adi et al. 2018: 315)

Media Studies, then, should resist the idea that the task is to teach students the difference between fake news and the real thing. Instead, critical media literacy will facilitate healthy cynicism about and resilience to *all* media. Furthermore, where possible, media literacy education should seek to enable a porous 'third space' knowledge exchange using pedagogic 'scaffolding' approaches, from Vygotsky (see Daniels 2005) between academic perspectives on critical thinking about media and students' 'lifeworld' engagements with collective civic media literacies, such as they already exist.

Sarah Newstead is a Media Studies teacher 'at the chalk face' in a rural secondary school in the north of England. She is also the Principal Examiner for an A Level theory element of Media Studies. She graduated from university with a degree in English and Media Studies in 2001 and has also worked as a journalist, for the *Richmond and Twickenham Times*, the *News and Star* and *the Cumberland News* as a news reporter and features writer. Prior to her current post, she *"taught for four years in state secondary schools and a sixth form college, teaching media almost by default as the subject was, and sadly still may be in some institutions, considered to be the preserve of English teachers who fancied a bash at something different."*

Sarah's views are important as a key context at this point because her profile spans the pedagogy, assessment and curriculum design of the version of Media Studies most young people experience *and* professional journalism. The A Level examination she leads is Critical Perspectives in Media, which includes topic choices on media regulation, media and democracy and media in the online age—for all of which students routinely choose news case studies. So what does she think about our false binary?

I think that the term fake news itself is problematic and open to abuse and notably the term has been used to denigrate information that may be contrary to a political agenda. Can we define 'fake news' as information that is factually incorrect or as information that may be deemed propaganda? Is it information circulated with malicious intent? What about parody and satire? Yet the muddier the waters, the more fascinating an area of debate 'fake news' becomes. Another interesting part of the phenomenon is that it can indicate divisions within communities, local and global, often springing up over points of ideological debate which provide an insight into the moral and political conflicts at the heart of populations. As a former journalist, obviously I am concerned that 'fake news' adds a further dimension to worries over maintaining quality journalism in the face of declining print circulation, fewer resources available to genuine news organisations and pay-walls. Whilst public trust in news spread via social media has been damaged, we must still seek to explore the ways in which audiences receive and process news online. How can we protect freedom of expression and maintain a credible free press whilst also acknowledging economic forces and the appetite for 'click-bait'? Finally, the on-going discussions over legislation are of particular interest. Will more centralised laws constitute 'liberticide' and will social media sites evolve to the status of news providers or publishers? As ever, more questions are raised than answered!

In her own teaching, she describes a combination of 'business as usual' with a focus on new examples:

> Encouraging students to form critical, objective standpoints and judgements about media and its sources have always been at the heart of any media teacher's agenda. However, I have been introducing elements of the debate in relation to the 2016 US elections and the Trump campaign. If I can appropriate the idea of the 'digital native' for a moment, I feel that many of my students view 'fake news' items as entertainment and already have an inherent instinct for sensationalised mis-information constructed to serve political or moral ends.

And on this book's manifesto—for a long overdue recognition of Media Studies as a good place to locate a response to fake news?

> Media Studies has always been considered to be a 'soft option' in some quarters. As the body of academic study grows and the importance of media in our daily lives becomes undeniable, this perception is changing. However, anecdotally I believe it is changing more rapidly at the grass roots – with students and, interestingly, parents – rather than amongst policy-makers.

Context: Bias

> Bias sells. (Buckingham 2017b: 4)
>
> False media, we don't need 'em do we? (Public Enemy, 1988)

December 2018. I'm at the Reuters Institute for the Study of Journalism for a panel at Lady Margaret Hall in Oxford, reflecting on a European Commission action plan on disinformation published the day before. In the contexts of both political disinformation and bottom up, often unwitting, viral dissemination of false media, the challenge of positioning real journalism as the defence at a time when the profession is in crisis is laid bare by the Director of the Institute, Rasmus Kleis Nielsen, declaring *"There's nothing less than a war on journalism taking place across the world."*

The panel agreed about two urgent responses to the problem. Firstly, journalism is under attack across the world and "fighting back is mission central", in the form of a robust re-booting of professional and ethical values and practices within the industry to reclaim the lost ground. And secondly, media literacy education is essential in schools, so that young people can be taught to distinguish between fake news and the real thing, to understand the concept of 'verifiable information in the public interest' and to value it.

But there's an elephant in the room. We are in the rarefied environment of Oxford University. No prospective student with the qualification in Media Studies that *already exists* in UK schools—the very education for resilience through media literacy that we are all calling for as the antidote to the crisis presented for this 'Oxford debate'—would get anywhere near the door to an Oxford degree.

The European Commission's Action Plan against Disinformation (EC 2018) excludes parody, satire and mistakes and defines its reference point as *"verifiably false or misleading information that is created, presented and disseminated for economic gain or to intentionally deceive the public and may cause public harm"*. Such harm includes threats to democratic processes.

Definition and distinction by verification are only part of this, though.

Context: Austerity

Politics changed in 2008. The political response to the economic crash was a decade of austerity. Adam Tooze's analysis of the decade we've just lived through, *Crashed* (2018), is presented as both "economic analysis and political horror story". As politics changed, the public's attitudes to politics changed. The 'chicken and egg' question about whether media discourse represents or frames these public attitudes is well rehearsed. But it's hard to understand what's happening with fake news from a Media Studies perspective, without paying attention to the economic crash as the most formative context. If fake news is a product of a polarised public discourse, of an era of extremes, of the centre failing to hold, this hasn't just happened because of a change in mindset, or a disillusionment with politicians, the media, experts and the liberal elite. It's happened because people are getting poorer. They are getting and staying poorer for longer. And there is no end in sight.

Fake news has its variants, or subgenres. Political fake news is *intended* to misinform and influence. A subgenre of this subgenre is strategic cyberwarfare by one nation on another. Commercial fake news, on the other hand, is manifested in clickbait, which seeks advertising revenue like more conventional media with the added element of the trading of user data. The digital giants operate on a business model that includes this activity. Sometimes these subgenres overlap, or the intentions are harder to identify as only related to one area (see Nielsen and Graves 2017, for audience perspectives on these categories).

And fake news is old. Posetti and Matthews provided a timeline to make this case (International Center for Journalists [ICFJ], 2018: 2–16), from which we can trace the Marc Antony smear campaign, circa 44 BC. The timeline continues to the proliferation of Boer War propaganda at the end of the nineteenth century, on to the Russian Revolution, World War 2 and Vietnam and the Cold War, South Africa and apartheid misinformation from the 1970s to 1990s, and in this century, weapons of mass destruction, the Syrian information war and to Trump, Brexit and contemporary Russian influence. This is a selection from more than fifty cases on the ICFJ timeline.

What's new is the scale and speed of it now in the context of the destabilisation of the mainstream media—and this state of *information disorder* (Wardle and Derakhshan 2017; Derakhshan 2019) is also probably new. Additionally, the powerful intersections, in our era of austerity-caused polarity, between disinformation and oppressive practices, racism, misogyny, the exploitation of the vulnerable, the discursive power of partisanship:

> The current crisis includes the 'weaponisation' of information by many governments, as well as abuse by an industry of public relations companies often under contract to political entities and actors. This risks an 'arms race' of disinformation efforts, which is arguably a recipe for

mutually assured contamination of information environments in general as well as high potential blowback. (Posetti and Matthews 2018: 2)

The propaganda machine of the Nazis, for instance – you take away all the hideous horror and that kind of stuff – it was very clever, the way they managed to do what they did. In its pure marketing sense, you can see the logic of what they were saying, why they were saying it, and how they presented things, and the imagery. (Andy Wigmore, former Communications Director of Leave. EU, quoted by Briant 2018: 2)

Context: Capitalism

The benefits of capitalism as a way of organizing the world are open to debate. Since the inception of capitalism in the sixteenth century, we have traded things with each other on a supply and demand basis. The industrial revolution in the eighteenth century led to the more systematic organisation of, and division of labour. Human beings have thus been divided into those that own and those who work for those that own. Aligned with production and trade is the financial system, with banks and investment. International trade enables us to sell things to countries who need them to come from abroad. The role of national governments in this trajectory has been to manage the country's relationship with the global market with minimal intervention in the private sector, a process we now call 'neoliberalism'.

When the Soviet Union was dismantled in the 1990s, the battle between capitalism and communism/socialism appeared to have been concluded. The market would dictate politics and governments would be judged on the extent to which their economic policies served the national interest. This consensus was founded on low inflation and high growth, with the market-forces mentality pervading to the extent that public services were outsourced to private companies without opposition. The long-term view was that trickle-down economics would, over time, reduce inequality. The economic crash revealed the extent to which this period was really defined by excessive debt. The austerity response took away any notion of that reduction in inequality. The relatively stable politics that had pervaded for decades was suddenly challenged by both the inability of politicians to agree on an economic response and the growing sense of injustice among populations. In this climate, polarisation is likely, if not inevitable, as there is no compelling centre-ground solution. Instead, it is easier to articulate a solutionist discourse at either end of the scale—either a socialist redistribution of wealth and huge raising of taxes on the rich or a protectionist rejection of multiculturalism and migration, whereby the small remaining budget for services is ring-fenced for the legitimate citizens. Both positions challenge the previously accepted tautology of global capitalism, by returning to a concept of the nation state, but clearly the rise of the digital corporations and their networking of the planet are inconvenient for these arguments, a fact which uses these networks to mobilise for the very political ideas they may be seen to render as obsolete or at least complex, if not outright contradictory. Here's Yanis Varoufakis:

> Our market societies will not evolve naturally into the good, *Star Trek*-like society that the giant technology corporations insist they are bringing about. I fear that something more like *The Matrix* awaits us, controlled not by machines but by the fantastically wealthy and powerful heads of those companies, If so, it is not just matter a waiting patiently until the Googles, the Apples, the Teslas, the Amazons and the Microsofts of today and tomorrow deliver a brave, new, wonderful world to us on a silver platter. So what should we do instead? (2017: 124)

Paul Mason (2015) has predicted 'post-capitalist' economics, a logical episode, he argues, in long wave economic theory (upturn and downturn cycles), citing digital technology as a driver. Three elements are foregrounded—the blurring of labour with free time; the abundance of online information and the proliferation of collaborative, peer production in digital spaces. This is a much more optimistic analysis. Fuchs observes the inherent tensions:

> The digital law of value has created new forms of exploitation as well as contradictions that allow the creation of new spheres of non-commercial, alternative, co-operative production and a solidarity, commons-based and peer production economy outside the realm of capitalism that undermine

the law of value. But the aim and tendency of destroying the law of value is not an automatism that follow from information technology. It can rather only be achieved in conscious political struggles for the decommodification of information, the economy and the world. (Fuchs 2016: 237)

So, it's pretty important for Media Studies to facilitate an understanding of how capitalism works, as it seems we are validating Natalie Fenton's argument, or at least that power and the economic system need to be assessed together with the representational practices and conventions of media. It's not just political opinion, as Picketty (2013) observed, that the 'trickle down' theory has always been an illusion; and that social mobility is always limited by the need for those with a stake in the inequal system to maintain their distance from the poor (see McGarvey 2017) and economic mobility can be in conflict with greater difficulties in acquiring cultural capital:

More powerful than 'merit' are drivers rooted in the misrecognition of classed self-presentation as 'talent', work cultures historically shaped by the privileged, the affordances of the 'Bank of Mum and Dad', and sponsored mobility premised on class-cultural similarity and familiarity. (Friedman and Laurison 2019: 229)

As we will explore further in the chapter devoted to the internet, we're still at only just over 50% of access to the web for the human race and digital capitalism is devoted to colonising and monetising every aspect of our online experience for the pursuit of profit:

One of the historical sources of world inequality under capitalism was the uneven adoption of technology. The Big 5 Silicon Valley firms wield increasing power and influence over our lives that, if unchecked, will gain rapidly as the digital economy becomes more significant. (Field 2018: 125)

So the inconvenient truth for this book is about the extent to which teaching young people about media and news, enabling them to be more resilient to misinformation through the kinds of critical media literacy that they'll get from Media Studies (my core argument) is, to be blunt, 'pissing in the wind'. I don't think it is, or I wouldn't be writing this book! But the folly of looking at media in isolation from the workings of global capitalism at the point of study should be obvious. It's more than *just* one of our contexts, let's agree.

TOOLKIT#2 The Public Sphere: Analogue vs Digital

The concept of the 'public sphere' is important to Media Studies, usually attributed to Habermas (1992) as a space where the public express opinion and impact on politics, a cornerstone of democracy. The development of mass media, according to Habermas, contributed to this, with a free press as conduit between citizens and the political class—the 'fourth estate'. Livingstone and Lunt, 'set theorists' for Media Studies, trace the failure of mass media to live up to this potential—'instead of being a source of creative disorganisation that promoted public autonomy and public life, the press had become a vehicle for established power' (2017).

Livingstone and Lunt, however, argue that media students should now explore the practices of mediation in enabling; authentic and diverse dialogue between government and citizens' (ibid.: 27), potentially consisting of active engagement with ideas from representatives of civil society and tolerance for diverse ethical positions within a definition of public interest.

Working with this more optimistic conception of digital media and networked publics, a Media Studies approach will require students to find examples, beyond the 'moral panic' of a new, *digital* public sphere—this is a direct link from the Media Studies canon to the recent work of scholars such as Paul Mihailidis, who we will hear from later.

Context: Journalism

Back in Oxford, the Reuters panelists cover trust (why it matters, what is means); information disorder—and the important distinction between falsity of all kinds and the intention to harm (mal-information); transformations in news and threats to the safety of journalists (see Council of Europe 2019). These may be separate issues, but they are brought together by one of the new intersections cited above; various modes of fact checking and variability and, hence our interest here, the role of 'Media and Information Literacy' (MIL) in damage limitation. Mapping this to the longstanding conceptual framework for Media Studies in the United Kingdom, they are 'part and parcel' to a large extent with the exception of two elements—the broader objective, critical thinking, is here aligned with 'healthy scepticism' and the specific ability to 'weigh the veracity' of information. This is an important departure from the legacy of Cultural Studies and Stuart Hall as its 'founding father' for media education. Whereas the Birmingham School's influence on Media Studies has been to teach the critical awareness that 'all news is fake news' (see the chapter devoted to this), this journalism-led derivative seeks a clear distinction between journalism, 'flawed journalism' and 'fraudulent news' (Ireton and Posetti 2018: 79):

> With MIL, participants can learn to recognize that even authentic news is always constructed and consumed within authentic narrative frameworks which give meanings to facts, and which implicate broader assumptions, ideologies and identities. This means the ability to recognize the difference between diverse journalistic attempts to capture and interpret salient reality on the one hand, and on the other, instances of deception that exploit the format of news while violating professional standards of verifiability. (2018: 78)

I caught up with Julie Posetti after the Oxford event. She has a thirty-year career in journalism and training journalists, so far, including some prominent roles with the World Editor's Forum in Paris, the Australian Government, Fairfax Media and recently UNESCO and the Reuters Institute in Oxford. Our meeting point is media literacy: how has this topic come into her field of vision and what difference has it made to her identity as a journalist?

> In that role in Paris my interest in what I now understand to be media literacy was really fostered and that was partly because of NGO facilitated funding work with school-age children to upskill their media literacy in the context of digital disruption. Then I made the step again back to a role which fortuitously sits at the intersection of journalism and research which is here at the Reuters Institute and I was contracted to a UNESCO project recommending curriculum development for countering disinformation

and misinformation in the context which became known as the Fake News Crisis. It's now clear to me that the capacity to withdraw from daily journalism practice and spend considerable time thinking about and researching issues at an academic level provides you with capacity for critical reflection and critical engagement with the media in a less tribal way. There's a tendency towards tribalism within journalism that really favours practical journalistic experience over other sorts of knowledge and I think it becomes often a position of defensiveness on the part of journalists (and me included, historically). So there's a lot of camaraderie and respect for difficulties in field work as a journalist and the risks that journalists take that sometimes I think causes issues to be interpreted differently, so I'm not saying that's true of all journalists but I can assume the way that many journalists would disregard serious concerns about political interference and derailment of democracy, press freedom threats and so on might be less nuanced than say an academic who's had journalistic experience who might be more prepared to be critical of certain media tropes and news media narratives. I can think of the fine line between misinformation identifiable in tabloid newspapers that are particularly partisan, taking a particular position on an issue like mass migration or refugees and there's a political line that's being followed, whereas some journalists might draw a line there and say 'well I'm not going to criticise other news organisations, no matter what they do and I'm not going to accuse them of misinformation because to do so would be to break away from the profession', does that make sense? But on the other hand, I would also say that it's the reverse too, it goes the other way also, so having been a journalist I do genuinely feel that the professional insight that that brings and the way that it influences my research is extremely valuable too. I just don't want to create the impression that it all goes one way.

I want to delve into the detail of what she thinks her work with UNESCO and its resources are offering the world as practical 'resilience-building' tools in the era of fake news. She offers the modules in the training handbook as examples of material that Media Studies teachers can use:

I think the contextual information at the front of each module would be really useful as a way of allowing students to have an appreciation for things like the dramatic disruption of the media field, the ways in which things have changed so significantly in their lifetime. Students could build their own timelines in their own communities and think about doing some research around events that have involved accountability journalism, where there might have been outcomes which changed local government, for example. In terms of the specific modules, the two things I would flag that I think could practically be adapted would be the fact checking module where there's a discipline of fact checking as a subset of verification principles where students could be given a text broken up into colour-coded traffic lights, segregated bits of information and taught to appreciate the difference between opinion and fact and between hyperbole and verifiable information, each of which you might be able to establish as fact. I think starting at school level is vital to have students of media across the board and better equipped to deal with the digital era threats around security and engagement with broad publics. I just don't think there's nearly enough of that, we talk about safety of kids online and we think in terms of their ability to protect themselves against predators, but as they participate as active audiences members who are now part of agenda-setting, interacting with news organisations or potential sources of information I think we need to give them the skills to ensure they are able to protect themselves in a scaled way, so you're not going to teach kids in school necessarily how to do end-to-end encryption but you might highlight an awareness of the need to have secure communication or the absence of privacy online as a starting point because one of the things we know is that there is a real correlation between state sponsored disinformation campaigns and online abuse and so as we see these sorts of orchestrated mass dissemination of disinformation involving bots and a whole other range of actors, I think you need to have a community who are at least broadly aware, and that starts at school level.

I think one of journalism's real gifts is its ability to weave a narrative around credible, reliable, verified and verifiable information and I think if you can incorporate creative ways of treating information as being a potential source of journalism and actually engaging kids who are studying media at school in being able to identify for themselves at what point factual reporting turns into dramatics or fiction, those are the sorts of exercises that would be useful and if children are tasked with identifying a story that provides some sort of solution to a problem and they're going to write that based on an assessment of what's factual and what impact this particular bit of information could have on their local community, anything you can do that encourages school students to think of themselves as we now know them to be as not only creators of media but actual participants in the co-creation of journalism and as active engaged publics, this necessarily means that they have to be better equipped to deal with disinformation, mal-information, misinformation. So hopefully programmes like media literacy will find themselves being strengthened as a result of the impact of this current crisis.

Noam Chomsky's *Manufacturing Consent* (1988) is a 'legacy text' for Media Studies. Des Freedman, Natalie Fenton's colleague at Goldsmiths and author of *The Contradictions of Media Power* (2014), describes Chomsky's intervention to "*equip media audiences with a way of talking about bias, ownership, control and politics that related to the experience of growing numbers of people that - generally speaking - established media outlets were not talking truth to power but instead sacrificing truth for power*" and, reflecting on the use of the book in his own teaching now:

> What makes it 'canonical' is that I find it so hard to avoid. When I want to discuss concepts of bias and theories of objectivity, MC provides such a consistent and provocative toolkit that it is often the best place to start though not always the best place to end up. It provides a wonderful account of the pressures and routines that skew media agendas towards those of the most powerful interests but isn't perhaps as useful in thinking through some of the tensions and slippages that exist in the media. (Freedman 2015: 92)

Manufacturing Consent, published thirty years ago, argued that news media reproduce elite discourses and manufacture the illusion of our acceptance of this in the way that particular agendas are normalised to appear neutral in, particularly, coverage of war and terror, poverty and austerity, power and resistance. The work of the contemporary *Media Lens*, endorsed by Chomsky, is a current and vivid example of the application of this approach to the more complex media landscape of today, whilst resisting the argument that this complexity does anything to challenge the longstanding media bias towards the powerful and elite, with the liberal media (in the United Kingdom, *The Guardian* and the BBC) being part of the problem.

So, looking back at Chomsky's 'canonical' text for Media Studies with an eye to his alliance with Media Lens and Freedman's adaptation with the Goldsmiths undergraduates, we would look at the UNESCO label of 'flawed journalism' as an apolitical distraction from the sacrifice of truth *for* power.

According to Paul Bradshaw (2018), fake news should fundamentally be understood in the context of 'mobile-first' publishing and that we should focus our attention on three battles in this arena—commercial, political and cultural. Fake news has clearly disrupted the optimism for mobile media to increase diversity and plurality, but the commercial part of the battle started half a decade ago at the point when mobile consumption of news overtook desktop engagement, so that professional journalism via traditional news organisations faced yet another 'adapt to survive' challenge. This not only required new formats (e.g., video for vertical screens) but also new kinds of journalists who could understand how to tell stories in new ways to fit these formats and audience expectations, taking the lead from BuzzFeed in this regard. The political battle *is* more recent and the consensus is building that alleged Russian activity relating to other nations' democratic processes constitutes a new form of international conflict in which, according to research findings from *New Knowledge* (RiResta et al. 2018), the giant technology corporations were at best slow and clumsy in response and at worst complicit, with Russia's influence spanning YouTube, Tumblr, Instagram, PayPal, Google, Facebook and Twitter. The Russian Internet Research Agency sustained false personas and communities of hundreds of thousands in the United States over several years in order to exploit existing societal tensions.

All of the messaging clearly sought to benefit the Republican Party - and specifically Donald Trump. Trump is mentioned most in campaigns targeting conservatives and right-wing voters, where the messaging encouraged these groups to support his campaign. The main groups that could challenge Trump were then provided messaging that sought to confuse, distract and ultimately discourage members from voting. Social media have gone from being the natural infrastructure for sharing collective grievances and co-ordinating civic engagement, to being a computational tool for social control, manipulated by canny political consultants and available to politicians in democracies and dictatorships alike. (RiResta et al. 2018)

And from the journalists' perspective on this political battle:

> This information war could prove to be the most significant for modern journalists: by turning our territory into a battlefield it risks turning us all into war reporters: verification skills are no longer the preserve of the hard-bitten hack, and information security is everyone's concern when news media are a target for state hackers. (Bradshaw 2018: 4)

The third battle is cultural, concerning the war for attention and professional journalism's stake in news agendas in the immediate present and near future, in the era of 'Post-Truth'. This is where media literacy has a role to play.

Following this thread, Karen Fowler-Watt, a journalist, who sets out the case for 'New Journalisms, New Pedagogies':

> So, time for a radical rethink: The Internet age requires vibrant, engaged journalism that builds connections. Experimentation might involve close scrutiny of journalism's normative values to foreground notions of journalism that is 'fair (with its sources and readers), participative, community oriented, and finally, giving priority to untold stories'. (Neveu 2016). Within the current challenging context, could re-imagining journalism education provide a starting point for a re-imagined journalism practice that prioritises the human aspect of journalism as a craft? (2019).

Context: Post-truth

> Fake has become an omnipresent feature of both our daily lives and a globalized, ultra-connected culture: it is in the way we dwell and break free from spaces and ideas. (*Excursions* Journal 9.1, call for articles, 2018).

McIntyre (2018) concludes a deep-rooted study of the conditions for 'post-truth' with a call to arms—"If our tools are being used as weapons, let's take them back" (p. 122).

This is a burgeoning field. Kakutani writes of 'Truth Decay', looking back to Hannah Arendt (1951) and the ideal subject for propagandists—that where the distinction between fact and fiction no longer exists, or matters. The progressive writing of the 1960s on the micropolitics of truth and postmodern arguments for such (radical deconstruction of normative power for some, dangerous relativism for others) have been hijacked by the Alt-Right. We can find warnings to this effect, 'pre-post-truth'; in the work of Andrew Keen on the cult of the amateur (2007), Tom Nichols on the death of expertise (2016) and Adam Curtis on hyper-normalisation (2016). These ideas, more or less dystopian, seem to converge in the mainstreaming in the language of 'red pilling', from *The Matrix*—content with convenient untruth, and, the argument goes, once we have taken the red pill with lower stakes, we are more open to extremism in the future or at least once 'Orwellian' becomes the zeitgeist, as when the President of the United States uses language to convey the opposite of what he means. If so, then:

> A disregard for facts, the displacement of reason by emotion and the corrosion of language are diminishing the value of truth. (Kakutani 2018: 7)

Taplin, in *Move Fast and Break Things*, an account of the digital destruction unleashed by Napster and harnessed by Silicon Valley, describes how, virtually unchallenged, "an old and largely discredited form of robber-baron capitalism took on a new form in the digital age" (2017: 108), drawing an analogy with the monopolistic colonialism of the British East India Company. And back to Rusbridger, from his experience of editing a print newspaper during this time, describing the shock and awe of watching it happen:

> Information chaos was, in itself, frightening enough. What made it truly alarming was that the chaos was enabled, shaped and distributed by a handful of gargantuan corporations, which – in that same blink of an eye – had become the most powerful organisations the world had ever seen. (2018: xviii–xix)

Fake news is, then, a symptom of something much bigger and the impact of the economic crash of 2008 is a significant context, if not a direct cause, of post-truth, rather than thinking of it as a media, technological or 'cyber' phenomenon. The polarisation of social media would then be a manifestation of human behaviour in response to the extremes of a crisis in economics. It isn't just that the de-centering impulses of postmodern mediation led, fifty years or so later, to a relativism that would be, inevitably with hindsight, utilised by powerful agents and extremists—a dystopian 'Uses of Literacy' (Hoggart 1957). It's also hard to deny that the conditions of possibility for post-truth are to do with the failure of neoliberal politics to avoid or respond to the economic crash, at the same time as it has succeeded in dismantling traditional conceptions of the public sphere, putting the seemingly natural and neutral workings of the market in its place. One important aspect of all this is that we no longer have a shared view—however contested it might have been—of the role of journalism, the concept of public interest, holding power to account, power and responsibility.

We need to take a step back and separate media literacy from its uses; to separate the nouns of media from the verbs, the tools from our hands.

While working on this book, I co-edited a special issue of the journal *Cultura y Educación* on the same theme. The published articles are used to form another dataset in the final chapter, along with the outcomes from the US Embassy project. David Buckingham's contribution to that journal offers some stepping stones to an educational response to fake news as a symptom of the broader issue of bias that Media Studies has been dealing with for a long time. He proposes a deconstruction of the concept of bias itself, an acceptance of it as part of life and a subsequently reflexive approach to students' own 'prejudices, assumptions and preconceptions', then refining the focus to look more rigorously at processes of framing and agenda-setting, both classic elements of the Media Studies curriculum, as well as developing a critical understanding of the institutional and economic drivers of bias.

There are some significant pedagogical problems in how we might deal with fake news. There's a danger here of assuming that we are dealing with a rational process – or at least one that can, by some pedagogical means, be *made* rational. But from an educational perspective, we surely have to begin with the question of why people might believe apparently 'fake' news in the first place. By no means all media use is rational. Where we decide to place our trust is as much to do with fantasy, emotion and desire, as with rational calculation. All of us are inclined to believe what we *want* to believe. This is arguably much more complex at time when we can exercise much greater control over the media and sources to which we are exposed. In terms of digital media, this has led to growing concerns about the 'filter bubble', or the 'echo chamber effect'. We can easily filter out things we dislike or do not agree with, and thereby remain in a comfortable world where everything appears to confirm our existing world-view. Research suggests that people positively *want* to remain in such filter bubbles – and, more generally, that news that plays to already-established positions or prejudices is much more inclined to be liked (and hence to generate more income for social media companies). While this is partly a consequence of the proliferation and fragmentation of media, it is also a symptom of growing political polarization, and of diminishing trust in authority much more broadly. (Buckingham 2019: 215)

If partisanship is obvious on the one hand, and a business model has evolved on the other that develops from clickbait to misinformation, from financial motives to political manipulation, are we kidding ourselves if we resist the more alarming term 'propaganda'? Or are we in an historical transition, one which might be possible to change the course of?

True authoritarians do not need your consent. If post-truth really is pre-fascism, maybe fake news is merely an early tactic, whose purpose is to soften us up for what comes later. Fake news confuses us and makes us doubt whether any source can be trusted. Once we don't know what to believe anymore, this can be exploited. Perhaps true propaganda comes later – once it doesn't matter whether we believe it – because we already know who is in charge. (McIntyre 2018: 116–117)

There's a danger lurking here, a paradox, that Media Studies might 'backfire' in this regard. Dannah boyd speculates that 'too much media literacy' has had this effect:

Media literacy asks people to raise questions and be wary of information that they're receiving. People are. Unfortunately, that's why we're talking past one another. (boyd 2017)

In Russia, a recent media literacy project with teenagers led to a direct correlation between increased critical thinking about news media and a distrust of all journalism: *"they often turn away from all sources instead of checking or making critical comprehension"* (Kachkayeva et al. 2017: 406). In Acatlán, Mexico, two men were burned to death by a crowd after the circulation of *noticias falsas* (fake news) on WhatsApp. The men were wrongly accused of intent to kidnap children. The messaging platform has also been the site of widespread political misinformation, leading to the development of a WhatsApp fact-verifying account, to which anyone can submit requests for debunking stories. Most of the requests are from users under 25 (see Oprea 2019). Meanwhile, the *India Digital News Report* (Reuters Institute/The Quint) reported a decline in trust in news media among over 1000 internet users and a move to accessing news on smartphones, including WhatsApp, now cited as a major source of disinformation in the country and linked to a rise in nationalism (Chakrabarti 2018):

> 57% of our respondents are worried whether online news they come across is real or fake, and when asked about different kinds of potential disinformation, many of our respondents express concern over hyper-partisan content (51%) and poor journalism (51%) as well as false news (50%). (Aneez et al. 2019: 7)

Buckingham's argument, noted above, that understanding this kind of 'bigger picture' is at the heart of resilience, takes us back to Natalie Fenton's 'opening gambit' for this book—Media Studies as a subject, our media literacy project for the US Embassy (and all the others that came before it) and the open access toolkit produced from the findings, the research journal Buckingham was writing in, these can only ever be micro. With such interventions, we can only control so much, or offer so much agency, as part of a contained domain. The macro contexts are either too big to deal with, or simply act as the framing determinants of the micro domains, depending on the media educators' perspectives and, probably, their politics.. We kicked off with Fenton's very strong assertion that we start with an understanding of power and it's already very clear that fake news can only be understood, never mind made less dangerous through 'resilience' developed in education, in broader social, economic and cultural contexts. Now, we can add to these external drivers—power, economics and politics—some even bigger philosophical macros—truth and knowledge, questions of ontology and epistemology.

> Even our sense that, whether or not we have knowledge, we do have justified beliefs weakens if we take seriously the possibility that what we accept as justification is no final guarantee of truth. For one cannot decisively prove something – or demonstrate it – from insecure premises, or by making merely inductive and hence fallible steps from even the most trustworthy premises. But why should proof be our standard of the kind of justification (or perhaps certainty) appropriate to knowledge? We are not talking about what is required to show conclusively that there is knowledge, but about whether there in fact is any. (Audi 2010: 335)

Epistemology is the process of knowing what knowledge is but in the era of post-truth and alternative facts, the relationship between reality (ontology) and knowledge (epistemology) is either more complicated than before or we can just see more clearly how complicated it always was. Language, rather than direct experience of reality 'in essence' describes the world to us and by us, as soon as we've learned to use it. So truth is always already encoded in language and by and with other people—"*We know because we live in a world with others who know*" (Peim 2018: 41). When Donald Rumsfeld, at the time the US Secretary of Defence, said "*Reports that say that something hasn't happened are always interesting to me because as we know, there are known knowns; there are things we know we know. We also know there are known unknowns; that is to say we know there are some things we do not know. But there are also unknown unknowns – the ones we don't know we don't know*," he was mocked. Since then, however, a lot has changed, and now it might be considered a fairly astute observation of epistemology clash.

So, is bias inevitable? An interesting intervention in the zeitgeist comes from Rosling et al. (2018), on the need for factfulness. Rosling argues that it is possible, and of course desirable, to be, first, mindful of, and then actively resist, a set of instincts that we are drawn to in our pressurised lives. These are the gap instinct; the negativity instinct; the straight line instinct; the fear instinct; and other instincts to do with generalization; destiny; singular perspective; blame and urgency. In practice, subverting these instincts through this factfulness involves:

> … being aware of how difficult your instincts can make it to get the facts right. It means being realistic about the extent of your knowledge. It means being happy to say 'I don't know'. It also means, when you do have an opinion, being prepared to change it when you do have new facts. (Rosling et al. 2018: 249)

The building blocks to this argument are scaffolded through a dataset of beyond first appearances examples. For this project, our attention might be caught by the need to put lonely numbers in media reports into comparative contexts. This is not quite the same as understanding news agendas from a critical media literacy perspective or the various models for fact-checking being offered by journalists at the time of writing. Linking this intention to the importance of seeking fake news as part of something much bigger is important in the broader post-effects framework of media literacy:

> Our elites are having none of it. Their fake news narrative is itself fake: it's a shallow explanation of a complex, systemic problem, the very existence of which they still refuse to acknowledge. The ease with which mainstream institutions, from ruling parties to think-tanks to the media, have converged upon "fake news" as their preferred lens on the unfolding crisis says a lot about the impermeability of their world view. (Morozov 2017: 2)

If we accept this, it might be quite straightforward for the conceptual framework of media literacy to deal with, by re-building the political economy model. Students would need to understand first the geo-political and economic situation in which this has happened and then apply theoretical devices such as ideology theory and representation to mainstream media and social media texts alike, a kind of taking back control, at least of how we understand things. However, there is a problem now with the notion of agency that would propel such a project:

What is common to the Brexit campaign, the US election and the disturbing depths of Youtube is that it is ultimately impossible to tell who is doing what, or what their motives and intentions are. It's futile to attempt to discern between what's algorithmically generated nonsense or carefully crafted fake news for generating ad dollars; what's paranoid fiction, state action, propaganda or Spam; what's deliberate misinformation or well-meaning fact check. (Bridle 2018: ch 9, para 51)

We can see, then, a problem with trying to apply the classic conceptual framework of Media Studies to this situation. But within the discipline, attention is turning to a non—media-centric approach and there are opportunities here for a more nuanced media education. Rather than separating the media from everyday life, and thus spending our time trying to work out who or what these media are, who or what is behind a text and who or what stands to benefit from our reception and engagement, a non—media-centric way of looking at things is all about contexts, places and performances for and of media engagements; for example, *The newspaper is transformed into a place (there is nothing surrogate or less than real about it) through habitual practices or movements, as a habit-field is gradually formed* (Moores 2017: 70).

This is important since social media exchanges—including fake news proliferation—are inherently locative, spatial, to do with feeling a sense of belonging, hence the now accepted metaphors of chambers and bubbles that we use when disclaiming our practices in these environments. Moores is pointing out that the idea of the media as disconnected from movement, place, settings and habits was always problematic. Therefore, a non—media centric approach is a new way of thinking *about* media rather than anything new in how we engage with media in our everyday lives. Our cognitive responses to media are part of the story; the remainder has to do with movement, place, physicality. Perhaps the way that fake news circulates is just a more obvious, visceral manifestation of what was already happening, then?

However, this doesn't mean that a non-representational approach would avoid questions of power and social justice, as Bridle reminds us:

Fibre-optic connections funnel financial transactions by way of offshore territories quietly retained through periods of decolonisation. Empire has mostly rescinded territory, only to continue its operation at the level of infrastructure, maintaining its power in the form of the network. Data-driven regimes repeat the racist, sexist and oppressive policies of their antecedents because their biases and attitudes have been encoded into them at their root. (2018: ch 10, para 14)

And going further, another layer of complexity obliges us to recognise that the kinds of counter-representational media activist practices (see Feigenbaum and McCurdy 2018) that media literacy education might want to harness for resilience-building are, arguably, now differently configured in this current conflict:

> Today, the bottom-up techniques of guerrilla media activists are in the hands of the wealthiest corporations, politicians and propagandists. (Rushkoff 2019: 35–36)

Going Forwards

Ryan Broderick is Deputy Global News Director at BuzzFeed—in his words a "long and wanky title"—the global news and entertainment organization with headquarters in New York. Based in London, Broderick says his expertise in web culture, formed in his teenage years (he's now 29), is now in demand since "now we just call it everything culture" and "now that the world is now by 4Chan trolls". He connects to me from his desk in London via Google Hangout and I ask him how what he does relates, if at all, to long-standing Media Studies' models of news agendas:

> We cover the local news of what is on social media. Our point of view is that when you are 22 years old and you wake up in the morning and you open social media and there's a bunch of stuff happening, our role is to make that all make sense. For us, social media sets the agenda.

Turning to questions of audience, it strikes me that his product is consumed by more young people than most forms of news; as such does he have a different view of their vulnerability to disinformation to the Reuters panel, for example?

It's a demographic shift, old people don't have any media literacy but unfortunately because of the way the world works, old people have a lot of power. And on the other hand, you have extremely cynical opportunistic millennials in Gen-Z who know they can culture-jam. This sort of information fight happens with any sort of new technology. The main difference with the internet vs the printing press, say, is that it's invisible, all-encompassing and immediate. So for a young journalist, you have to understand you're going into a world which is pretty much constantly having its own referendum about something all of the time.

And on the strand of Media Studies that deals with the nurturing of the next generation of journalists:

> It's so much easier than people make it out to be. I think a lot of the styles of journalism are the same as they used to be, but the types of tools are different, you need a debunking course, it's pretty easy, there are lots of easy tips, using open source information to triangulate when and where something happened, this isn't complicated for college students and then it's the first thing junior reports will be doing nowadays. But I think there might be something else that's needed, the chances are that a graduate reporter won't work on anything over 900 words and won't work on any original reporting for a year or two.

I tell him he sounds more optimistic than most of the people I've interviewed about young people's media literacy, so I wonder what he thinks about the idea of education coming to the rescue.

> The issue with young people is they know it's fake, but they do it anyway. For old people, I'm worried about media literacy, for young people I'm worried about media morality. A 13-year-old understands that it's wrong to steal someone's photos and put them on an Instagram page and pretend to be that person. With young people, it's not about whether they fall for fake news, it's about them knowing it's fake and weaponising it. That's pretty similar to how every young person figures out ways to hurt other young people on the internet. But the real society-collapsing garbage that happens right now, that's on the other side of it, because young people can't vote, I'm more worried about the effect of conspiracy theories

that people who can vote shouldn't even be aware of. The influence of that on how young people understand right and wrong is the bigger problem, we're stuck in a bad cycle right now.

Broderick's perception that young people are better at discerning fake news stacks up. A 2018 Pew Research Institute study asked US adults to categorise factual statements and opinion statements. A third of younger participants correctly identified all five of the factual statements as factual, compared with 20% of those over 50. For opinion statements, it was 44% against 26%. But the interpretation challenges our essential binary:

> This stronger ability to classify statements regardless of their ideological appeal may well be tied to the fact that younger adults – especially Millennials – are less likely to strongly identify with a political party. Even when accounting for levels of digital savviness and party affiliation, the differences by age persist: Younger adults are still better than their elders at deciphering factual from opinion news statements. Two other factors have a strong relationship with being able to correctly classify factual and opinion statements: having higher political awareness and more trust in the information from the national news media. Despite the fact that younger adults tend to be less politically aware and trusting of the news media than their elders, they still performed better at this task. (Gottfried and Grieco 2018: 2)

Maria José Brites *is* hopeful. I know Maria from various EU networks and projects. She's Professor at Universidade Lusófona do Porto and the Centre for Research in Applied Communication, Culture, and New Technologies (CICANT). She's the Portuguese coordinator of the European project *Media in Action*, the *RadioActive* project and she coordinates the Digital Literacy Team for the European Literacy Network. But before all this, she was a journalist:

> I was a journalist for over ten years and at a certain point I thought that maybe I didn't want to continue, for several reasons, one was that I was always doing the same thing, just changing the content. So, I was doing my masters degree also so at the end of that I thought 'maybe I

could apply for a PHD and also for a grant'. And then I got both, so that changed everything. But in Portugal you keep your press card after 10 years as long as you are not doing anything that breaks the rules of journalism, such as PR or working with politicians. So I like that I can keep my press card but don't have to do journalism!

I ask the obvious question about all her projects and the challenge of making a difference in the wake of so many challenges:

I was an activist on East Timor when the Portuguese left the country. Other activists didn't believe that we would be successful, but I can say I was part of the start of a new country. And in media literacy, I think the same way. I myself have believed fake news, so I don't think it will be easy, but maybe now the problem is so serious, then the European Commission are addressing the issue and funding programmes. So yes, it's a bad situation, but it's also an opportunity, as media literacy gets new visibility.

Inevitably, as so often when I talk to my counterparts in the EU network (for now, at least!), the conversation turns to the irony that the United Kingdom has by far the most established media education presence in the school and university curriculum in the form of Media Studies, but by far the least political or economic support for the subject or teacher training (i.e., none):

Media literacy is not addressed directly in the school in Portugal. Maybe I am a bit old fashioned but I think we need it as a discipline, like you have in England. OK, its's transversal, but that means it is always on the margins, so I think at least one year in the curriculum would be important. But the question is who would be teaching that, experts in media literacy or subject teachers? We are now starting to train teachers on this but they are not confident.

Following this thread, we discuss *Media in Action*, the project Maria led to raise awareness among teachers of media literacy pedagogies, and her suggestions are included in the resources below.

Summary and Links to Next Chapter

This opening chapter has, necessarily, complicated matters. We needed to map out the terrain in which Media Studies *can* make a difference. Putting the statements from the teachers, researchers and journalists included so far in dialogue with the subject's core learning objectives, there are three areas to take forward—(1) *critical analysis of the interaction between media language and audience response*; (2) *critical debates around the political and economic contexts for media* and (3) *knowledge and understanding of the digitally convergent nature of contemporary media.*

Onward Journeys (Applications)

App 3   BuzzFeed's weekly Fake News Quiz (*Duped by the Internet?*) is more likely than other resources cited in this book to be familiar to students. It's a simple set of True/False responses to social media posts, some from randoms, some from politicians and some from news providers. The obvious Media Studies task would be to flip this to have students set the questions, along with some set criteria—of ten cases, five should be from media sources, two should be retweets, and the other three are free range. The learning objective is to assess the process of selecting the examples which students found the most difficult to discern and look for patterns. What, then, are the conventions of a well constructed piece of fake news, based on the evidence of this exercise? To avoid the activity reinforcing the idea that fake news is harmless, though, students should be required to look for at least one example of potentially damaging manipulation, providing this can be facilitated with some pedagogic skill, attention to ethics and safeguarding.

Follow up: https://www.buzzfeed.com/tag/fake-news-quiz.

App 4   Maria José Brites offers up *Media in Action*. MIA is a European project producing learning materials in the 'confluence of media literacy, news literacy and digital storytelling' (MIA 2018). A useful resource for the focus of this book is 'Nutritional Labels for News'. This is informed by work by the Credibility Coalition (2018) and Clay Johnson (2010). As the background context to the activity shows, the analogy with food nutrition criteria presents an open brief for students to arrive at their own equivalents for news, so this is not about giving them a set of principles to apply to media texts. Instead, they negotiate the news health indicators themselves, in the constructivist tradition.

Follow up: http://mediainaction.eu/pt/class-activity-nutritional-labels-for-news/.

App 5 Sarah Newstead uses a BBC World Service documentary, *The Fake News Challenge to Politics*. She says *"I find this serves to open students' eyes to the importance and reach of the 'fake news' phenomenon.* The programme was recorded at the World Economic Forum in Davos and includes perspectives from *The New York Times*, RT and Wikipedia. The value of this resource for Media Studies is in mapping the various discourses that operate around fake news, specifically for the learning objective about critical debates as, obviously, this is itself an example of one. A helpful learning strategy here might be to use a Top Trumps' framework for each of the panelists—the categories students might use could include Strength of Argument, Use of Examples, Clarity of Communication to Audience, Objectivity and perhaps two wildcard criteria they come up with themselves. The added value of this approach, as opposed to just having them listen to the piece and discuss it afterwards, is that they should come to realise they are flipping their own assessment criteria to judge a panel of experts on a topic they are studying. That said, like so many aspects of this topic, it's likely that the teacher will need to provide the students with some background information on the cases discussed as preparation.

Follow up: https://www.bbc.co.uk/programmes/w3csvvdy.

App 6 Julie Posetti points me to Module 5 of the UNESCO handbook she co-edited. This is *Fact-Checking 101* (Mantzarlis 2018). The methodology offered differentiates between fact-checking, verification and debunking.

Students use colour coding to categorise statements in media texts, to identify statements which can be fact-checked (green) from those that can't (red) and those in between (orange). For green statements, groups can work together to source evidence that verifies or challenges them. But a set of criteria are also provided as a framework for choice of sources—proximity to the data; expertise; rigour; transparency and reliability. Putting these things together, students can use the Politfact ratings to assess claims on a scale between true and Pants on Fire. Alternatively, they can produce their own less linear scales to suit the mode of text under scrutiny and/or use more fluid formats such as GIFs. All this is different than journalistic fact-checking, which would be conducted before publication. Instead:

> This form of 'ex-post' fact-checking seeks to make public figures accountable for the truth of their statements. Fact-checkers in this line of work seek primary and reputable sources that can confirm or negate claims made to the public. (2018: 86)

Follow up: https://en.unesco.org/fightfakenews.

References

Adi, A., Gerodimos, R., & Lilleker, D. G. (2018). "Yes We Vote": Civic Mobilisation and Impulsive Engagement on Instagram. *Javnost, 25*(3), 315–332.

Aneez, Z., Neyazi, T., Kalogeropoulos, A., & Nielsen, R. (2019). *India Digital News Report*. Oxford: Reuters Institute for the Study of Journalism.

Arendt, H. (1951). *The Origins of Totalitarianism*. Berlin: Schocken Books.

Audi, R. (2010). *Epistemology: A Contemporary Introduction to the Theory of Knowledge*. London: Routledge.

Bennett, P., Kendall, A., & McDougall, J. (2011). *After the Media: Culture and Identity in the 21st Century*. London: Routledge.

boyd, d. (2017). Did Media Literacy Backfire? *Data and Society: Points*. https://points.datasociety.net/did-media-literacy-backfire-7418c084d88d.

Bradshaw, P. (2018). Journalism's 3 Conflicts: And the Promise It Almost Forgot. In S. Hill & P. Bradshaw (Eds.), *Mobile First Journalism*. London: Routledge.

Briant, E. (2018, April 17). Cambridge Analytica and SCL: How I Peered Inside the Propaganda Machine. *The Conversation*.

Bridle, J. (2018). *New Dark Age: Technology and the End of the Future*. London: Verso.

Buckingham, D. (2017a). *The Strangulation of Media Studies*. https://davidbuckingham.net/2017/07/16/the-strangulation-of-media-studies/.

Buckingham, D. (2017b). *Can We Still Teach About Media Bias in the Post-Truth Age?* https://davidbuckingham.net/2017/02/01/can-we-still-teach-about-media-bias-in-the-post-truth-age/. Accessed 29 September 2019.

Buckingham, D. (2019). Teaching Media in a 'Post-Truth' Age: Fake News, Media Bias and the Challenge for Media/Digital Literacy Education. *Cultura y Educación, 31*(2), 213–231.

Bulger, M., & Davison, P. (2018). *The Promises, Challenges and Futures of Media Literacy*. New York: Data and Society Research Institute.

Chakrabarti, S. (2018, November 12). *Nationalism a Driving Force Behind Fake News in India, Research Shows*. BBC. https://www.bbc.co.uk/news/world-46146877.

Council of Europe. (2019). *Democracy at Risk: Threats and Attacks Against Media Freedom in Europe*. Strasbourg: Council of Europe.

Curtis, A. (2016). *Hypernormalisation*. London: BBC.

Daniels, H. (Ed.). (2005). *An Introduction to Vygotsky* (2nd ed.). London: Routledge.

Department for Education. (2016). *Subject Criteria for Media Studies*. London: Department for Education (DfE).

Derakhshan, H. (2019, May 9). Disinfo Wars: A Taxonomy of Information Warfare. *Medium*. https://medium.com/@h0d3r/disinfo-wars-7f1cf2685e13. Accessed 9 May 2019.

European Commission. (2018). *A Multi-Dimensional Approach to Disinformation: Report of the Independent High Level Group on Fake News and Online Disinformation*. Luxembourg: Publications Office of the European Union.

Feigenbaum, A., & McCurdy, P. (2018). Activist Reflexivity and Mediated Violence: Putting the Policing of Nuit Debout in Context. *International Journal of Communication, 12*, 1887–1907.

Field, J. (2018). *Is Capitalism Working?* London: Thames & Hudson.

Fowler-Watt, K., & Jukes, S. (2019). *New Journalisms: Rethinking Practice, Theory and Pedagogy*. London: Routledge Research in Media Literacy and Education.

Freedman, D. (2014). *The Contradictions of Media Power*. London: Bloomsbury.

Freedman, D. (2015). Laughey's Canon: Review of Manufacturing Consent, by Edward S. Herman & Noam Chomsky (1988). *Media Education Research Journal, 6*(1), 92–93.

Friedman, S., & Laurison, D. (2019). *The Glass Ceiling: Why It Pays to Be Privileged*. Bristol: Bristol University Press.

Fuchs, C. (2016). Henryk Grossmann 2.0: A Critique of Paul Mason's Book "PostCapitalism: A Guide to Our Future". *tripleC, 14*(1), 232–243. http://www.triple-c, at CC-BY-NC-ND: Creative Commons License.

Gottfried, J., & Grieco, E. (2018). *Younger Americans Are Better Than Older Americans at Telling Factual News Statements from Opinions*. Washington, DC: Pew Research Center. https://www.pewresearch.org/fact-tank/2018/10/23/younger-americans-are-better-than-older-americans-at-telling-factual-news-statements-from-opinions/.

Habermas, J. (1992). Further Reflections on the Public Sphere. In C. Calhoun (Ed.) & T. Burger (Trans.), *Habermas and the Public Sphere*. Cambridge, MA: MIT Press.

Herman, E., & Chomsky, N. (1988). *Manufacturing Consent: The Political Economy of the Mass Media*. New York: Pantheon.

Hoggart, R. (1957). *The Uses of Literacy*. London: Pelican.

Ireton, C., & Posetti, J. (Eds). (2018). *Journalism, Fake News and Disinformation: Handbook for Journalism Education and Training*. Paris: UNESCO.

Kachkayeva, A., Shomova, S., & Kolchina, A. (2017). Education and Media Literacy in Russia: Genesis and Current Trends. In *Multidisciplinary Approaches to Media Literacy: Research and Practices* 媒介素养的跨学科研究与实践 (Ch. 31, pp. 401–408). Hong Kong: Communication University of China (CUC) Press.

Kakutani, M. (2018, July 14). Truth Decay. *The Guardian*.

Keen, A. (2007). *The Cult of the Amateur*. London: Hodder.

Mantzarlis, A. (2018). Fact-Checking 101. In C. Ireton & J. Posetti (Eds.), *Journalism, 'Fake News' and Disinformation*. Paris: UNESCO.

Mason, P. (2015). *Post-capitalism: A Guide to Our Future*. London: Allen-Lane.

McDougall, J., José Brites, M., Couto, M., & Lucas, C. (Eds.). (2018). Digital Literacy, Fake News and Education. *Cultura y Educación, 31*, 203–212.

McGarvey, D. (2017). *Poverty Safari: Understanding the Anger of Britain's Underclass*. London: Picador.

McIntyre, L. (2018). *Post-truth*. Cambridge, MA: MIT Press.

Merrin, W. (2014). *Media Studies 2.0*. London: Routledge.

Mihailidis, P. (2018). *Civic Media Literacies: Re-imagining Human Connection in an Age of Digital Abundance*. New York: Routledge.

Moores, S. (2017). *Digital Orientations: Non-media-centric Media Studies and Non-representational Theories of Practice*. New York: Peter Lang.

Morozov, E. (2017, January 8). Blaming Fake News Is Not the Answer. *The Guardian*.

Neveu, E. (2016). On Not Going Too Fast with Slow Journalism. *Journalism Practice, 10*(4), 448–460.

Nichols, T. (2016). *The Death of Expertise: The Campaign Against Established Knowledge and Why It Matters*. Oxford: Oxford University Press.

Nielsen, R., & Graves, L. (2017). *"News You Don't Believe": Audience Perspectives on Fake News*. Oxford: Reuters Institute for the Study of Journalism.

Oprea, M. (2019, February 25). The Spread of Fake News Has Had Deadly Consequences in Mexico. *Pacific Standard*.

Peim, N. (2018). *Thinking in Education Research: Applying Philosophy and Theory*. London: Bloomsbury.

Picketty, T. (2013). *Capitalism in the Twenty-First Century*. Harvard: Harvard University Press.

Posetti, J., & Matthews, A. (2018). *A Short Guide to the History of Fake News and Disinformation*. Washington, DC: International Center for Journalists.

RiResta, R., et al. (2018). *The Tactics & Tropes of the Internet Research Agency*. New Knowledge.

Rosling, H., Rosling, A., & Rosling, O. (2018). *Factfulness: Ten Reasons We're Wrong About the World: And Why Things Are Better Than You Think*. London: Sceptre.

Rusbridger, A. (2018). *Breaking News: The Remaking of Journalism and Why It Matters Now*. London: Canongate.

Rushkoff, D. (2019). *Team Human*. New York: W. W. Norton.

Taplin, J. (2017). *Move Fast and Break Things: How Facebook, Google and Amazon Cornered Culture*. London: Macmillan.

Tooze, A. (2018). *Crashed: How a Decade of Financial Crises Changed the World*. London: Random House.

Wardle, C., & Derakhshan, H. (2017). *Information Disorder Toward an Interdisciplinary Framework for Research and Policymaking*. Strasbourg: Council of Europe.

Varoufakis, Y. (2017). *Talking to My Daughter: A Brief History of Capitalism*. London: Vintage.

3

Democracy

There is broad agreement that fake news presents a particular kind of *new* challenge for democracy and that this has to do with the complicated, intersecting techno-cultural environments in which misinformation circulates. The objective of this book, to re-state, is to argue that Media Studies provides a critical framework for such an adequate defense, so rather than creating a new educational project in the form of media literacy as an antidote to fake news—the false binary—we should put Media Studies to work on these challenges and advocate for every student to take the subject as a civic entitlement and as part of the broader project of doing democracy in school.

But it would be foolish to see these new challenges as a threat to a level playing field when one of the first things media students work out is how *un*representative the (traditional) media are of our society. Therefore, fake news presents a new twist, or a rebooting, of an ongoing failure of media in democracy, it can be plausibly argued.

In 2019, the Media Reform Coalition's report *Who Owns the UK Media?* offered an update on its assessment from four years before. The research found that three companies control over 80% of the UK newspaper market, a 10% increase from the previous report and this

© The Author(s) 2019
J. McDougall, *Fake News vs Media Studies*,
https://doi.org/10.1007/978-3-030-27220-3_3

increases only to five companies when online news is included. As has already been established, the domination of digital capitalism by a small cluster of huge corporations (the most powerful the world has ever seen, we are told) does not deliver on the hope for a democratic, citizen media that the internet had seemed to promise.

Democracy is rarely understood in all its complexity by media students. Why would it be? The relationship between democracy as a principle and its manifestation in political systems has been exposed as fragile in recent times. Just as our political representatives are not representative of the public, neither are our media:

> What does it mean to have a 'free' media when the nation's social media platforms, TV channels, news outlets, radio stations and search engines are owned by a handful of giant corporations? What does it mean to have 'independent media' when many of our most influential news organisations are controlled by individuals and boards that are so closely connected with vested interests? (Media Reform Coalition 2019: 4)

Holding Power to Account

We meet Fergal Keane at the BBC, which he joined in 1989 as Northern Ireland correspondent. He's now Africa Editor. Keane is famous for both award-winning reporting from the bleakest of conflict zones and for his deeply reflective, personal writing about his experiences, most famously his 'Letter to Daniel' and his account of the Rwandan genocide, *Season of Blood*. He's talking to my colleague, Karen Fowler-Watt (who is also interviewed for this book), Head of the Journalism School at Bournemouth University, from which Keane has an honorary doctorate. We're about to run a media education event in Hong Kong, with Keane as a keynote speaker. This is significant as he reported on the handover to China just over twenty years ago, and his famous letter to his new son was written there. He also holds it up as, during his time there, a beacon of open media and diversity, with the vibrancy and positivity of the city helping him to heal from the trauma of Rwanda. So, he was reflecting on his time in Hong Kong, but also in Rwanda and South Africa and offering perspectives for this project about challenges for journalists and questions of accountability, responsibility, freedom, diversity, democracy and, of course, the notion of fake news.

> On the day of the elections in South Africa, I talked to a man who had been tortured by the security police. One of his children had been killed. I asked him, 'what does democracy mean to you' and he said 'today, I became a human being once more'. That stayed with me ever since and if you ask me about my role as a journalist, it is about that. It's about amplifying, deepening and respecting our humanity in everything I write and broadcast.

Keane links his formative experiences in the three countries together around "the use and abuse of media". He describes a radio station and newspaper in Rwanda calling for murder and 'preaching hatred', leading to "the normalisation of hate and the subversion of people's better instincts".

> If you look at our changed media landscape, there is certainly more freedom in much of the world than before, social media has ensured that. But if you look at the environment in which future journalists are going to have to operate, it is going to be tough in the years ahead and it is going to take courage. Journalists have one fundamental obligation, to speak truth to power. But they also have responsibilities as people, to practice the craft of journalism.

If this may seem too easy for an established BBC journalist to convey to a Chinese audience, Keane also has plenty of reflections to offer on the colonial register and 'othering' discourses of Western media. This is, of course, what makes the landscape so fraught with danger—all news is fake news when we look at it this way. What can be said in defence of the BBC? He talks about verification units at the institution, the great lengths being gone to in order to protect the credibility of this most divisive of media institutions, and his message is ultimately hopeful, as was the case with many of the people I interviewed. To add weight to this point, in Karen's film, review Keane's comments while he is standing in front of the statue of George Orwell outside the BBC's headquarters:

You could look at the modern media landscape with the amount of fake news that is everywhere and become depressed. But I would counsel some optimism. Why? Because I think there is a great fight-back going on, and there are huge opportunities. Orwell famously said, and it's inscribed in the stone beside his statue, if liberty means anything at all it means the right to tell people what they do not wish to here. And that's certainly true if you're challenging the Government of China, or Donald Trump, or Putin. But it's also important that you challenge yourself. All too often now I encounter people in journalism who think all that matters is that you have an opinion. No. What matters is that you vigorously investigate your own opinions, that you take what you believe and you subject it to forensic examination, when you critically see things from the point of view of the other person, with empathy. In the media market place as a journalist, you are assaulted by fake news, manipulation and the seductive offer of power, the relentless lying and scheming and manipulating of governments. From where I stand now, I see a media landscape full of pitfalls and dangers but I'm also fundamentally an optimist because of the human decency I see, the goodness of humanity. The role of journalism is to uphold that goodness.

Let's take these statements as a framework for this chapter, for looking first at the relationship between journalism and democracy, then at the role of media education in providing a critical understanding for citizens about their entitlement to the kind of journalism Keane describes.

The Crisis

Some questions for the broader society given the challenges of fake news: Should social media be more tightly regulated? Should the public demand that journalism once again operate in the public interest? How can democracy be sustained and renewed in light of such challenges, and is education even capable of offering an adequate defense for new media environments? What role does media education play within civics and democratic education? These questions and more should arguably become part of the exploration that must be grappled with by both media literacy advocates and their students given the challenges surrounding fake news. (Mason et al. 2018: 7)

Recent accounts of our 'crashed democracy' offer a sobering antidote to Keane's outlook, and in the responses to the film at our conference in Hong Kong, there were echoes of Natalie Fenton's arguments about the role of journalism in the problem it now self-appoints itself to resolve. Baldwin (2018) comments on this paradox in relation to Brexit:

> The contempt, even hatred, felt by many people towards the mainstream media in Britain did not suddenly appear in 2016. Its roots can be found in the behaviour of newspapers and journalists over the past three decades as they have stirred fear, prised looser a fragile grip on truth and generally spread distrust of every institution, including the media itself. (2018: 224)

Baldwin's assessment is that the fragile state of democracy can be partly attributed to the fact that the business model of digital capitalism requires resonance to take priority over 'reason' (p. 209) and what is required, therefore, is far more than a return to respect for professional news reporting. Rather, "*Western democracy must mend its thirty-year abusive relationship with the new information age*" (p. 293).

There is, though, an element of convenience to some of this, as those of us on the losing side in recent elections and referenda lay the blame at the door of disinformation. Here's Morozov:

> Will the fake news crisis be the cause of democracy's collapse? Or is it just a consequence of a deeper, structural malaise that has been under way for much longer? While it's hard to deny that there's a crisis, whether it's a crisis of fake news or of something else entirely is a question that every mature democracy should be asking. Our elites are having none of it. Their fake news narrative is itself fake: it's a shallow explanation of a complex, systemic problem, the very existence of which they still refuse to acknowledge. (2017: 1)

If so, then there are two elements of denial at work here. First, fake news is an easy distraction from the more difficult economic problem and second, the desire of the political establishment, academics and other inhabitants of the privileged expert class to see the problem as being mostly to do with 'the masses' being lied to, as opposed to them rejecting their expertise.

The moral panic around fake news illustrates how these two denials condemn democracy to perpetual immaturity. The refusal to acknowledge that the crisis of fake news has economic origins makes the Kremlin—rather than the unsustainable business model of digital capitalism—everyone's favourite scapegoat. Morozov's case study for this is the preference of experts to blame the Kremlin rather than Google. At the very least, he argues, the former could not spread fake news so effectively were it not profitable for the latter. And linking back to the argument from Natalie Fenton:

> To hear professional journalists complain about this problem without acknowledging their own culpability further undermines one's faith in expertise. Democracy may or may not be drowning in fake news, but it's definitely drowning in elite hypocrisy. (Morozov 2017: 2)

Democracy is under threat, but rather than just making citizens more resilient to disinformation, an urgent brake on digital/surveillance capitalism is what's needed. Then, along with children protesting over climate change, it is perfectly reasonable to consider the school as a good place to start with a critical response to our economic system. Education is often cited as the arena for democracy's protection. But this also requires the important acceptance that democracy is not something we are born to desire, rather democrats are 'made' (Biesta 2018). Classroom subject epistemologies, including Media Studies, do not necessarily include democratic values, or the kinds of social and community values that might be required for democracy to flourish. Civic education is generally annexed to a cross-curricular or more peripheral context. Further to this, the notion of who counts as a citizen is now up for grabs, some argue. If so, then the question of who democracy includes, and who it excludes, how walls are constructed to represent this (either metaphorically or physically) and what we mean when we talk about common values and the public sphere are serious and difficult questions that students should understand before we can even begin to teach about the relationship between democracy and media.

Values, Whose Values?

Brussels, November 2018. I am reporting to the European Commission on a large field review looking at media literacy education. The event is about shared European values and so it's a bit strange being there in the lead-up to Brexit. Gert Biesta is the keynote speaker and he's offering a provocation—that education for democracy is more about teaching *un*common values. He breaks down his argument: Firstly, democracy is not natural, or rational; instead it is historical, political and thus a paradox. Secondly, the values that are required to enable democracy are also specific and cannot be taken for granted—a particular notion of desirable plurality: liberty, equality and rights. Thirdly, this is formed by the transformation of what people in a society agree is desired into collective criteria for the public interest. Therefore, in a democracy, people have to limit their own personal identities, to an extent, in the interests of political relationships. Biesta cites Hannah Arendt on the challenge of trying to be at home in the world. If we go with this formulation/hypothesis, then we will see a democratic pedagogy as being the dialogue between what our students want for themselves and "to arouse the desire for the democratic way of life." (see Biesta 2017), Crucially, and awkwardly for the European Commission, since the event is framed by a discourse of common values, this approach fundamentally prioritises plurality, as the alternative is totalitarianism. This is a view of democracy as a common world but not a common ground:

> The defence of democracy is therefore not about teaching 'our' values to 'them' but about showing what makes it possible to 'have' values in the first place. The values of democracy are therefore not someone's values but are *un*common in relation to all the values individuals and groups have. (Biesta 2019: 19)

In John Lanchester's satirical dystopia *The Wall* (2018), a concrete wall surrounds Britain. Rising sea levels caused by global warming (The Change) combine with the need for The Defenders to protect the country (as mandatory national service) against The Others by patrolling the wall. Citizens are supported by The Help (migrants). Reading the novel, I'm reminded of *1984* but with a far shorter leap from where we are now, it seems, than would have been the case in the late 1940s when Orwell published. Or at least, if Orwell was warning readers about the dangers of one version of the organisation of the state over the other, Lanchester's fiction reads more like an inevitable end-game to where we are now. The important point for the focus of this chapter is that, unlike *1984*, the society depicted in *The Wall* is a democracy—the requirement of everyone to take their turn as defenders to keep out others and the acceptance of domestic help as an entirely different sub-species of human, by virtue of ethnicity, does not contradict the versions of democracy seemingly favoured by British, American and Russian governments at the time of writing. Indeed, what is being defended *is* a form of democracy, and this resonates with Biesta's argument that the notion of common values excludes those that we can claim do not hold them—they are citizens of nowhere, on the other side of the wall. It is, then, only this more enclosed definition of the citizenry that is 'futuristic', but we are arguably down that road already.

A more comedic take on British society divided by Brexit comes from Jonathon Coe's *Middle England* (2018), which provides another useful reflection on the precarious nature of democracy. Take this exchange between two characters with differing positions on the (forthcoming) referendum:

> That's the beauty of our parliamentary system. It keeps the fruitcakes, loonies and closet racists from having any real influence. I mean, think of all the fruitcakes, loonies and closet racists up and down the country, and imagine what would happen if they were given an equal say with everyone else on matters of national importance. But that's exactly what this referendum is going to give them'.

> Nigel sighed. 'Negative thinking, Douglas. Always with the negative thinking. Negativity, negativity, negativity. We're about to embark on an amazing experience in direct democracy. Now come on – you live and breathe politics, don't you? It's been your lifelong passion. Don't you want to see that passion shared with your fellow citizens? (Coe 2018: 268)

Zagreb, April 2019. I'm speaking about media education and resilience to disinformation and hate speech at another European Commission event. Markus Prutsch, from the European Parliament, is talking about the challenges in fostering a common European identity and historical memory. It's especially complicated and fraught in Croatia and the surrounding region, as I'm aware from presenting on the uses of media literacy in Sarajevo two years before. The Brexit journey is still truncated and perilous, as it was when I was in Brussels, so that adds another layer as I am listening to Prutsch. He describes the tensions between assumptions about belief in freedom and democracy as 'large topoi' and the high levels of abstraction required to foster collective identity. He cites examples of this abstraction, in combination with highly specific and selective historical references to iconic events, both at nation state and European levels. These events are elevated to create myths and they inevitably marginalize more diverse representations of the past, whilst ignoring issues like European colonialism (see Prutsch 2015). He departs from Biesta's analysis, however (or, perhaps, Biesta departs from his), in positing the need for a sense of collective identity and values as a 'sine qua non' for any political project. And because the locus for such, as so often, is the classroom, Prutsch calls for a 'dynamic civic culture', to be fostered by history and citizenship teaching. The links to the kinds of 'dynamic literacy' enabled by Media Studies are clear.

TOOLKIT#3 Regulation vs Free Press

News media is dominated by powerful organisations in the West, with ownership patterns that are far from pluralistic. This oligopoly controls the means of production for 'real news'. The current situation is that four publishers own 75% of regional and local titles. Four newspaper groups dominate national and daily newspaper sales and this is about to be three. Media students will understand this and assess the degree to which this makes this part of the mainstream media much different from the digital corporations who pose such a threat to them. Put simply—*Who and what are we defending, and for whom? Discuss.*

UK newspapers continue to argue that *self-regulation* is preferable to statutory, government or independent scrutiny, to protect the investigative practices of 'the free press', posited as essential to a democratic society, to hold those in power to account.

Media students will weigh up this undisputable principle against the economic reality that, in the analogue/print news era, the freedom to publish was restricted to millionaires. They will then consider the paradoxical situation that free news (to the consumer) really can be produced by anyone, online, and so it has turned out that the free press really coming to fruition has created the current 'crisis', whereby 'the free press' is at risk of extinction at the hands of another 'free press'. Again, discuss.

The General Council was born in 1953 and was replaced a decade later by the Press Council. In 1991 this became the Press Complaints Commission and then, since 2014, the Independent Press Standards Organisation. Every time the status of the regulator changes, it is a result of government pressure to self-regulate better or lose the right. The latest, and most serious of such pressure points came about after the phone hacking scandal, leading to the Leveson Inquiry in 2011. That inquiry led to the following recommendations: Self-regulation of newspapers should continue without government interference; a new body with a new code of conduct should replace the Press Complaints Commission; this new body should be underwritten by legislation to ensure that regulation of the press is independent and effective.

Media students will look at the non-implementation of the third recommendation, understand the reasons, and come to an informed, academic position on how they feel about it.

Power, Responsibility, Accountability

The late Tony Benn offered these five questions to ask of anyone in power, as a kind of benchmark for democracy (2010).

What power have you got?
How did you get it?
In whose interests do you exercise it?
To whom are you accountable?
How do we get rid of you?

Going back to Fergal Keane's optimism, professional journalism would be key to asking these questions to the powerful on behalf of the public, this is the nature of the free press as a 'fourth estate' in a healthy democracy. Media Studies has always asked these same questions to 'the media'. It's important that any new application of this framework is not reduced to mere fact-checking but is also agile enough to generate the answers, whether the media text in question is shared on social media by a politician or broadcast by *The Guardian*.

Notwithstanding Biesta's challenge to the notion of a democracy as natural and necessarily inclusive, a democratic society is generally taken to be founded on principles of representation by elections and account-ability. Put simply, if we don't like the decisions made by people with power over us, we have the opportunity to replace them with other people, through a transparent and open process.

On Civics

Paul Mihailidis is generating something of a paradigm shift for media education. He is an advocate of, and researcher into, media literacy for civic engagement, in the same school of thought in this regard as other American academics such as Renee Hobbs and Henry Jenkins. He's at Emerson College in Boston, MA but also runs the Salzburg Academy for Media and Global Change.

I met with him in the serene surroundings of the Academy's venue, Schloss Leopoldskron, a rococo castle built in 1736 in a seven-hectare park, location for *The Sound of Music*, and subject of Nazi occupation for a period. The academy is here because of a random encounter on the New York subway about a suitable venue for a Marshall Plan of the Mind as a critical element of recovery from the war. I'm interested to know more about Paul's journey.

My family emigrated from Greece in the 1960s and I grew up in an industrial, middle-class industrial space outside of Boston, Massachusetts in a very rich Greek cultural diaspora in the United States and I think I was always interested in the ways in which my upbringing and my work came together. I saw a lot of ways in which cultures tried to integrate and connect with their larger communities and what the points of tension and connection were around how diverse communities function and I think as a five-year-old, it was learning what it means to be inside and out of the community. As I went on through university I started writing for alternative press and really kind of pushing on this idea of what makes communities work, what makes people want to participate in things. And I think from my youth I was interested in that and it just kind of took off into my adult life, as I saw challenges that my family faced, some of my peers faced, that I faced, and then when I was travelling as a young person abroad, also. And then the role of the media became more central in that problem, what information people have, how they create stereotypes, so this has been something that I have been personally motivated for and it's kind of taken over my professional life.

I know Paul pretty well. He's a visiting professor in the research centre I run, he's hosted our annual conference at Emerson, we've co-edited an international collection on media literacy education and I've been out to Salzburg a couple of times. I've always championed the politics of his work—this is clearly not just Media Studies, whilst expressing my anxiety about any assumption that media literacy education will automatically generate civic action for making the world a better place. After all, as I often say in keynote speeches, if only to wake the audience up, the most media literate people in the world are using it mostly for very bad things. His new book directly addresses this issue, so we turn to that.

I say from day one to colleagues, peers and students that these personal narratives in our lives are normally the things that frame our media literacy and media representation work. I think that the Salzburg project and the graduate programme at Emerson and my work in the Engagement Lab all really have the same umbrella theme, around looking at media literacies as explicit forms of civic action-taking. Salzburg is a labour of love more than anything else, I think, that project started in 2005, all these new technologies were emerging and a lot of people were talking about their impact on media and journalism. We had this idea about what if we could bring people together from around the world to really understand how these tools are going to impact us and then start to build responses that could strengthen social and global networks? And so we've been thirteen years into this project and what's emerged is the intersection of media literacy and action taking. We have this network of institutions and universities and organisations that feel compelled every year to send their students and faculty and it serves two purposes. One is we are we are building capacity, we're building research, we're building exchange programmes, we're building organisations and off-shoots, all around this idea of can we strengthen the role of media literacy as a civic framework. And then the second part of it is helping grow the network. So we had over a thousand young people so far who have come through this that are doing amazing things across media fields as teachers or as journalists or filmmakers and artists and working in the non-profit sector and we continue to cultivate that network. So what started as this novel idea has grown into this robust space for institutions and individuals for scholars and activists and practitioners to come together and have meaningful exchanges and immerse themselves in dialogue and experimental, transformative media pedagogies. So Salzburg has provided us academics with spaces to do things that universities often don't allow us to, right? Just taking the pedagogical risks and seeing how they work and that's been such a source of energy for our group and it's become much more of a centre-piece.

So what does this offer for the 'battle' against fake news?

So, I've written about this recently and I think the long and short of it that fake news itself is a phenomena specifically of this technological age, when people say 'fake news has happened and this is nothing new', I mean I understand that sentiment and I understand where they're coming from but I think if we can just extract the phenomenon of what we're calling fake news right now it's really a phenomenon of this specific technological age where you have this kind of digital capitalism that is not regulated, that you have these tools that are designed to promote spectacle, to breed distrust, designed to channel attention and they do that through increasingly sensational content and you have politicians that are able to use these tools to be very effective in advocating for ideas. So I think the combination of this lack of regulation and these digital platforms and infrastructures that are not designed to do anything but increasingly grab our attention has created this landscape where truth is kind of obscured, so I think we've always had these issues but now they're a product of this age. And so when we see this idea of alternative sets of facts and truths being much more compelling and being able to scale much more than before, I think the media literacy response side has so far just been like, 'oh, if we just had more media literacy we could solve this current crisis' and I guess my response to that would be quite cynical. I agree that we don't have media literacy, at least in the case of the United States, in enough formal pedagogy programmes and maybe that's a problem but I also think that scapegoating fake news as a lack of media literacy is a problem. In fact, you could argue that media literacy skills and dispositions kind of contributed to this fake news phenomena as much as they've taken away from it and I would argue that the problem of fake news is not one of a lack of people being able to kind of decipher media but really just a lack of people being able to have human connections and dialogue and engagement. So in media literacy for a long time we've been teaching these skills of deconstruction and analysis and then assuming those lead to better civic engagement. Whereas my argument has always been that media literacy as a response needs to prioritise civic intentionality or it risks just giving more people the skills and the dispositions to advocate for the values that they want to without ever needing to have them challenged in the context of other people.

Agreed. I ask for an example.

I'm always interested in this idea of hyperlocal media, like the local journalism landscape and community engagement, we've been working a lot on this here in Boston. The idea that media literacy had a reductionist lens to it, trying to make these grand statements and these points about systems and structures and at the same time communities often get dragged into narratives and structures that are misrepresentative or don't paint the complete picture, not that they ever could, but media literacies, if they're going to respond to these current problems of digital culture, they need to start by thinking about value systems or civic values so you talk about things like care and persistence so the models that we've been experimenting with lately ask about communities and how we understand them and how we form deep sets of relation and then from there you can start to build media that bring us together with others in the world.? I guess it's kind of an inversion that we've been working with lately, so we're doing a project in Boston now that takes our civic media students to hyperlocal journalists and does a bunch of community engagement workshops which are playful and creative, pop-up newsrooms and these kind of, like, really cool public press stations and these are media literacy interventions, working between education, communities and local journalists to better connect them and as a pedagogy it's really powerful when you approach media literacy through that angle rather than just through talking about 'the media'.

TOOLKIT#4 Pointless Blog vs The Canon

DesiMag and *PointlessBlog* are set texts in Media Studies. They are not 'hyperlocal' but they are different examples of 'new entrants' to the mainstream and the way that the subject deals with them is informative for the broader topic at hand here, the interplay between 'classic' media theory and new modes of media production and engagement. *DesiMag* is an Asian lifestyle magazine and *Pointless Blog* is the pseudonym of a YouTuber.

A revision aid for one of the Media Studies specifications focuses on media representation and identity as the core business of analysis:

> Online media products like DesiMag and PointlessBlog arguably provide audiences with a much wider range of representations than traditional broadcasters. Where traditional media uses fixed schedules and broadcast technology, online media relies on peer-to-peer distribution to generate product visibility. The subsequent proliferation of media has led to a blossoming of identity construction and expression online. While we have identified some complex representations and constructions of identity in the set products, there is also some evidence of established representations and stereotypes in relation to gender and ethnicity. (Eduqas, 2017)

Mapping set theories from the classic Media Studies 'canon' to contemporary texts is an important skill in the subject—students need to understand that theories can be 'old' and still relevant for today's textual landscape. Here is how the exam board suggests this mapping be undertaken for these examples of contemporary media:

Summarise your analysis of the products in relation to Hall's ideas.

Suggested response: *DesiMag can be seen to be forging some powerful alternatives to established stereotypes, whilst PointlessBlog offers, to some extent, a less subversive representation of masculinity.*

Write two or three sentences that provide detailed examples of how Gilroy's ideas link to *PointlessBlog*. Give examples to support your points.

Suggested response: *PointlessBlog's marginalisation of non-white participants supports a segregated view of UK society—a view that associates*

> *expressions of mainstream culture as belonging to white only groups. The almost total absence of non-whites from the blog potentially constructs an imagined version of UK society in which whites and non-whites live and work in mutually exclusive communities, however contemporary Britain is in reality much more integrated and inclusive.*
>
> Follow up: http://resource.download.wjec.co.uk.s3.amazonaws.com/vtc/2017-18/17-18_3-22/_eng/unit04/revision-activity-applying-theories-to-desimag-and-pointlessblog.html.

Mass Literacy, Mass Media, Media Literacy: Uses and Abuses

For MacPherson (1966), the liberal-democratic state (such as the United Kingdom and United States, currently) is characterised by a balance of freedom, welfare and regulation. The state provides basic services to all but regulates us more than would be the case if we were left to survive without those things. How news media are located within this equation is open to debate. The classic Media Studies questions on this would be about how free news outlets can be from the state, who else gatekeeps the flow of information and in whose interests? In a *purely* capitalist system, media is like any other industry and media providers can do whatever they want to make money. In an unelected dictatorship, media will be explicitly controlled by the state and used to convey one view of the world, to justify and promote the actions of government. But in 'neoliberal' democracies, again, *it is neither all of one nor all of the other* (Fenton 2016: 101). The question now, of course, is whether the rise of fake news takes us back to a classic paradigm, where we need old school Media Studies tools to deconstruct news bias more than ever, or whether the media landscape is now so rapid and fragmented that we need a new analytical framework altogether.

Either way, within Media Studies it is clear that understanding the relationship between power, media and democracy is *only* possible if students have an advanced critical perspective on the idea of democracy in the first place.

Sticking with the old school for a while, the ideas of Richard Hoggart in the United Kingdom and John Dewey in the United States, both commenting on the development of the mass media, firmly back in the analogue era, remain formative for Media Studies. For Dewey, the extent to which media are open and accessible for citizens to be represented is crucial to the everyday workings of a democracy:

> Dewey believed that the emergence of a modern mass media had the potential to improve the conditions and operations of American democracy, if structured with those ends in mind, but he worried that the particular shape of the American media system, governed primarily by commercial interests, would have a much more negative influence. (Press and Williams 2010: 75)

Dewey provided a kind of 'yardstick' for media students to use when looking at the extent to which media in a society at any given time is democratic. What is the balance between public interest and political or commercial imperatives?

In *The Uses of Literacy* (1957), Richard Hoggart wrote about how his working-class community, in the North of England, was at once using the new 'mass literacy' for self-improvement, education, social mobility and civic engagement and, at the same time, the powerful were also seizing the opportunity to use this expansion in literacy, through the new popular culture, for commercial and political ends. This, then, is the double edge of civic democracy. Hoggart wrote about the role of popular culture in the "vastly complicated interplay of social, political and economic changes" and the reductive force of mass media and collective audience-making (p. 138):

> What a phoney sense of belonging this all is, this which is offered by the public pals of this publicly gregarious age; it would be better to feel anonymous; one might then be moved to some useful action to improve matters. (1957: 162)

The question is whether Hoggart's anxiety over 'group passivity' holds, sixty years on and whether it is challenged or reinforced by the internet and by the idiosyncratic blending of 'the group' with anonymity? His conversion of Forster's Only Connect into Only Conform seems to be both complicated and amplified by the new connected conformity. The role of mainstream media, 'fake news, data harnessing and social media in both the election of Donald Trump and the Brexit situation offer rich territory for contemporary re-application of Hoggart's *counting of heads as a substitute for judgement*' (p. 146).

Doing *Colombo*

These days, academics are judged on the impact of their research on public policy. In this field, Divina Frau-Meigs is one of the most impactful agents. Born in Morocco to Spanish parents, she graduated from Sorbonne University, Stanford University (Palo Alto) and the Annenberg School for Communications (University of Pennsylvania, Philadelphia) and is now Professor at Sorbonne and UNESCO Chair for "know-how in the era of sustainable digital development" as well as a major player in media and information literacy across the European Union.

Typically, she's managing various 'transversal' Skype calls around the slot I've booked and before we get into the core business we catch up on various threads of activity for cross-EU media literacy projects which I've been hesitant to throw myself into because of Brexit. One question I've never asked her, during the various EU and UNESCO events we've attended and when she keynoted at our Summit in Prague, is how her academic background fits with media literacy.

> It's complicated. At a personal level I am in media and information literacy because I believe in multiple intelligences and multiple ways of learning, based on how we process information and how this information is conveyed to us, which is a communication dimension. So I don't come to media literacy like some other French scholars from a perspective of decoding the press. I come to it from a perspective of information as a necessary condition to access knowledge. And with the full understanding that the way you communicate that information is part of how people

can understand it. On a professional level, I've realised that it's also a political project. It's about democracy and citizenship and that explains why I have been putting a lot of energy into NGOs to push this political project at civil society but also at a political level where it can change things, so that's why I'm invested in public policies on media literacy, that's why I'm the European chair of the global alliance partnership in media information literacy of UNESCO - that's why I participate in the EU expert teams about media literacy, to try to make sure that the political project part of media literacy gets incarnated in laws, in policy guidelines and all possible directions.

Clarifying terms is interesting and important with Divina, whether it's to do with media and information literacy—a relationship we've wrestled with when working together on the UNESCO declaration or, in this case, about fake news and its variants.

I think in the history of media literacy and its epistemology, mal-information, as I like to call, it is part of a series of issues that scholars think about as behaviour disorders related to media. I've always been careful to balance the notion of information content disorders with empowerment and creativity but when you're dealing rights and a political project, of course the disorder is what is going to catch the attention of the politicians. Not so much when everything is going fine and then people are enjoying themselves!! So for me this comes after a long train of these content disorders like the violence issue, for example, and what's interesting is that these prior disorders were more focused on fiction. So I think there is a shift here, the advent of fake news for me is a turning point, also because it really shows what we had a hard time seeing before, which is what the internet and data are doing to media and what social media are doing to media. And so for me we're not just in the old-fashioned pre-digital world of rumour and then false information, which has always existed, and propaganda, whatever. We are really into something new that is more than media driven but has an impact on the way we perceive information. I don't buy the post-truth business, you know. But definitely, it's more about cognitive decision making really. It's not problematised enough at the moment when people talk about fake news. So we as researchers have still a lot of work to do to problematise this.

Moving from the research response to the educational/pedagogic work for so-called 'resilience' to fake news?

I'm teaching for the holistic response, not a 'one-shot' response which is why I have a very ambivalent attitude to fact checking, per se, which has been emerging and framed into the media literacy answer to fake news and it's enough to do some fact checking and you send journalists to schools so that they show how they verify their sources. For me, that's a very narrow understanding of the issue and it sends us back to the pre-digital world of media literacy being about the press. So it's the risk of sending media literacy back to the pre-digital and I think you and I and others are trying to make this about a more holistic approach to information.

OK, so can we look at examples of the approach we are favouring?

One of the strategies I've been able to use working with a European research project is 'INVID'. It is a fact checking process developing an app for detecting fake manipulated videos, so it's kind of a forensics of video. It was a tool first developed first for journalists in particular, but I'm using it with them for different pedagogic scenarios where we also use it to understand how an image works, to analyse better how you construct an image or you deconstruct it or you manipulate it, a larger spectrum of analysis. And so, instead of staying in fact checking as an echo chamber for journalism, we move more towards the media literacy of trying to understand what social media does to media and what advertising does to the business model of fake news, a more critical perspective. It can be downloaded by young people to use it on their own or teachers can use it in the classroom with them, and for our last 'Internet Governors Forum' that took place in Paris, we had a hackathon around that where we encouraged young people to work with us towards different scenarios. It was more like the *Colombo* series, you know (this is a welcome, old school, reference!) You know who the murderer is from the start and then you look at the workings of the mind of Colombo, so if you transpose this to journalism, we know from the start it's fake news and we are going to look at journalists and how they solve the problem and where the forensics of fakeness are, but that was only possible because we were working with these young people who themselves are consumers of fake news and trolls themselves telling us: 'You have to change your perspective, it's not like this". And the other example would be 'SMILE' (Synergies in Media and Information Literacy in Education) – it's a totally awful acronym, but we've just received big funding from the French Development Agency to start our second SMILE centre in Tunisia. And the idea is really what I think you and I perceive when we think about media literacy projects, in that it has several partners and a multi-stakeholder approach where you have the ministries, you have research, you have the private sector, media and information platforms and you have civil society and you bring them together to elaborate projects that are very localised. Because fake news in Tunisia is not the same problem as fake news in France. So it's interesting for me because it really allows us to bring back a lot of elements of media literacy from the perspective of representation, audiences and communities in the context of the whole chain of values and actors around information that I consider very pedagogical in fake news and regarding information disorder.

I pick up on the relationship between legal/state regulation and the more neoliberal mode of self-regulation that has recently pervaded around media.

I deeply think that it's a democratic issue. And don't get me wrong, I think some of the communities that bring out fake news do it because they don't trust the information they are receiving and so they're pushing rumours and fakes in the hope to generate more acceptable news or they are very ironic and satirical are this is contributing to the debate on democracy and on trust, if not truth. But some are not and some are belligerent and hold aggressive attitudes towards democracy and for this reason France has finally decided to regulate, but it's the last resort to me and the way we've gone with the EU has first been trying self-regulation. Hence the idea that we were going to give a chance to platforms to produce their codes of good practices and good conduct. But we're going to check that they're not developing it alone, they're developing it with other stakeholders. And I will push the next step, for me in my mind this will be accompanied by training and workshops for these platforms' developers, the way we did with the self-regulation of video games, self-regulation as a first step, But fake news has kind of reset everybody's GPS, if you want, all the professions - the librarians; the journalists;

the researchers; the data scientists; the teachers - it's reset things that we thought were established and engraved in marble, yes? We have to revise our values for the digital world.

And the challenges of doing this in the classroom, though?

So, these are not the usual actors of the school, no, but they can bring new tools to the schools, which are supposed to be places for debate but where this has totally gone down the drain with the sort of approach of schools that have deadlines and evaluations over all else. The choice we made in Riga about moving to this new paradigm, for this we are going to need to think about a curriculum, like the research you and your colleagues have conducted, and I agree we still have to put long-term, high scale sustainable things there, not just good practices.

The *Production* of News

The ownership of news outlets, the political and regulatory infrastructure in which they operate and the journalistic codes of conduct in place all make a difference to news 'as a thing' in any context. Where news is still bound by national borders, we can still apply a comparative framework from Oates (2008) which defines the US system as 'libertarian' (a small percentage of news media is publicly funded); the Russian news media as state regulated and the UK system as in between (though much closer to that of the United States). Oates' criteria are political environment, media norms, regulation, ownership and journalistic practices:

> Examining these elements of the News Production Model reveals a range of constraints that will shape news content. These constraints start long before a journalist arrives at her desk in the morning to begin the task of covering events and gathering news. All of these elements will dictate the shape, direction, and final form of news coverage. That, in turn, will influence the citizens and the public sphere. (Oates 2008)

When Barlow and Mills (2015) offered the following distinction between liberal and Marxist 'lenses' on news media, things were arguably more 'black and white' than now:

Liberal theory argues that the press – and mass media in general – serve democracy in three ways. They play a key role in informing the electorate. They provide a means of overseeing and 'checking' in government – the watchdog role. They articulate public opinion. A Marxist perspective holds that as mass media organisations are owned and operated by ruling, or elite groups in society, the individuals running them will ensure that these institutions reinforce the dominant ideology in a way that appears to be 'common sense', thus helping maintain class inequalities. (Barlow and Mills 2015: 41)

But how much of the media still exists to hold politicians to account? This is at the heart of everything we've discussed previously from Fergal Keane and Tony Benn and it would be important to a Media Studies curriculum informed by the ideas of Gert Biesta about 'grown up' plurality. Comparing an old school case study with a '3.0' phenomena, we would view Rupert Murdoch as Big Media: proliferating a right-wing, capitalist, Republican agenda through traditional news outlets, versus Mark Zuckerberg's extraordinary, but seemingly uncontrollable, power. Zuckerberg claims to have no political project, so his answer to Tony Benn's question—in whose interests do you exercise this power—would be his own profit motives only, or some form of the Frankenstein myth 'because we can' experiment or even, if we accept the Facebook mission statement, 'Bring the world closer together', as ours.

Facebook has a power and reach that is unprecedented. As Chief Executive Officer and a major shareholder, accountable only to an advisory board, Mark Zuckerberg has control over the information exchanged by over 2.2 billion people every month. Facebook is accused of exposing the personal data of 87 million people in such a way that the UK European Referendum was skewed towards one side of the campaign—those who accessed the data—and which facilitated a Russian infiltration of the US election in 2016. The combination of the scale of Zuckerberg's power and the lack of accountability can lead once to conclude that *he* is a greater threat to democracy than Trump, Putin or any dictator.

But back to the mainstream media. During Trump's tenure, the US network Fox News has become openly partisan, whilst its competitor, CNN, has been labelled Fake News by the President. At the start of

2019, Trump had given 41 interviews to Fox, considerably more than all the other networks combined.

The Media Studies view of media in democracy is that when the plurality is lessened, the hegemony increases:

> A state of hegemony is achieved when a provisional alliance of certain social groups exerts a consensus that makes the power of the dominant group appear both natural and legitimate. Institutions such as the mass media, the family, the education system and religion, play a key role in the shaping of people's awareness and consciousness and thus can be agents through which hegemony is constructed, exercised and maintained. (Watson and Hill 2003:126)

The Closed Shop

In a revelatory account of journalism in the Hacked Off era, but prior to the emergence of fake news as a new moral panic, Nick Davies' *Flat Earth News* (2009) exposed deals between journalists and politicians with the news being, in these cases, at the service of the powerful. There was also a damning account of discrimination in newsrooms:

> A district reporter told me he would call up from Manchester to tell the news desk a story, 'and they would always ask: 'Are they our kind of people?' i.e. Are they white, middle class?' Or more often it would be: 'Are they of the dusky hue?' And if they were of the dusky hue, they didn't want the story. (Davies 2009: 371)

Peter Jukes' journal of his experiences reporting the phone hacking trial of 2013 'followed the money' to the collusion between journalists and politicians in stark terms. His version of events concludes with optimism for a re-balance of power in the near future:

> Thousands of people were targeted by hacking, and hundreds of relationships, friendships and marriages were badly damaged by the cruel publication of private secrets. This has nothing to do with a free press or exposing public interest scandals. It's a display of power designed to

intimidate and silence. Yes, thanks to interactive media, we're no longer passive consumers of news, entertainment and opinion, but can share countervailing information – and answer back. The press had tried to shape public opinion with its take on the hacking trial, but other forces are now in play. (Jukes 2014: 231)

Indeed. Fake news being one such 'other force', rather complicating matters more than Jukes may have foreseen.

Professional journalists are still no more representative of the general public than politicians. According to data from research produced by the Sutton Trust, Social Mobility and Child Poverty Commission and academic studies published in the last five years, over half of the UK national journalists went to private schools (43% more than the general population), whilst less than 20% had a comprehensive education (70% less than the public). According to these reports, in 2016, 94% of journalists were white and 55% were men. Less than 1% of journalists are Muslim and only 0.2% are black. The gender pay gap is stark, and senior roles are dominated by men (see Sutton Trust 2016; Social Mobility and Child Poverty Commission 2014; Thurman 2016). Owen Jones has traversed the difficult landscape of attempting to challenge this hegemony without attacking the free press. Adding compelling evidence of nepotism and networks of privilege operating around internships and recruitment to the mix, Jones accuses the professional media of a kind of 'groupthink':

> Groupthink is partly a consequence of how socially exclusive the British media is. Our backgrounds inevitably have an impact on how we see the world, particularly if we are in denial about our own privilege. If you have so many people from such similar backgrounds—from a small and relatively privileged slither of British society—then similar prejudices and worldviews will reinforce each other. There will be a similar approach to which issues are selected as priorities and which are ignored, and the angle with which certain issues are approached. (Jones 2018: 2, see also 2014)

If we accept the increasing concern that the decline in the print news industry is bad for democracy, we must be careful not to ignore these problems with the representation and accountability of the 'mainstream media'.

But returning to Jukes' optimism, and looking ahead to the claims for 'Media 2.0' we will explore later, are *we* 'the media' now?

In 2004, Dan Gillmor, founder of the Centre for Citizen Media published a book called *We, The Media*. His prediction was clear, and at the time, noting that 'Big Media' (the huge corporations, such as News Corporation, CNN, the BBC) had for decades enjoyed unrivalled control over who could produce and share media, leading to a 'concentrated' media 'oligopoly'. This ecosystem was profoundly unrepresentative of the population of society. It was therefore undemocratic for media to be configured in this way. Gillmor saw 'web 2.0' as a catalyst for an uprising against this hegemony as ordinary citizens would use blogs and other forms of 'citizen journalism' to produce their own news. We would then be 'the former audience'. At the time, examples were proliferating in the form of blogs from Iraq during military operations, which offered an alternative to the Western media's accounts: a range of collaborative Wikispaces, children's news blogs and Persian networkers using the internet for a collective voice in a country where free speech was restricted:

> The spreading of an item of news, or of something much larger, will occur- much more so than today – without any help from mass media as we know it. The people who'll understand this best are probably just being born. In the meantime, even the beginnings of this 'shift' are forcing all of us to adjust our assumptions and behaviour. (Gillmor 2006: 42–43)

The question now is whether this came true, and is that good or bad?

Arab Spring, Russian Winter?

This is James Baldwin's slogan (2018: 151), describing the practices of the Internet Research Centre and the alleged manipulation of Western democracy by Russian troll farms and bots, the moral panic around which is partly the reason we're here. But a more detailed account is offered by Timothy Snyder, who warns in *The Road to Unfreedom* where we are headed. Again, the argument would thus be that Media Studies can offer a crucial diversion. Snyder writes about 'the politics of eternity' (ch 5, para 1), whereby Russian state TV combines with the international RT network to construct a paradoxical mindset from which audiences accept that all media is fake news but sees Russian output as more honest by 'virtue' of being openly false. This is typical of a pervasive Russian strategy of 'baroque contradiction', according to Snyder, whereby doubting everything, a kind of manufactured consent of hyper-cynicism leads to an ironic trust in open distortion in the national interest (the contradictory claims of the Russian government and Russian media over events in both Ukraine and Salisbury are case studies to this effect).

> There is now overwhelming evidence that Russia is engaging in an orchestrated, strategic campaign whose purpose is to erode liberal democracy in Europe and the United States, and to weaken NATO and the European Union. This campaign uses what has become known as hybrid warfare with the emphasis (in the case of western countries) being on: launching cyber-attacks against government agencies, utilities, companies, universities, media and individuals; exercising political influence in domestic audiences; spreading misinformation; engaging in character assassinations; and interfering in domestic politics, elections and referenda, by directly and indirectly funding and supporting political parties of the far right and the far left. (Gerodimos 2017: 1)

In Gerodimos' report, case studies of this Russian campaign are cited in Germany, France, the Czech Republic, the United Kingdom, Finland, Greece, Ukraine, Georgia, Moldova, Estonia, The Netherlands, Hungary, Austria, Italy, Montenegro, Bulgaria and the United States. All of these are viewed as acts of war on democracy through a dilution of citizens' capacity to distinguish fact from fiction.

Starbird (2018) described an accidental study of Russian disinformation, starting out as a framing analysis of *#BlackLivesMatter*. The data from the study provided an unexpected trail from Twitter accounts posting about the campaign to the Internet Research Agency. The researchers discovered IRA-generated accounts which were acting as caricatures of Americans using social media for political activism. Some of the accounts were extreme, but others were seemingly liberal. This is seen as more sinister because it looks like the IRA strategy was to build trust within online discourse communities, in order to use that trust to then provoke dissent and sow division, it is assumed to destabilize the community as fertile ground for fake news. The same strategy appears to be at work in IRA-generated Tweets about gun rights and immigration in the United States:

> Russia likely does not care about most domestic issues in the United States. Their participation in these conversations has a different set of goals: to undermine the U.S. by dividing us, to erode our trust in democracy (and other institutions), and to support specific political outcomes that weaken our strategic positions and strengthen theirs. Those are the goals of their information operations. One of the most amazing things about the internet age is how it allows us to come together—with people next door, across the country, and around the world—and work together toward shared causes. We've seen the positive aspects of this with digital volunteerism during disasters and online political activism during events like the Arab Spring. But some of the same mechanisms that make online organizing so powerful also make us particularly vulnerable, in these spaces, to tactics like those the IRA are using. (Starbird 2018: 2)

The importance of all this is that, whilst Russian propaganda was hitherto an international case study for Media Studies in the West, the clear and present relevance for the subject and this project is currently manifested in the alleged pursuit of a project of information destabilization in the West:

> To end factuality is to begin eternity. If citizens doubt everything, they cannot see beyond Russia's borders, cannot carry out sensible discussions about reform, cannot trust one another enough to organize for political change.......As social mobility halts, democracy gives way to oligarchy.... As distraction replaces concentration, the future dissolves into the frustrations of the present. The oligarch crosses into real politics from a world of fiction, and governs by invoking myth and manufacturing crisis. In the 2010s, one such person, Vladimir Putin, escorted another, Donald Trump, from fiction to power. (Snyder 2018, ch 5–6, paras 3 and 2)

In this quote, whether or not we accept the tautology of the Putin-Trump 'takeover', we can see the perfect storm for fake news: economic hardship, austerity politics, the subsequent failure of centrist politics to satisfy disenfranchised publics, the erosion of trust in democracy and the opportunity provided by this erosion for oligarchs to offer hope through an attack on both mainstream media *and* politics.

A real issue for Media Studies now, of course, is where do we draw the line—this is really about geopolitics and philosophy, rather than just media. But if we see the internet as a medium, then it counts because it crosses geographic borders. The de-regulated web is pivotal in this account of Russian operations. In the quote below, Twitter is not merely the platform for something bigger or external, but rather, to paraphrase Marshall McLuhan, social media *is* the medium that is the message:

> The polarization of politics in the West, notably in the United States but also in the European Union, has provided the opportunity to import the uncertainties and obfuscations routine in Russian politics into Western politics, by cheaply importing narratives, arguments and conspiracies using the power of bots. For instance, Russian bots and trolls regularly tweet about vaccination in divisive terms, linking the issues to controversies in American politics. The tweets are both pro- and anti-vaccination, but the purpose appears to be less to establish a position as to create, by the volume of tweets, the impression of strong and partisan debate, and to recruit partisan campaigners by associating vaccination with the several other wedge issues in America's dysfunctional politics. This is not just a Russian tactic (although the term "disinformation" was indeed originally a Russian term, coined during the Stalin era). No doubt all nations indulge in deliberately propagating falsehood. However, disinformation is a particularly potent weapon against the West, where speech is freer (and it is easier to spread ideas), and where controlling the public sphere is seen as rather alien. (O'Hara and Hall 2018: 19)

But with Russia, another angle on all this suggests an obsession with 'Putinology' that verges on conspiracy theory, which itself serves to strengthen Putin's power in Russia—a kind of conspiracy theory about Western conspiracy theories (see Yablokov 2018). Further to this, it is also argued that our obsession with Putin reflects on a liberal identity in crisis. This thesis suggests that we deflect our local problems to Russia, and Putin specifically, to defer dealing with them in the here and now. An example would be the obsession with explaining the election of Trump and Brexit as the product of Russian interference, as Snyder lays out as a 'fait accompli' above. This narrative from Putinology, according to Gessen (2017), describes '*the production of commentary and analysis about Putin and his motivations, based on necessarily partial, incomplete and sometimes entirely false information*' (2017: 1). Taking Russian disinformation and the impact of this on democracy as a Media Studies topic will require students to consider the possibility, also, of fake news purporting as liberal critique about 'honest' fake news.

First World Problems?

Jad Melki runs the Digital Media Literacy Academy of Beirut (at the Lebanese American University) and works with Paul Mihailidis at the Salzburg Academy. We've also worked together with Paul recently at another media literacy forum in Stockholm. The conversation cited is partly a more considered, recorded version of various threads we've started already. His research is at the intersection of digital media literacy conflict and journalism education. In 2006, he was awarded for his reporting on the Lebanon-Israel war and in 2015, he won the UNESCO-UNAoC International Media and Information Literacy Award for advancing media literacy education in the Arab region. I went to Beirut in 2017 to work at DMLAB. That experience, combined with reading his work on a Media Literacy of the Oppressed was formative in raising my awareness of the issue of media literacy as a 'first world problem'—here's a quote I often use in my talks as a kind of 'disclaimer':

> I often facetiously tell my US- and EU-based colleagues that some emerging media literacy issues they tackle are First World problems that we would love to deal with once we get rid of… say ISIS and dictatorship. While their issues merit the genuine attention of media literacy scholars, it's hard to see them as priorities in our context. (Melki 2018)

Melki lives on campus at the American University of Beirut, where he worked before moving to LAU. I walked and talked with Jad and Karen Fowler-Watt in the beautiful grounds with an outlook to the Mediterranean, during our visit to DMLAB. Later, he tells me his story:

> I was born in Lebanon and when I was two years old, civil war broke out so I had to go with my parents to Australia as refugees. Some time around 1982, my parents thought the war was over so we came back and then almost right away the Israeli invasion took place.

He describes a rich and varied academic background, starting in Computer Science and moving on to film, TV and journalism, across Lebanon, Australia and the United States. Returning again as a post-doctorate, he built up the digital media literacy academy at AUB, to bring media literacy into the Arab region, but due to resistance to expansion, took it with him to LAU. I pick up on the obvious question, at least from a Westerner's perception, perhaps fraught with assumptions, about how these experiences of migration and return have framed his work:

> You develop multiple mind-sets and sometimes you switch between them. On one hand, I have lived enough in Western countries to feel like a Westerner but on the other hand, I've lived for long enough with war and conflict and the problems of third world countries to understand at a visceral level and have that character, so an advantage is to see through two different lenses but at the same time it creates a schizophrenia – where do you stand, especially where there's conflicts of interest. I think the common ground often, when it comes to media literacy, is about being part of this oppressed world whether you are in the West or not, it's like a different priority list depending on where you are.

So, is 'fake news' another first world problem?

> Whatever you want to call it, we've always had this and we can go back to the British Government spreading lies about eating carrots in the second world war, people still believe it now. I think what has changed is the power of the individual to do this in a more credible way because of the

low bar in learning how to use the technology and widespread literacy. So it's no longer political or military, it's now a way to make money for individuals, that's the key shift.

Can it ever be justified to spread fake news?

Ah, so now we're into some moral and philosophical questions. Growing up in Lebanon, when I was a kid I was taught by my mother not to tell the truth in certain circumstances, to be smart about it. So if someone asks if your father is part of this political group, your answer is "I don't know". Same if they ask if he has weapons in the house. So I was raised to lie, as a defence mechanism, rather than an ethical, cultural or moral thing in the Arab world, it's just necessary. So could fake news serve a good purpose, yes of course! Just like nuclear weapons can serve a good purpose, as a deterrent, you could put any evil to a good purpose, even to the extent that Nazi crimes led to the invention of some medicines. Or is it permissible to take photos of people dying or in terrible circumstances as a journalist so that people know about it? Where do you draw the line? I guess you can balance cost and benefit, but can you ethically permit yourself to do anything to say that the greater good outweighs the damage?

Working with aspiring journalists at LAU and across the region with DMLAB, do the cohorts he works with in Beirut see the same opportunity as those in the West, to revalidate the profession through the threat of fake news?

There are some really nice windows of opportunities opening right and left. We have students and graduates working on new initiatives here, for example to strive for high quality, credible, objective news with particular objectives, such as the experiences of women. But at the same time, there are a lot of newspapers in Lebanon closing, so this opens up leeway for accepting new ideas and new companies emerging and employing our students and prioritizing objective news for multiple audiences rather than the politicized news which is still here but not as dominant. So sometimes students fall back into the old traditions of partisan press and when I see them, they can't look me straight in the eye because of what they wrote. MDLAB really encapsulates everything I have worked for and everything I believe in, my multiple identities, experiences of war and my passion for social justice in this part of the world. And I think that what the lab does is already the kind of work you're thinking about for your project.

Indeed, MDLAB. Since 2010, with support from the Open Society Foundation, participants from Iraq, Syria, Yemen, Algeria, Tunisia, Egypt, Jordan, Palestine, Oman, UAE, Morocco and Lebanon have come together in Beirut each year, joined by Western academics and journalists. Writing with Lubna Maalaki in a 2017 article for a US journal on the role of the event in fostering agency among media literacy educators and activists, Melki was at pains to establish a context for the Western reader:

> Each academy, participants tell their travel stories: the participants from Palestine who braved the agony of crossing Israeli checkpoints – including a guy who snuck through a Gaza tunnel to make it into Egypt – only to face enough more discriminatory treatment by the Lebanese border police; the woman from Northern Iraq who had to drive 12 hours through dangerous militia-held towns to reach Baghdad airport after ISIS occupied her region and shut down the nearby airport; the cohort from Damascus who dodged mortar attacks on their drive to Beirut and spent eight hours at the Lebanese-Syrian border; the Yemeni participant who, after Sana's Airport was bombed, had to board a cattle-ship from Aden to Digibouti, where he spent 48 hours in detention, then flew to Jordan to face another 8 hours of interrogation and abuse before arriving three days late to Beirut; the Egyptian cohort, each of whom had to prove that they carry $2000 in cash at Beirut airport before being allowed in; and the Palestinian Professor from Ramallah who spent over 12 hours maneuvering Israeli checkpoints and Jordanian security only to be turned back home after the border officials noticed an Israeli stamp on his passport. Somehow these stories of Arab countries discriminating against their own people unify the diverse mix of participants. (Melki and Maalaki 2017: 57–58)

MDLAB works on three levels—building a critical mass of media educators in the region towards the facilitation of a resilient culture;

promoting media literacy in schools (with the help of UNESCO) and production of local texts, resources and pedagogical materials to reduce the reliance on cultural translation from Western contexts. It strikes me that, whilst the quote above illustrates a very different and difficult environment for this work, the struggle to promote media education for social justice and to 'resist any attempted perversion of its mission' (2017: 60) is shared with the project at hand.

Going Forwards

A plausible future requires a factual present. (Snyder 2018, ch 5, para 3)

This thinking has left us in no doubt that democracy is neither stable nor natural and that we can't assume that media students will necessarily understand its formulations or find it desirable without some educational work. In the next chapter, we'll spend more time on the difference the internet has made and will make to democracy and also to Media Studies, as "*When a society develops new technologies of information and communication, we might expect political changes as well. This applies even to a concept as venerable as democracy.*" (Susskind 2018: 224).

And to restate, to teach media students that fake news offers a challenge to a hitherto open, democratic media would be to mislead them. What the moral panic over misinformation does offer is an urgency, as the proliferation of new forms of propaganda and the widespread *abuses* of media literacy are seen by the wider public, policymakers, the liberal media and (some) politicians as more of a problem than long-standing inequalities in media representation. The Media Reform Coalition reminds us, however, of the need to keep our eyes on media ownership, while worrying about troll farms and algorithms:

It is time for an open and honest debate about the impact of media concentration on our democracy and our wider culture…. media plurality is not a luxury in the digital age but an essential part of a media system in which vested interests should not be allowed to dominate. We want to see independent media that are able to hold power to account and to serve their audiences and the public in general as opposed to shareholders, proprietors or politicians. In order to achieve this, we need a rebooted system of regulation that gets to grips with the complexities of media ownership in the twenty-first century; one that encompasses top-down measures to check the dominance of individual or corporate interests as well as bottom-up measures to support genuinely independent and not-for-profit media on the ground. Above all, we need a new system of regulation that addresses both the enduring (and in many ways intensifying) grip of legacy media on public debate as well as the control over news and information 'flow' wielded by tech giants. (2019: 4)

Media Studies is at the heart of this debate.

It is clear that there's no *one* type of democracy and the issues raised for media students about civic engagement, technology and mediated information require them to come to judgements about 'flavours' such as direct democracy, people's assemblies, referenda and more convoluted forms of political representation, and how they are related to media representation. For Varoufakis (2017), markets are in conflict with democracies. He paraphrases Churchill's famous hypothesis, that democracy is a bad form of governing but it's better than all the others, to suggest that one of the others is now our 'order of things'. I think it's appropriate to end this chapter with his question to his daughter, because I think it's a central question for media students as well:

Your era will be typified by the momentous clash between two opposing proposals: 'Democratize everything' versus 'Commodify everything'. Take your pick. The clash of these two opposing agendas will determine your future well after I have gone. If you wish to have any say in that future, then you and your contemporaries will have to form an opinion on this matter and articulate good arguments with which to win others to your point of view. (2017: 180–181)

Onward Journeys (Applications)

Media Studies has its key concepts, as outlined earlier: genre, representation, narrative, audience, ideology, effects. It also has a set of key contexts—Social, cultural, political, historical and economic. A Media Studies approach to a text will ask about the characteristics of the society in which the text was produced and circulated. This will raise questions about gender equality, class divisions, the extent to which the society is open, tolerant, democratic. It will take into account political events and history—how is the text representing conflict, economic conditions, protest movements, change? The economic conditions also include the industrial situation of the media text—is it a thriving sector or is it struggling? How are new technologies and shifting audience behaviours impacting the 'cultural industries' (Hesmondhalgh 2019) from which the text is generated, or is it produced outside of 'the media' and potentially disruptive in this sense?

Summary and Links to Next Chapter

> Once we searched Google, but now it searches us. Once we thought of digital services as free, but now surveillance capitalists think of us as free. Democracy has slept while surveillance capitalists amassed unprecedented concentrations of knowledge and power. These dangerous asymmetries are institutionalised in their ownership and control of our channels of social participation … and a stark inequality in the division of learning. They know more about us than we know about them. These new forms of social inequality are inherently antidemocratic. (Zuboff, in Naughton, 2019: 20–21)

Assessing the relationship between media and democracy is fundamental for meeting learning outcomes such as *the capacity to act and engage in citizenship through media, to become political agents in a democratic society* and *debate critically key questions relating to the social, cultural, political and economic role of the media*. This chapter has demonstrated the need for Media Studies to support a deep and critical understanding of democracy as a starting point for learning objectives such as *demonstrate appreciation and critical understanding of the media and their role both historically and currently in society, culture, politics and the economy* and *engage in critical debate about academic theories used in media studies,* since many of those theories relate to the over-arching political and philosophical questions about power, society, rights and the limits of freedom. This is, of course, overlooked in the discourse of derision about Media Studies, but let's not go there. Zuboff's alarming assessment requires us to apply these 'old school' critical questions to a relatively new context—the uses and abuses (including fake news), by humans, of the affordances of the internet. If 'democracy has slept', as she claims, then Media Studies needs, more than ever, to be 'woke'.

Onward Journeys (Applications)

App 7 During our filmed conversation with Fergal Keane, he gives the example of the BBC's *Africa Eye*'s technical analysis of social media video footage from Cameroon, showing the murder of women and children by soldiers, which the government had claimed to be 'fake news', casting doubts over where it was actually filmed. The BBC was able to utilise geo-technology to prove that the murders did take place on Cameroonian territory. For Media students, this takes us to the heart of the debate about artificial intelligence (AI), media and ethics. Whilst there is growing concern over the ability for people to use AI to produce deep-fake videos, this example shows technological forensics revealing the truth and holding power to account, the bedrock of free, democratic news media.

Follow up: https://www.cemp.ac.uk/summit/2018/ (Fergal Keane keynote, from 26:15).

Full piece: https://www.bbc.co.uk/news/av/world-africa-45599973/cameroon-atrocity-finding-the-soldiers-who-killed-this-woman.

App 8 The *InVID* platform enables journalist and media content creators to integrate social media content into their news output as verified and rights-cleared content, therefore "protecting the news industry from distributing fakes, falsehoods, lost reputation and lawsuits". This application (literally) is more for Media students' production work or experiential learning, though this is always-already a case of theory into practice. So either as a coursework project feeding back into understanding of the *social, cultural, political and economic role of the media* or as a stand-alone enquiry-based learning element of an 'exam topic', students can use the *InVID* verification plug-in and evaluate its function to debunk fake news.

Follow up: https://www.invid-project.eu/.

App 9 This chapter has been about the challenge fake news presents to democracy. We considered the role of media in democracy more broadly and challenged our assumptions about them. This all hinges on media plurality and diversity of representation. *The Engagement Lab* and *Civic Media Project* draw together a range of hyperlocal projects in which people either reimagine media for civic activism or take back control of media tools to connect and tell their stories. One example is *Access Dorset*, a platform for disabled people to produce citizen journalism. This is one of a huge range of such projects in the world, where underrepresented groups represent their lived experiences to audiences as familiar strangers. Media students should research this example, look at others from the Civic Media Project, then explore their local area for such activities and ideally start their own new civic media project. Again, this is enquiry-based active learning, in what we call a 'third space' (in between school and commu-nity, but where learning flows back and forth across the boundary and takes people forward on both sides). Most importantly, such a project will enrich the study of media and democracy and facilitate a more crit-ical gaze on the false binary between 'real' and 'fake', mainstream and alternative.

Follow up: http://civicmediaproject.org/works/civic-mediaproject/citizen journalismandcivicinclusionaccessdorset.

App 10 *Get Bad News* vs MDLAB: Get Bad News is an interactive game which offers an experiential 'learning gain' through role play—*"Drop all pretence of ethics and choose the path that builds your persona as an unscrupulous media magnate"*. It's a very good example of an approach that, later, we call 'Teaching about fishing'—part-way between fact-check-ing (Giving a Fish) and 'teaching to fish'—that's the full version, critical media literacy for sustainable, civic engagement in a mediated reality.

The best example of teaching to fish that I have encountered on my travels is the Media and Digital Literacy Academy of Beirut, led by Jad

Melki. This is a simple but important exercise—play the game, watch the MDLAB video and take a look through the open access curriculum resources. Reflect on the differences in approach, and whether MDLAB verifies the hypothesis this book is building.

Follow up: https://getbadnews.com/#intro and https://mdlab.lau.edu.lb/.

References

Baldwin, J. (2018). *Crt, Alt, Delete: How Politics and Media Crashed Our Democracy*. London: Hurst.

Barlow, D., & Mills, B. (2015). *Reading Media Theory: Thinkers, Approaches and Contexts*. Harlow: Pearson.

Biesta, G. (2017). Touching the Soul? Exploring an Alternative Outlook for Philosophical Work with Children and Young People. *Childhood and Philosophy, 13*(28).

Biesta, G. (2018). *Teaching Uncommon Values: Education, Democracy and the Future of Europe*. Neset II and EENEE Conference, Brussels, 22 November 2018.

Biesta, G. (2019). *Obstinate Education: Reconnecting School and Society*. Leiden: Brill Sense.

Coe, J. (2018). *Middle England*. London: Viking.

Commission on Social Mobility and Child Poverty Commission. (2014). *Elitist Britain*. London: Gov.UK.

Davies, N. (2009). *Flat Earth News*. London: Vintage.

Eduqas. (2017). *Online Media Revision Activity: DesiMag and Pointless Blog*. https://resource.download.wjec.co.uk.s3.amazonaws.com/vtc/2017-18/17-18_3-22/_eng/unit04/revision-activity-applying-theories-to-desim-ag-and-pointlessblog.html. Accessed 30 August 2019.

Fenton, N. (2016). *Digital, Political, Radical*. London: Polity.

Gerodimos, R. (2017, February 16). Russia Is Attacking Western Liberal Democracies. *Medium*. https://medium.com/@romangerodimos/russia-is-attacking-western-liberal-democracies-4371ff38b407.

Gessen, K. (2017, February 22). Killer, Kleptocrat, Genius, Spy: The Many Myths of Vladimir Putin. *The Guardian*.

Hesmondhalgh, D. (2019). *The Cultural Industries* (4th ed.). London: Sage.

Hoggart, R. (1957). *The Uses of Literacy*. London: Pelican.

Jones, O. (2014). *The Establishment: And How They Get Away with It.* London: Allen Lane.

Jukes, P. (2014). *Beyond Contempt: The Inside Story of the Phone Hacking Trial.* London: Canbury Press.

Kirkby, P. (2016). *Leading People 2016: The Educational Backgrounds of the UK Professional Elite.* Sutton Trust. https://www.suttontrust.com/wp-content/uploads/2016/02/Leading-People_Feb16-1.pdf.

Lanchester, J. (2018). *The Wall.* New York: W. W. Norton.

MacPherson, C. (1966). *The Real World of Democracy.* Oxford: Oxford University Press.

Mason, L., Krutka, D., & Stoddard, J. (2018). Media Literacy, Democracy, and the Challenge of Fake News. *Journal of Media Literacy Education, 10*(2), 1–10.

Media Reform Coalition. (2019). *Who Owns the UK Media?* London: Goldsmiths Leverhulme Media Research Centre/Media Reform Coalition. https://www.mediareform.org.uk/wp-content/uploads/2019/03/Who_Owns_the_UK_Media_2019.pdf.

Melki, J. (2018). Towards a Media Literacy of the Oppressed. *Media Education Research Journal, 8*(1), 5–14.

Melki, J., & Maalaki, L. (2017). Manouvering Entrenched Structures of Arab Education Systems: The Agency of Arab Media Literacy Educators and Activists. *Journal of Media Literacy, 64*(1–2), 56–60.

Morozov, E. (2017, January 8). Blaming Fake News Is Not the Answer. *The Guardian.*

Oates, S. (2008). *An Introduction to Media and Politics.* London: Sage.

O'Hara, K., & Hall, W. (2018). *4 Internets: The Geopolitics of Digital Governance.* Ontario: Centre for International Governance Innovation.

Press, A., & Williams, B. (2010). *The New Media Environment: An Introduction.* Oxford: Wiley-Blackwell.

Prutsch, M. (2015). *European Historical Memory: Policies, Challenges and Perspectives.* Strasbourg: European Parliament. http://www.europarl.europa.eu/thinktank/en/document.html?reference=IPOL_STU(2015)540364.

Snyder, T. (2018). *The Road to Unfreedom: Russia, Europe, America.* London: Random House.

Starbird, K. (2018, October 20). The Surprising Nuance Behind the Russian Toll Strategy. *Medium.* https://medium.com/s/story/the-trolls-within-how-russian-information-operations-infiltrated-online-communities-691fb-969b9e4.

Susskind, J. (2018). *Future Politics: Living Together in a World Transformed by Tech*. Oxford: Oxford University Press.

Thurman, N. (2016). *Journalists in the UK*. Oxford: Reuters Institute for the Study of Journalism.

Varoufakis, Y. (2017). *Talking to My Daughter: A Brief History of Capitalism*. London: Vintage.

Watson, J., & Hill, A. (2003). *A Dictionary of Communication and Media Studies*. London: Edward Arnold.

Yablokov, I. (2018). *Fortress Russia: Conspiracy Theories in Post-Soviet Russia*. London: Polity.

Zuboff, S. (2019). *The Age of Surveillance Capitalism: The Fight for a Human Future at the New Frontier of Power*. New York: Public Affairs.

4

Internet

It's the internet's thirtieth birthday, which coincides with a deluge of revelations about how out of control it is. Tim Berners-Lee, its creator, is not in a celebratory mood, instead reflecting on the dysfunctional adoption of his invention and calling for us to change direction before it is too late: *If we give up on building a better web now, then the web will not have failed us. We will have failed the web* (Berners-Lee 2019: 1).

> Our digital town squares have become mobbed with bullies, misogynists and racists, who have brought a new kind of hysteria to public debate. Our movements and feelings are constantly monitored, because surveillance is the business model of the digital age. Facebook has become the richest and most powerful publisher in history by replacing editors with algorithms – shattering the public square into millions of personalised news feeds, shifting entire societies away from the open terrain of genuine debate and argument, while they make billions from our valued attention. (Viner 2017: 31)

How did we get here? Can we agree, yet, on the history of the internet? Actually, the internet has been around for longer, so what we are really talking about is our use of it in the form of the web. This revolution in

© The Author(s) 2019
J. McDougall, *Fake News vs Media Studies*,
https://doi.org/10.1007/978-3-030-27220-3_4

human existence, like all the others before it, is about connection. The web enables every 'bit' to interact with every other in digital form. And what we're also talking about here is the subsequent use of the web by people with the capacity to organize it on our behalf, imposing order on infinite freedom—in other words, Google. Next, we're talking about the rapid race to make money out of the web—its economic model, in the form of advertising in return for 'free' use, and then the use of our data. And what makes all this possible is the way that the web encourages and rewards very quick interaction—the new 'attention economy'—at the expense of more measured consideration—and these would be the conditions for 'fake news':

> What seems to Sir Tim to subvert the whole intention of the web has been its capture by the attention economy, in which the interest of the public becomes the only measure of success, however much damage this may do to the public interest. By shortening the loop between urge and action, the web has had a particularly infantilising effect on its users. This is reflected in the extraordinary degree of polarisation, and indeed cruelty, seen online. It is an impulse uncontroller. (Guardian Editorial, 11 March 2019)

It's important to put the internet into the mix with the other agents, using the term from actor network theory. Information disorder is a mix of online misinformation threatening democracy; mainstream media contributing to the problem by circulating 'poor quality information' sourced online; a weakened local media reducing plurality and narrowing representation; the use of data for demographic targeting and the use of bots to manipulate and influence. All five of these elements are because of the internet, but we can see here that information disorder is a particular configuration of the human and non-human 'actants' in each relationship (Wardle and Derakhshan 2017: 4). Derakhshan's recent updating of 'information disorder' by way of a taxonomy consisting of nine sets of state, agent and target takes this view to another level with regard to understanding the agents in the network:

Agent is the creator of dis-/malinformation, target is whom the agent wishes to influence or manipulate in order to reach a specific goal which intends harm. (Derakhshan 2019: 1)

Just after Berners-Lee's call to arms, Carole Cadwalladr published another reflection, this one only a 12-month retrospective, looking back at her investigatory reporting bombshell, *The Cambridge Analytica Files*, and the resulting lack of action it. Perhaps, she muses, this is due not to a lack of outrage, but rather to an inertia, a feeling of helplessness (see also Briant 2018). She talks about this to Martin Moore, author of *Democracy Hacked* (2018), who agrees with her thesis:

It's like a driver going past a car wreck; we're transfixed by it, but we have no idea what to do about it. We're just at the beginning of recognizing the scale of this. We're in the middle of a huge transition, the fourth great communications transition after speech, writing and printing. And even breaking up Facebook is not going to save us from this, it's so much bigger than that. (Cadwalladr 2019: 13)

This all seems profoundly depressing for those of us who were thinking and writing about the second phase of the worldwide-web from a Media Studies perspective a few years ago, during a period in the subject's genealogy referred to as the 'Media 2.0' debate.

The Web vs Media Studies

How much of the internet is fake? Studies generally suggest that, year after year, less than 60 percent of web traffic is human; some years, according to some researchers, a healthy majority of it is bot…. Everything that once seemed definitively and unquestionably real now seems slightly fake; everything that once seemed slightly fake now has the power and presence of the real. The "fakeness" of the post-Inversion internet is less a calculable falsehood and more a particular quality of experience — the uncanny sense that what you encounter online is not "real" but is also undeniably not "fake," and indeed may be both at once, or in succession, as you turn it over in your head. (Read 2018: 1)

Web 2.0 described a transition point whereby the web became more like Berners-Lee's vision, web 1.0 was a 'push down' mass media internet with producers making content for audiences, then web 2.0 allowed us to share media among ourselves—horizontal connection instead of vertical production and consumption. Web 3.0 responds to our needs and influences our actions, as well as extending into augmented spaces—'the internet of things'.

It was the web 2.0 moment that opened up a huge can of worms for Media Studies.

Back in 2007, David Gauntlett argued for a re-framing of the subject in which "*The view of the Internet and new digital media as an 'optional extra' is replaced with recognition that they have fundamentally changed the ways in which we engage with all media*" (Gauntlett, 2007: 2) and later, in a more overarching account of a new approach to the subject focused more on 'making':

> Media have changed from being primarily about watching, listening and reading to being about creating and discussing and so bringing about change in people, ideas and culture. (2015: 9)

Taken together, the various strands of the MS 2.0 thesis were that the academic subject needed to urgently respond to the digital age by working in the spaces of the new, transformed media culture, which are defined profoundly by interaction and networking, with a more fluid and de-centred ecosystem of production and new modes of 'produsage', a shift to an active audience and, ultimately, to a more democratic media. Here's Dan Tapscott in one of the many commentaries on 'digital natives'—the idea that a generation (*Y*) was emerging for whom broadcast, analogue media would be merely the stuff of history lessons:

> The print media company and the TV network are hierarchical organisations that reflect the values of their owners. New media, on the other hand, give control to all users. The distinction between bottom-up and top-down organisational structure is at the heart of the new generation. For the first time ever, young people have taken control of critical elements of a communications revolution. (p. 21)

Whilst we must stress that the advocates of a '2.0' curriculum were never proposing an uncritical, cyber-utopian celebration of all things shiny and new, they were stark in their assessment of the conventional practices of 'Media Studies 1.0':

> If digital media are the result of the meeting and merger of computing and mass media then we need to teach our students computing to enable them to produce software and products for themselves. One thing at least is certain: filling students' time by teaching them how to use a video camera or making them pretend to be a newsreader in a fake studio is a waste of their fees and an inadequate training for the 21st century. (Merrin 2014: 186)

Gauntlett (2015) more recently described the reformulation of Media Studies after the internet as a *"diminished blob of the old themes, but with two new peaks of exciting and vital activity, everyday making and data exploitation and surveillance"*. So not quite where we'd want to be if we fully embraced Henry Jenkins' 'transmedia learning principles' to the extent of 'a post-disciplinary, epistemological reboot', but getting there.

So, Media Studies 2.0 never quite happened, and some of the different arguments made for both returning our focus to political economy and for celebrating 'quality journalism' are pretty 1.0.

If Only Something Could Be Done in Schools?

The widespread consensus that schools should be the 'safe space' for fostering resilience to fake news is uncontentious. As with everything, if you talk about it openly, it's easier to deal with, goes the logic. Furthermore, if a critical understanding of what's fake, and why that is bad, is developed in the classroom, then we are less likely to raise a generation of hyper-cynical citizens with no trust in any information, in effect tuning out of the public sphere and leaving the big decisions to those who have created this situation in the first place—a perfect storm of abusive power and compliance through disengagement. So this more generic educational approach would cover the subgenres of fake news, zoom in on the more serious and subtle issues and then teach approaches such as source-checking; lateral checking of links and examples; reverse image searching; triangulation by mainstream media and the risks of passing on dubious information prior to conducting those safeguards (see Hewitt 2017) (Fig. 4.1).

As we have established, fake news isn't new and Media Studies deconstructs all media, including 'real news'. But the internet is a new challenge for all of us – governments, teachers, lawyers, everyone! The very precarious balance between control of content and freedom of expression has enabled social media platforms to evade regulation. Currently, the UK press sector is self-governed by IPSO, working to an editors' code of practice. Article 1 of this code prohibits *inaccurate, misleading or distorted information* or images. Where this is proven, apologies are usually printed later. The Broadcasting Code is managed by Ofcom, and compliance includes *due accuracy and due impartiality* with legal and financial penalties for violations.. Social media falls between, or outside of, these codes. The same is largely true of European Union directives. Article 10 of the European Convention on Human Rights protects free expression, and much of the material posted on social media that we would want to live without is covered by this convention. It is very difficult to see how greater regulation of the internet can be achieved without curtailing free speech.

Structure and Agency

Sonia Livingstone, OBE, is at the intersection of all these strands. I believe that *The Class,* her deep ethnography with Julian Sefton-Green (2016) is *the* single most important piece of research published into young people, technology and education and I insist every doctoral researcher I work with now reads it. We've worked on an EU report together and she's keynoted at our Summit, in Rome. Her day job is Professor of Social Psychology in the Department of Media and Communications at the London School of Economics and she's very widely published on media audiences, media literacy and regulation. Her academic work has impacted the UK government, European Commission, European Parliament, Council of Europe and other

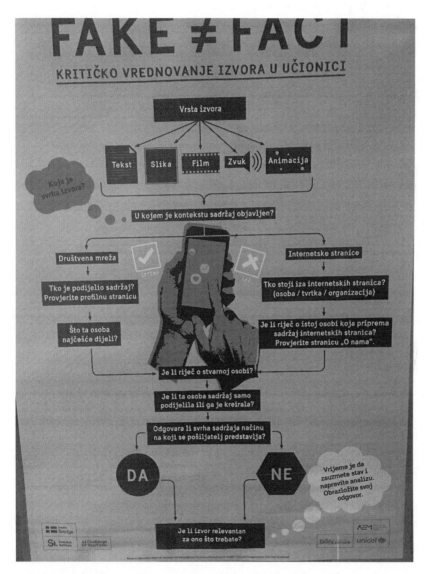

Fig. 4.1 Fighting fake news, Croatia (*Source* Author)

national and international organisations on children's rights, risks and safety in the digital age. Her OBE was awarded for 'services to children and child internet safety.' Recent projects of note include *Global Kids*

Online (UNICEF and EU); *Parenting for a Digital Future* and the *Truth, Trust and Technology Commission*.

She comes to all this from a different trajectory to me and most of the other educators I am interviewing, being more informed by psychology, initially:

> I was trained as a social psychologist at a time when the media environment was changing dramatically and interestingly. And so in trying to put psychology in a place that seemed to have something to contribute and seemed part of a wider social change, the study of audiences was the obvious way to bring the two together and then somewhere about halfway through my career I became increasingly interested in not only the descriptive and explanatory, in other words how people live in a mediated word, but also the normative, which is how could people's lives be made better by and through media and that took me into media literacy as a sort of label for policy and practice interventions or another strand of regulation. So if I imagine ordinary people living in a mediated world, which is where I began, then how could their lives be better or different? Media literacy is one kind of solution and media regulation is another. And I'm really interested in the inter-dependence between them and I guess I see them as a kind of structure-agency interplay.

How has this 'way in' marked her out as thinking differently about all this stuff, I wonder?

> I'll start by saying of course it's terribly complicated but I think the question for a social psychologist (and I insist on social because it's precisely at that interface) is the longer term question about social influence, in other words how do we come to understand ourselves and the world that we are part of in a social environment and through social relationships and so the question of unequal uses and abuses of power within those social relationships has always been crucial and the fact that the media, especially the big platforms, have become a very rapid intervention into what was a very delicate balance, if you like, of what we understood about the influences upon us, the fact of the sudden arrival of these big platforms has disrupted and made very apparent and very problematic all the different influences that people are experiencing and the challenge they must face in deciding what to believe, what to trust and what is going to be in their

interests. So I would say that for a social psychologist, there's nothing new about fake news, we've been studying propaganda since people first started opening their mouths and speaking to each other and seeing that there's something to gain by pulling the wool over someone else's eyes, so it's one of the oldest topics, but in a fantastically complicated media environment where the commercial interests are just so huge and the potential for manipulation is so enormous, the burden on ordinary people to be media literate is overwhelming and actually too much for anyone to be expected to manage, which is why I come back to the necessary balance between media literacy and media regulation - which is where we say, as a society, there is a limit to what people can know and learn and manage for themselves and at that point we need to take a structural intervention in the public interest.

At this point I throw in the observation from my *BuzzFeed* interview about the distinction between literacy and morality.

Well, I've been interviewing young people about where their data goes and their sense of privacy and that's a related thing, people keep saying young people have no sense of privacy, but when I say that to these kids, they are outraged. They have an absolute sense of privacy and similarly they have a very strong sense of fairness, in fact I'd go so far as to say every child is born with a very strong sense of what's fair and the first thing your three-year-old says is 'it's not fair!' so of course they have a morality. But we have created a world for them in which their morality doesn't get them very far and isn't terribly beneficial to them and we have also, as an older generation, increased the amount of competition around them and pressure on them so they've got to play a very fast game in which they compete or they lose and that is also very different. I grew up with a less competitive environment, a welfare state, a slower pace of change and greater tolerance for mistakes and for recovery. So young people are living in a high-risk environment, trying to protect their sense of morality in this media landscape is intensifying all of those problems.

So, the role of teachers?

Educators can never try one thing and have one magic intervention. We've just launched our 'Truth, Trust and Technology' report and one of the things we've said is that it may be hard to teach people to identify the truth but we can certainly teach them to identify lies. I mean we teach one point of education as to make judgement and to provide a criteria for doing that, we are not going to be able to produce a rule of thumb that says 'this is fake and this is real', in any simple sense, without young people being taught about the larger network of information flows behind anything that they happen to see. So, we've got to start teaching about network effects, about the operation of algorithms and automated processes, about the international nature of the internet so how what teenagers do in Nigeria or Macedonia can, through these network effects, have disruptive consequences in completely different contexts. I'm a rationalist, so maybe something about the process of having to argue and defend your case, teaching them as it were the kind of transferable skills of critical media literacy which can apply to many things – how strong is the argument, have you considered the counter-argument, have you considered the evidence, how does this argument stack up against the alternative, processes of dialogue and debate. Will it be enough? No, I'll say again, education can only go so far and some things have to be regulated out of the system, so in another context I might say let's break up Facebook, let's strengthen the electoral commission's role in relation to regulating political advertising and let's ban bots from Twitter. We can't expect kids to deal with all of that but we can teach them to understand the internet better, through critical media literacy.

Isn't that just making Media Studies compulsory, then?

I think it would be a brilliant thing to do. We do say that in the T3 report, if this is going to be addressed in the curriculum, is it a PSHE (Personal, Social and Health Education) question, is it a citizenship question, but why shouldn't it be Media Studies? But you know that the difficulty, once we are where we are, is that very few kids take Media Studies but I agree with you because until young people understand the nature of representations, the nature of networks, about the major organisations behind the management of both the representations and the networks, without understanding that, they're not really going to grasp either the nature of the problem or the solution. But it's just been a really bad history for Media Studies and it's a peculiarly British history. It's a peculiar legacy of British education that that media has seemed like leisure and

Britain has the most weird kind of 'back to basics' moral ethos, other countries seem to have adjusted to a different notion of media education without it being trivial or 'what the working classes do' and 'we want kids to learn their times tables properly and put their kings and queens in order'. We've never had a notion of education as social, we've never really embraced critical pedagogy, we've always preferred to beat little boys!

The T3 report (*Trust, Truth and Technology*) was produced by the London School of Economics. It sets out a policy framework for 'Media System Resilience' by identifying five elements that require an urgent policy response—confusion (over what to believe); cynicism (loss of trust in information); fragmentation (echo chambers, division of citizens into discrete 'truth publics'); irresponsibility (organisations working outside of ethical codes and transparency) and, arising as the sum of these parts, citizen apathy (disengagement from the public sphere and loss of faith in democracy). (see LSE 2019: 10).

As part of a holistic, integrated strategy for 'rising above the fray' (2019: 2) to address these 'five giant evils' of the current information crisis, the educational proposal mirrors this book's agenda:

Media literacy is a complex and demanding topic to teach and learn. It is vital that this is thoroughly embedded in classroom education and also that it extends well beyond the classroom to enable civic and political engagement of diverse kinds, for adults as well as children. In a crowded curriculum, neither Media Studies nor Citizenship education have been prioritised, with the former studied by only a minority and the latter barely finding space in the curriculum. Neither receives the cross-curricular attention required, and there are concerns about the level and quality of media literacy teaching resources. Information literacy is in the Citizenship curriculum and that is compulsory, but there is little time for critical digital literacy. As a subject, Media Studies has been marginalized. (2019: 26)

On Regulation

The 3T report calls for an Independent Platform Agency (IPA) *to "Monitor whether all relevant parties are fulfilling their responsibilities to ensure that the UK information environment is one in which citizens can contribute to democracy effectively, and making policy recommendations to address problems that arise."* (p. 36). Soon after my discussion with Sonia, Mark Zuckerberg called for both regulators and governments to intervene more in regulating the internet, going as far as to provide a framework, with four areas highlighted as requiring such attention. These are, according to Facebook's CEO, harmful content, election integrity, privacy and data portability. His proposal would be cross-platform, with common rules for all social media to comply with. It also suggests a requirement for Facebook and other digital corporations to adhere to new standards of transparency, with regard also to political content prior to elections. Zuckerberg set this out in a piece for the *Washington Post*, perhaps strategically using an 'old media' text to get the message out:

> The rules governing the Internet allowed a generation of entrepreneurs to build services that changed the world and created a lot of value in people's lives. It's time to update these rules to define clear responsibilities for people, companies and governments going forward. (Zuckerberg 2019: 2)

In April 2019, the UK Government published a White Paper on the regulation of online content, via a statutory 'duty of care', to be monitored by an independent regulator such as OFCOM. This would be retrospective punishment for breaches of this duty, with financial and personal liability for companies and executives, respectively. The duty will apply to platforms, search engines and hosting services. Where specific concerns arise, such as terrorism or exploitation of children or vulnerable groups, the government will have the power to direct the independent body. Social media companies will be obligated to publish transparency reports (as suggested by Zuckerberg). Of direct significance here, *"The code of practice is also likely to include the steps companies will be expected to take to combat disinformation, including by using fact-checking services, particularly during election periods, and improving the transparency of political advertising."* (Stewart and Hern 2019: 2).

This is a major departure from three decades of the free web and was, thus, met with concern:

To bolster its case for censorship, the government conflates activity that is already illegal both online and offline – including terrorism, child abuse and modern slavery – with more subjective and perfectly legal harms. The White Paper even acknowledges this, listing harmful content it plans to tackle which, in its words, have an 'unclear definition', such as 'cyberbullying and trolling', 'extremist content' and 'disinformation' (aka fake news). These areas are entirely subjective: one man's extremism is another woman's sincerely held belief. 'Trolling' can extend from playful banter to persistent harassment. The 'fake news' label is often wielded to denounce uncomfortable truths and unpopular opinions. (Myers 2019: 2)

Then, in May 2019, news breaks of Singapore's Protection from Online Falsehoods and Manipulation Bill, passed by a large majority in Parliament and condemned by the United Nations as an 'Orwellian' infringement of the principle of free speech, with the law covering social messaging apps as well as social media.

Back in the United Kingdom, aside from the political and ethical debate over free speech versus protection from harm, the big question is over enforcement of the White Paper's recommendations. Can the regulator's algorithm be outsmarted by those it is trying to 'catch', and will the 'grey area' in which a lot of the online material with the greatest negative impact (for example, cyber-bullying, the promotion of self-harm and, yes, 'fake news') be in the net, given much of this is not illegal?

But Buckingham questions this 'trust in trust' (my phrase) by first reminding us that an apparent decline in trust, and the attendant moral panic about the societal implications, is nothing new, and second, offering a critical take on the assumption that trust is positive. At the very least, when assessing the 'five giant evils' of the information crisis that frame the 3T report, it's important to distinguish between trust in media and trust in the people they represent:

As ever, there is a danger of shooting the messenger here. Amid the chaos of the UK's Brexit debate, it's hard to see what politicians have done to earn or deserve our trust – and that's not the fault of the media. However, the growing spread of disinformation, and the cacophony of 'alternative truths' that are spread online – which some have called 'information pollution' or 'truth decay' – have almost certainly undermined people's trust in the media themselves. And arguably, the more we understand about phenomena like invisible algorithms and filter bubbles and online surveillance, the more distrustful we are likely to become. (Buckingham 2019: 3)

Empirical work from journalism studies also raises critical questions about trust. Karlsson and Clerwall (2018) worked with thirteen focus groups to explore cornerstones in citizens' ideas about quality journalism, using Bourdieu's concept of 'doxa' (2013), through which we can understand normative values about the essence of 'good journalism':

> The findings suggest that the respondents' views about good journalism are quite in accordance with the traditional norms of the journalistic field; however, there is more emphasis on stylistic and linguistic qualities. Few calls are made for transparency. The results suggest that a remedy to the decreasing trust in news may not lay in the changing of norms, but rather in how already established norms and values of the journalistic field are performed. (2018: 1)

TOOLKIT#5 4 Internets vs 3 Theories

The *4 Internets* report by the Centre for International Governance Innovation (CIGI) observes these competing versions of the internet—the *open* internet, the *bourgeois* internet, the *authoritarian* internet and the *commercial* internet (O'Hara and Hall 2018).

The published theoretical framework for A Level Media Studies includes *Media Industries: how the media industries' processes of production, distribution and circulation affect media forms and platforms* and theories from Curran and Seaton, Livingstone and Lunt and Hesmondhalgh.

So, this is a difficult activity. To be honest, more difficult than would be needed to get through the A Level exam. But for progression to University, or just generally for an even more resilient media literacy armory, students should apply the three theories to the four internets and decide which internet will prevail, under the terms of reference of each theory.

Doing Media Differently vs *Doing Greggs*

Sarah Jones and Dave Harte run the Birmingham Media School. Its Parkside campus is the most expensive in the United Kingdom and BCU proudly boast of its use by the creative industries as well as by the students progressing on to them. As such, we can consider Jones and Harte at the vanguard of developing the next generation of media creatives and journalists, but with a twist. Framed by their *#domediadifferently* mission statement and 'Rethinking Media' conference, the school is about a critical dialogue with media industries. I wanted to get into the question of how much of doing media differently is different because of the internet.

First, their trajectories, which I know are also interestingly different:

> *Sarah*: I was a journalist, in television news as a correspondent, reporter and producer, on local, national and international news, in the UK and US and then I moved into the University world, teaching journalism and then on to management and research.
>
> *Dave*: After 21 years here I now feel more like a professional media educator than someone from a profession coming into that, in fact my pre-University life was in community media, with a project in Handsworth which was set up actually to address gaps in media provision for black and working class communities in inner city Birmingham. Citizen media and hyperlocal media have remained an interest, into my PhD and a large AHRC (Arts and Humanities Research Council) project, I've always been interested in the media stuff people do as hobbyists as well as because they are riled up about something.

So how is doing media differently more different in the context of fake news misinformation, post-truth for 'thought-leaders' in their sub-fields of virtual reality journalism and hyperlocal media, respectively?

> *Sarah*: When you look at immersive journalism and virtual reality, we speak of this as an empathy machine, allowing you to feel a story and then switching the perspective from hearing to feeling, you realise the

power you have as a journalist, what is it that a story is trying to make someone feel? I worry about aspects of the 'hacktivism' movement in this regard, 'news for good', heralded as the antidote to fake news but actually it's similar. An approach where you are trying to get people to think in a certain way to donate to a cause, it changes journalism fundamentally.

Dave: it's striking if I look back at the transcripts from research we did with community journalists, that term (fake news) doesn't appear, but what they do talk about are ways in which mainstream media are representing them as fake, or false. So people living in spaces which were being misrepresented by mainstream media, running a hyperlocal news blog as a response to reading mainstream media stories about what a nightmare it is to live in the area, so wanting to redress unrepresentative claims about their area, countering it with a different mix of stories. That became a theme, that the mainstream local press doesn't tell the truth about where people live. So not accusing mainstream media of doing fake news about particular issues, but about a lack of balance. Another theme was from members of the public, that there's a bit too much truth! For example, in Castle Vale in Birmingham, it's a white working class area, that had a community newspaper run by a trained journalist who would tell it like it is, but members of the public were uncomfortable with stories about crime on their streets and they wanted more information about day to day services and activities, more banal stuff if you like, that should be the emphasis. Then we ran a workshop and gave participants a newspaper layout to show what they'd like to see reported and they made up stories, they had this imagined story about a homeless person being rescued and doing amazing things for the community, the function of this in their eyes was to counter a narrative about Castle Vale. From that, I got the sense that even though the discourse of 'fake news' hadn't hit at that time, the idea of truth and authenticity, those issues were always in play, the issue of countering dominant myths about the place where we live. That really challenged the journalism practitioners working on the project, the assumption that crime is something you should report in the paper and the argument that you shouldn't.

Sarah: that's another play on the Trump narrative, it's really interesting, another version of 'it's fake news'.

Dave: or another version of 'telling it like it is', as in 'it's OK round here, it's really quite nice actually'.

I move on to the question of why media education is viewed as the 'go to' for all this everywhere except in the United Kingdom? I've heard answers on this from many of my participants, but these two are really 'in the mix' with such a large media school and such clear and present industry partnerships. Why is it and is there hope that out of all this cyber-anxiety might spring some hope for what we're doing?

> *Dave:* well, partly there's some technological determinism about the current narrative, a belief in tools, like the resources produced by the industry being favoured over education, the idea that the digital got us into this so it can get us out again. There's a sense that we can solve this problem by loitering on the internet and hunting down falsity, either by broadcasters or agencies identifying economic opportunities to solve the authenticity problem. But I agree with you that the Media Studies literature from the 1980s and 1990s applies to this, Greg Filo's 'Bad News', picking apart reporting of the Miners' Strike, so it's surprising when you think about it that instead of going there we get this simpler narrative of solving a digital problem with digital tools. And also, in class, we talk about why you might want to spread fake news, we look at the example of David Attenborough's Facebook post about saving bees with sugared water on a spoon, and of course it wasn't Attenborough, but there's that thing about wanting it to be true, and students had saved bees through this method! It would have taken so little to check and find out it was posted by some geezer from Norwich. There's not much in the public discourse about us wanting things to be true so much that we help things go viral without checking, more out of hope than belief. Media education is a good space for that more complex discussion, but I have little faith in the idea that verification tools can save us.
>
> *Sarah:* The new terminology is frustrating, this been part of the news industry forever, this is just commonplace, whether it's "Freddie Starr ate my Hamster", or back to reporters being given stories by the Hollywood studios in the 50s, that's been the industry, there aren't that many big breaking stories that are real news, it's things on cycles, the news media churning all the time. In 2007, I was working a shift when the Haiti earthquake happened and it was around the start of Twitter and this was the first story I went to Twitter for. We found someone talking about Haiti, and we were really excited that we were using

social media to drive the story, and it turned out it was someone in Boston, and that was back then! So why now, is it just about a new generation of people wanting to believe stuff, or is it things going viral that's new, but even then wasn't that the case with something like Live Aid in the 80s? It's not new.

Dave: I don't see enough interest in the economics of fake news and its relationship with mainstream media. My starting point is local news, it's quite buoyant at the moment, it's had money via the BBC for local democracy reporters, a scheme that's working very well, more covering of local issues from councils and an interest in local democracy. But of course, the reason why you get a story about there not being a Greggs drive-through in your locality or last night's TV, these are a kind of clickbait, but the publishers' argument is that these stories are what people want, and we know that from the analytics, and then once people are at the site, they are drawn into read the stories about local council doing bad things, so there's an economics to this stuff, these aren't in the fake news realm, but these are banal stories drawing people in for more important stuff. But then what happens is that you then run a series of links underneath from third parties, and that's a grey space in terms of real or fake news, PPI claim sites, that kind of stuff. But there's a mixed economy, a political economy of fake news that's not getting enough attention from Media Studies either, the reliance on fake news by mainstream media, both to support its discursive position but also financially, it might need it to exist?

As the leaders of a huge Media School, their thoughts on how these discursive shifts around news, internet and core values, albeit not 'real' historical changes, are impacting on, or will be a catalyst for, curricular dynamics?

Sarah: at open days, I always talk about a student who went on to a job as a 'trending video reporter', it's specifically about clickbait, about driving traffic and there are lots of jobs now along those lines. Driven by analytics, totally.

Dave: Media schools have to come to terms with the split between what journalism studies is for and journalism training, from industry perspectives, so that's about holding power to account and I'll teach you how to do it. So that's valid, but there's real value in having students question at all times what it is that they are being taught, but these two things are difficult to hold within the same school. I made a pitch recently—why isn't there a module about sausage rolls? Because in their early career, these are the issues, having a strong sense of holding these two things together, the hardcore stuff, the ethics, but doing the Greggs story but also holding power to account, being both kinds of journalist, but that's the reality.

Sarah: in the UK, because we have the BBC and OFCOM we have this snobbery, we think we're above it all, and you see that on the parents' faces when I talk about the trending video reporter as a graduate employment route!

Dave: And the students are oddly uncomfortable with it as well. Really, we need a journalism satire module where students work on a hyper-local site where nothing is a real story, but I'm not going to be able to pitch that internally. But if students operated in that space alongside going to report on the courts, I think they'd get a more rounded sense of what journalism is about now. Satire seems to me to be unexplored in journalism education, a lot of satire uses the local as a signifier, 'satire in the suburbs', that's an unwritten paper with a great title.

On the question of why there is no module on a Media degree about sausage rolls, Harte shares his developing work on the importance of understanding…

…what we might call 'banal' news; forms of journalistic content that have become an ever-present feature within news ecologies. From local stories about lost animals on citizen journalism websites, news about celebrities undertaking everyday tasks, to stories about the opening (or sometimes non-opening) of shops, such content enters the readers' field of view whether they like it or not. The social spaces we now commonly use to read news come with the affordances to propagate such content, to the extent that its growth almost seems unstoppable. While it may be easy to dismiss this content as trivial and banal, for some scholars (Cable and Mottershead 2018) it is problematic, crowding out 'real' journalism by reducing quality in favour of the need for a click-through at whatever cost. Setting out the parameters for a critical engagement with clickbait and banal news content by taking a critical political economy approach supports a questioning of how normative news values ignore the "life situations of a large segment of population in any society" (Sonwalkar 2005: 261). (Harte 2018: 1)

As we'll discuss further when considering the implications and implementation of the 2019 *Cairncross Review*, the status of hyperlocal news media appears to be better understood by Media Studies than by government:

> Citizen journalists and hyperlocal news providers are perceived to add a valuable set of new voices to the news ecology, but the perceived democratic value of these voices is limited by their reach, motivations, professional values, and sustainability. My comparison of emerging forms of local journalism with mainstream news media has shown that new news forms are not yet seen as fulfilling or replacing any of the democratic roles of news that are in decline in the mainstream media (Firmstone, 2016, Firmstone and Coleman, 2015). New entrants online tend to be hyperlocal (serving very small communities), serve niche audiences, have aims and values that differ from professional journalists, and face far greater threats to their sustainability than the press. Any value that such entrants add cannot be relied upon to replace what is being lost due to the precarious nature of most of their funding models. (Firmstone 2018: 3)

Decontamination vs Algorithms

> The steady stream of "news" items on social media feeds may not seem like a Big Data problem because individual users generally only see one news feed at a time—their own—and the real-time procession of updates and postings appears superficially manageable, or at least ignorable. But aggregated, the propagation of user-generated content across billions of accounts worldwide on a 24/7/365 basis adds up, making the scope of activity vast but difficult to quantify, let alone verify. (Bucy and Newhagen 2018: 5)

Here's an example of the scale of 'contamination' (UNESCO's term for misinformation in the 'post-truth' context) and the effort it takes to clean it up. In the Philippines, Rappler is an investigative social news network that discovered over 300 websites disseminating fake news in the region, leading up to the 2016 elections. After three months of painstaking, manual checking of Facebook accounts, these were the findings:

> We found that one nest of twenty–six fake accounts is able to influence nearly three million Facebook pages. We also know that, as of November 2016, about 50,000 Facebook accounts can be used in targeted campaigns for or against politicians or individuals in the Philippines. Another fake account was linked to over 990,000 members of groups supporting one political leader, and yet another was connected to an estimated 3.8 million members of various overseas Filipino organizations and buy–and-sell groups. With about 54 million Facebook users in the Philippines, social media is a powerful weapon used to silence dissent and mould public opinion. (Resser 2017: 72)

The key distinction that Media Studies must make is this. We are not comparing like with like when we look at the 'news values' (Galtung and Ruge 1965) of a broadcaster or newspaper with that of Facebook. There may be no difference between those values, except that the editor of Facebook is not Mark Zuckerberg. Instead, the real editor is the algorithm. The algorithm gives a whole new meaning to 'power without responsibility' (Curran and Seaton 2018):

> Algorithms continue to shape the reading habits of one-fifth of the world's population. Facebook scans and analyzes all the information posted by any given user in the previous week, taking into account every page that he or she has liked, all the groups he/she belongs to and everybody he/she follows. Then, according to a closely-guarded and constantly evolving formula, the algorithms rank the posts in the precise order they believe the user will find worthwhile. (Yaloyan 2017: 18)

Michel Foucault has loomed large over Media Studies. In the chapter on 'post-truth', we'll look at how the theories of his that we've enjoyed applying to our subject have become reality in ways we weren't expecting and don't approve of! One of his major contributions to philosophy (1980) involved seeing how knowledge and power are related, as powerful *discourses* take on a life of their own in social reality. He didn't foresee Google, a corporation whose reason for being is to literally filter our discourse. The term 'filter bubble' is a good metaphor for Foucault's ideas. And the way we both accept, and often joke about, the way that these filter bubbles construct an 'echo chamber' to reinforce how we think and reduce our exposure to alternative ideas, would be an example of the normative functioning of discourse—it becomes everyday, we don't resist it. Following my viewing of *Citizen 4*, the film about Edward Snowden (Poitras 2014), I got spooked by Google and Facebook so I tried to live without them for a while. Finding alternative search engines which don't track you is easy enough, and I'm on Twitter 24/7 so I my social media needs are met. But it soon became impossible to function without Google's extensions—maps, document sharing, cloud storage for photos in particular, so I had to give up. I'm still off Facebook, and I can do my academic networking through Twitter, but I miss out on social stuff as a result! Anyway, the point here is that the boundaries we have created for ourselves are tangible only when we try to break out of them. Our 'data selves' (Lupton 2016) have a better life, it seems.

Are we digressing from the internet here, though? Is it possible, and important, still, to distinguish between the internet and 'the digital': algorithms, data, fake news and information disorder? Is the internet a medium? In which case a Media Studies course could, and arguably should, still cover it as one medium among others?

> It tends to feel like part of our lives to the extent that we don't think about when we are 'on the internet' or not…. From the perspective of media ecology, the internet – as an intrinsic part of digital society – is a medium because it is an environment. And conversely, it is an environment because it is a medium. (Lindgren 2017: 18)

If data really is 'the new oil', then the vocational modality of Media Studies will be remiss to ignore it, as the current specifications for schools do. Currently, big data is subject to a clamour by educational leaders, policy makers and commercial third parties for profitable utilisation. But in the curriculum? Williamson (2017) observes the challenge to education:

The field of education needs to involve itself in this new problem space. It needs to probe how young people are measured and known through traces of their data from an early age; how their tastes and preferences are formed through social media feedback loops; how these relate to entrenched patterns of educational and other social inequalities; and how their sense of their place and their futures in democratic societies is formed as they encounter the public pedagogies of big data and social media in their everyday lives. (Williamson 2017: 203)

Again, enter Media Studies.

Lindgren applies McLuhan's conceptual framework (1964) to the internet to distinguish between the internet as a medium and the messages it facilitates, not in terms of texts or content but in terms of the social transformations they create. It's pretty clear that the internet is transforming our ways of thinking and acting. So, Media Studies is about analysing how the web (as a medium) impacts social relations, compared to other media. In our terms of reference this has to do with the internet, news and the social actions we take when we share. In contrast with analogue media, the features of this relatively new medium—manipulation of time and space, modification enabled, open user-friendly tools for users to make content—are important in nudging us towards these new social relations. Pursuing this contrast a bit further, Media Studies also needs to break out of its own disciplinary insulations to be able to understand how these internet-transformed social relations are also emotional and affective. Sharing is the key, distinctive activity when we are comparing the internet with broadcast media. Sharing might be little more than a tangible, even visceral form of media reception as was always-already happening. Or it might be that sharing over the internet is different, more passionate and engaged, more *intense*. Ahmed (2004) calls this 'sticky'. Internet sharing is sticky when loaded with personal or social associations. This is also a 'two-way street', as Lindgren observes:

> People connect, disconnect, share and react because of emotions that they experience in doing so. These emotions might be both positive and negative, and are often much more intense that many early internet

researchers expected. The internet, therefore, is a space where affect is both activated and expressed. Not only does it arouse and transmit emotions, it also influences how those emotions are shaped and displayed. (2017: 132)

Summary and Links to Next Chapter

In these pages, the objective has been to pinpoint the significance of the internet, specifically, in matters at hand for Media Studies. Next, we will turn to news itself, and think through the extent to which a traditional Media Studies approach, involving news values, gatekeeping, selection and construction and the interplay of editors and owners, has 'stopped making sense'.

For this purpose, Divina Frau-Meigs, featured in the previous chapter, also offers us a clear link to the next:

It is important that media literacy exercises critical thinking against the media itself. It turns out that the top press organizations are among the biggest influencers and the ones who tend to push rumours, on Twitter for example, before they are confirmed. The fake news that circulates on Facebook, the first of the social media to spread it, draws its grain of truth from the fact that news professionals are overly responsive to the pressure of the scoop, transmitted before it is checked, in the same manner as the amateurs. And the denials do not generate as much buzz as the rumours! (Frau-Meigs 2017: 15).

But even this approach risks maintaining another 'false binary'— between fake news and 'the media'. Media Studies won't accept this. At the very least, it seems clear that the subject has to reappraise its internal relationship between media ethics and the micropolitics of clickbait in the realm of the hyper-local and counter-representational, as Dave Harte suggests. This critical deconstruction of the idea of 'the media' itself involves understanding that, in the sense of always being representational, gate-kept, ideological and subject to bias arising from commercial and political imperatives, 'all news is fake news'.

Onward Journeys (Applications)

App 11 The LSE's *3T* report sets up a number of reflective, enquiry-based learning activities. Students might directly relate the '5 evils' of the information crisis to their own lives—do they 'see no evil' or can they provide examples of their complicity in these problems? They might use a blog, or online forum space to comment on one another's reflections, adding a comparative element. Then, going back to the source, they might write a letter to Tim Berners-Lee, in response to his 30th birthday account of the state of the internet today, along the lines of *Dear Tim, on my role in the failure of your invention*. Third, stepping up more to the public sphere policy level, an analysis of Zuckerberg's proposal against the T3 framework—is he 'on message', is there some common ground, or is there tension between the two proposals?

Follow up: http://www.lse.ac.uk/media-and-communications/truth-trust-and-technology-commission/The-report.

App 12 Dave Harte's class on fake news offers an excellent mapping of the terrain, discussion of examples and critical embracing of the topic's complexities. For an example of how Media Studies deals with 'fake news' with neither moral panic nor complacently, it's a 'go to'. If using this with students, you might need to update it at some point. But at the time of writing, it does the job perfectly. The penultimate slide offers this learning strategy, for which students are given one of the categories from the typology on slide 15:

*Prepare a **PowerPoint** presentation about the type of fake news you have been given:*

*Identify **two** examples of this type of fake news.*
Explain the reasons for your choice in terms of:

Intention to deceive (high/low)
Level of facticity (high/low)

Discuss:
Whether you think audiences are deceived by this type of fake news?
What role might social media play in making this news more or less fake?

Follow up: http://daveharte.com/fake-news/.

App 13 Evolving Media: Team Human vs Long Form Drama vs Netflix Quantum Theory: *Stranger Things*, the 'Netflix Original' is a set text in Media Studies under the generic category 'Long Form Drama'. It's significant here because of the way in which Netflix's impact on our engagement with television is part of the same 'matrix' as Facebook's disruption of the news paradigm.

The text itself will be deconstructed in Media Studies, with an exploration of its generic conventions and playful, postmodern fluidity, hybridity, reflexivity and intertextuality.

Taking this further, where the story 'is', becomes a key learning focus. This kind of drama's diegesis is *platformed*. Whereas the broadcast era model was about developing narrative arcs over multiple series, thus hooking the audience into a channel or network for the long term, Netflix has created new modes of narrative and can offer more intensity over a shorter series run, set up for 'binge viewing', as the subscription economics liberate platforms from the need to carry advertising and thus 'deliver' viewers to paying companies for longer periods. This arrangement has, in turn, influenced the channels and networks to try new ways to compete—for example shorter 'mini-series'. *Stranger Things* is easy to analyse using postmodern theory, most notably Baudrillard's *America* (1981). We can see the text as hyperreal, as its representational world is intertextual, being lined to media representations rather than an external 'reality'.We recognise 1980s small town America from films and television mediation of the idea of it. But crucially, this diegetic world is extended over social media, with the narrative arc constructed to maximize social media trending. As the relatively new market of streaming television is dominated by a small number of companies – Netflix, Amazon and next, Apple, this is another oligopoly. The use of data and algorithms by Netflix to direct content to audiences can be understood as surveillance, even described as 'Netflix Quantum Theory':

> Using large teams of people specially trained to watch movies, Netflix deconstructed Hollywood. To understand how people look for movies, the video service created 76,897 micro-genres.They paid people to watch films and tag them with all kinds of metadata. This process is so sophisticated and precise that taggers receive a 36-page training document that teaches them how to rate movies on their sexually suggestive content, goriness, romance levels, and even narrative elements like plot conclusiveness. Netflix has built a system that only has one analogy in the tech world: Facebook's NewsFeed. But instead of serving you up the pieces of web content that the algorithm thinks you'll like, Netflix is serving you up filmed entertainment. (Madrigal 2014: 1–2)

The implications of this for media students go further. Just as social media has transformed the news cycle to 365, 24/7 (see Rosenberg and Feldman 2009), 'binge viewing' of long-form TV drama is enabled by streaming 'flow' with audience habits increasingly controlled by algorithms. As 'binging' is now common across both fictional drama and TV news, it is argued that the platform dynamics of streaming networks such as Netflix actually influence our political perspectives—essentially, another layer of insulation for our echo chambers. Horeck, Jenner and Kendall analysed the intersectional framing of Netflix bingeing:

> While research has explored the ways in which Netflix's 'algorithmic determinism' reproduces stereotypical identity categories based on reductive assumptions about race, gender and viewing preference (Arnold, 2016) more work is required on the gendered and racialised dimensions of binge-watching. To what extent does the 'user-directed' pull of a show, where 'each episode becomes a new level to be unlocked' (Poniewozik, 2015) depend on dominant gender and racial tropes? It is notable that a diverse range of Netflix hit series, from teen drama *13 Reasons Why* (2017) to true crime blockbuster *Making a Murderer* (2015), turn on the trope of the dead pretty White girl, with Caucasian male protagonists as the active heroes. In these texts, the calculated capture of audience attention through the use of cliffhangers and plot twists is designed to encourage viewers to hit 'play next episode' and is often dependent on familiar gendered scenarios. It is interesting to consider how the binge-able text – in which well-worn themes are extended across several episodes – allows scholars to freshly observe the problematic gendered and racialised mechanics of TV programmes. (Horeck et al. 2018: 501)

Whilst this appears more benign than the practices of Cambridge Analytica, it is part of the same processes of, first, filtering and thus gatekeeping and, next, influencing behaviour, that we find in the 'predictive data operations' of Russian trolls. Both Apple and Disney will offer TV streaming, like Netflix, which uses, and generates, algorithms to channel preferences into behaviour into new preferences and new behaviour. Thus, Media students should keep a convergent lens on the inter-relationships between 'disinformation' on social media and TV drama streaming, as both are developments in this new eco-system.

In October 2019, the BBC broadcast an episode of *Doctor Who* in which Jodie Whittaker's timelord was teleported to 1950s Alabama, where she witnessed Rosa refusing to give up her seat on the bus. The episode was very well received, in the public domain of television reviews and also on social media, by its 'fandom' and a broader public. However, there are some critical questions for media students to ask about the mediation of temporal displacement and the potential exploitation of historical memory "to revisit a period of grotesque and cruel white dominance in order to flatter ourselves with a sense of the rightness of our own, present-day racial politics." (Dix 2018: 2)

Doctor Who is an example of 'long form drama', a topic area within Media Studies. Studying this form of media requires textual analysis of moving image mediation, application of theories of representation and also, with this example as well as Stranger Things, postmodernism, and also an understanding of how long form drama is contextualized by disruptive technologies and industry transformations such as streaming and audience-generating algorithms. The BBC has the same status here as mainstream journalism in the wake of 'fake news'; it is part of the same ecosystem and is not at another, virtuous end of a false binary. An academic, Media Studies analysis of the Rosa Parks episode should include all of the above and consider whether, from another angle, it could be labelled propaganda, or even 'fake history'? There is no interest implied here in a racist position—one that would deny the importance of civil rights in the contemporary public imagination. Rather, through a decolonizing lens, could the narrative—in which the (white saviour) Doctor stops an attempt by another time-travelling character to prevent the incident—be considered to be, unintentionally, part of the problem it is setting out to address? This critical assessment is fundamental to the Media Studies' contribution to 'Team Human' and the problem of privileging one representational mode over others in the name of urgency.

Follow up: https://blog.lboro.ac.uk/news/art/time-travelling-to-the-civil-rights-era/.

References

Ahmed, S. (2004). *The Cultural Politics of Emotion*. Edinburgh: Edinburgh University Press.

Berners-Lee, T. (2019, March 11). The World Wide Web Turns 30: Where Does It Go from Here? *Wired*. https://www.wired.com/story/tim-berners-lee-world-wide-web-anniversary/.

Bourdieu, P. (2013). *Outline of a Theory of Practice*. Cambridge: Cambridge University Press.

Briant, E. (2018, April 17). Cambridge Analytica and SCL: How I Peered Inside the Propaganda Machine. *The Conversation*.

Bucy, E., & Newhagen, J. (2018). Fake News Finds an Audience. In J. E. Katz (Ed.), *Social Media and Journalism's Search for Truth*. Oxford: Oxford University Press.

Buckingham, D. (2019). *How Much Trust in Media Do We Need?* https:// davidbuckingham.net/2019/03/12/how-much-trust-in-media-do-we-need/.

Cable, J., & Mottershead, G. (2018). Can I Click It? Yes, You Can: Sport Journalism, Twitter, and Clickbait. *Ethical Space: The International Journal of Communication Ethics, 15*(1/2), 69–80.

Cadwalladr, C. (2019, March 17). The Cambridge Analytica Files. *The Observer*.

Curran, J., & Seaton, J. (2018). *Power Without Responsibility: Press, Broadcasting and the Internet in Britain*. London: Routledge.

Derakhshan, H. (2019, May 9). Disinfo Wars: A Taxonomy of Information Warfare. *Medium*. https://medium.com/@h0d3r/disinfo-wars-7f1cf2685e13. Accessed 9 May 2019.

Dix, A. (2018). *Time Travelling to the Civil Rights Era*. https://blog.lboro.ac.uk/ news/art/time-travelling-to-the-civil-rights-era/. Accessed 31 August 2019.

Firmstone, J. (2018). Saving the Local News Media: What Matt Hancock's Review Needs to Know. *LSE Politics and Policy Blog*. http://eprints.lse. ac.uk/88780/1/politicsandpolicy-saving-the-local-news-media-what-matt-hancocks.pdf. Accessed 31 August 2019.

Foucault, M. (1980). *Power/Knowledge: Selected Interviews and Other Writings 1972–1977* (C. Gordon, Ed.). London: Harvester.

Frau-Meigs, D. (2017). Developing a Critical Mind Against Fake News. *The UNESCO Courier—The Media: Operation Decontamination*, 12–15.

Galtung, J., & Ruge, M. (1965). The Structure of Foreign News: The Presentation of the Congo, Cuba and Cyprus Crises in Four Norwegian Newspapers. *Journal of International Peace Research, 2*, 64–90.

Gauntlett, D. (2015). *Making Media Studies*. London: Polity.

Harte, D. (2018). *'Imagine Doing a Journalism Degree and Then Being Asked to Write Trash Like This'—Considerations in Meeting the Challenges of Banal Journalism*. http://ajeuk.org/wp-content/uploads/2018/10/HARTE-AJE-banal-journalism-2018.pdf.

Hewitt, B. (2017, December 8). How to Spot Fake News—An Expert's Guide for Young People. *The Conversation*. https://theconversation.com/ how-to-spot-fake-news-an-experts-guide-for-young-people-88887.

Horeck, T., Jenner, M., & Kendall, T. (2018). On Binge-Watching: Nine Critical Propositions. *Critical Studies in Television, 13*(4), 499–504.

Karlsson, K., & Clerwall, C. (2018). Cornerstones in Journalism. *Journalism Studies*. https://doi.org/10.1080/1461670x.2018.1499436.

Lindgren, S. (2017). *Digital Media and Society*. London: Sage.

Livingstone, S., & Sefton-Green, J. (2016). *The Class: Living and Learning in a Digital Age*. New York: New York University Press.

London School of Economics. (2019). *Trust, Truth and Technology*. London: LSE Publications.

Lupton, D. (2019). *Data Selves: More-than-Human Perspectives*. London: Polity.

Madrigal, A. (2014). How Netflix Reverse Engineered Hollywood. *The Atlantic*. https://www.theatlantic.com/technology/archive/2014/01/how-netflix-reverse-engineered-hollywood/282679/.

McLuhan, M. (1964). *Understanding Media: The Extensions of Man*. Cambridge, MA: MIT.

Merrin, W. (2014). *Media Studies 2.0*. London: Routledge.

Moore, M. (2018). *Democracy Hacked: Political Turmoil and Information Warfare in the Digital Age*. London: Bloomsbury.

Myers, F. (2019, April 9). The Era of Internet Freedom Is Over. *Wired*.

O'Hara, K., & Hall, W. (2018). *4 Internets: The Geopolitics of Digital Governance*. Ontario: Centre for International Governance Innovation.

Poitras, L. (2014). *Citizen 4*. USA: Praxis Films.

Read, M. (2018). *How Much of the Internet Is Fake?* New York: Intelligencer. http://nymag.com/intelligencer/2018/12/how-much-of-the-internet-is-fake.html.

Resser, M. (2017). Fake News: Sound Bites on a Burning Topic. *The UNESCO Courier—The Media: Operation Decontamination*, 11.

Rosenberg, H., & Feldman, C. (2009). *No Time to Think: The Menace of Media Speed and the 24 Hour News Cycle*. London: Continuum.

Sonwalkar, P. (2005). Banal Journalism. In S. Allan (Ed.), *Journalism: Critical Issues* (pp. 262–273). New York: Peter Lang.

Stewart, H., & Hern, A. (2019, April 4). Social Media Bosses Could Be Liable for Harmful Content, Leaked UK Plan Reveals. *The Guardian*.

Viner, K. (2017, November 16). A Mission for Journalism in a Time of Crisis. *The Guardian*.

Wardle, C., & Derakhshan, H. (2017). *Information Disorder Toward an Interdisciplinary Framework for Research and Policymaking*. Strasbourg: Council of Europe.

Williamson, B. (2017). *Big Data in Education: The Digital Future of Learning, Policy and Practice*. London: Sage.

Yaloyan. M. (2017). Aftenposten Versus Facebook: Triggering a Crucial Debate. *The UNESCO Courier—The Media: Operation Decontamination*, 16–19.

Zuckerberg, M. (2019, March 30). The Internet Needs New Rules: Let's Start in These Four Areas. *The Washington Post*.

5

'All News Is Fake News': Discuss

In the late eighties, *Manufacturing Consent* (1988) provided Media Studies with a framework for understanding the ideological filtering that Herman and Chomsky saw as fake news by another name. The question now is, given that in the thirty years since that publication, the news industry has been transformed almost beyond recognition, can its way of seeing news media still apply? There are less employed journalists and the number will continue to decline as advertising revenue decreases. Readers sharing stories online have, arguably, more power than editors in all respects, in effect making clickbait a 'necessary evil' and the middle ground less viable.

Much of what we're dealing with here is on screen in the documentary "Trump's First Year: Reporting the Fourth Estate", an observation of *New York Times* journalists working in and reporting on the White House during the new tenure. If Media students consider it alongside *All the President's Men* and *House of Cards*, then the paradox is compelling—Trump changes the rules of the game, attacks the mainstream media (*You're Fake News*) but at the same time offers unprecedented riches for investigative reporting:

© The Author(s) 2019
J. McDougall, *Fake News vs Media Studies*,
https://doi.org/10.1007/978-3-030-27220-3_5

Trump is the best story they will ever have, and they are seizing it with both hands. Above all, you get a sense of how exhausting it must be. We often speak of the 24-hour news cycle, but most of us don't have to live in it. There are no clichéd shots here of papers rolling off presses. Nowadays, you push a button that says "publish", and instantly someone on TV starts talking about it. It never ends. (Dowling 2018: 3)

But there are grounds for optimism:

We have gone from a business model that manufactures consent to one that manufactures dissent—a system that pumps up conflict and outrage rather than watering it down. This sounds dire. Heck, it is dire. But the answer is not to pine for the days when a handful of publications defined the limits of public discourse. That's never coming back, and we shouldn't want it to. Instead, smart news operations are finding new ways to listen and respond to their audiences—rather than just telling people what to think. They're using technology to create a fuller portrait of the world and figuring out how to get people to pay for good work. And the best of them are indeed creating really, really good work. As the past 30 years of press history shows, everything changes. Great journalism helps us understand how and why things change, and we need that now more than ever. (Tanz 2017: 3)

Nearly forty years ago, the Glasgow Media Group drew this conclusion from a body of research into media representation in the United Kingdom:

The essential thrust of our critique is not against media workers as such, as if we could have better news simply by getting better journalists, editors and producers. Rather, it relates to the picture of society that the media construct with such remarkable consistency. We attribute this artificial and one-dimensional picture to the nature of organisations whose basic assumption is that our industrial, economic and social system operates to the benefit of everyone involved. Such a vision is given in the name of 'public interest', but unfortunately its construction involves the mass of this 'public' being misrepresented. (Philo et al. 1992: 144–145)

This work was the 'meat and drink' of Media Studies. Looking at 'fake news' in 2019, we're often encouraged to distinguish between professional journalism and misinformation and to trust the former. Doubtless, the situation is different. The Glasgow researchers were looking at a handful of daily newspapers and evening news bulletins from three organisations, with coherent, identifiable 'mass' audiences and limited rights to reply. This was the analogue, print and broadcast age. In this chapter, the question of trust in journalism today will be the focus, through the lens of 'old school' Media Studies, to see if we've really come so far from the problems the Glasgow Group were tackling.

A Different Space

We're in Stephen Jukes' office at Bournemouth University. The outlook is lots of 'new build' and graphics on the building site boundaries proudly boasting of the riches to come for 'the student experience' and the eco-credentials of the emerging new campus. It's a very different scene to the Stuart Hall Building at Goldsmiths, where we started this journey along our false binary. Cranes, scaffolding and 'fused learning spaces' in construction are a prominent feature of 'post-92' UK universities in the era of student fees. The we is Karen Fowler-Watt, Stephen, and myself. Karen is Head of the Journalism School and Stephen is Professor in Journalism and ex-Dean of the Media School. Stephen hired me to run the Centre for Excellence in Media Practice, a national centre accredited by the UK Government under Jukes' tenure and Karen is my Head of Department.

Moving to the Media School at Bournemouth was, for me, a big deal as it's the largest in the United Kingdom and has the 'excellence' designation, so it was outward looking and industry-facing, with impressive graduate employment and CEMP hosting the annual Media Education Summit, at which I had given a keynote. CEMP was setting up a new doctoral programme for media teachers, and my job was to get that up and running. That programme is now recruiting its seventh cohort and we have taken the Summit to an international audience. Stephen and Karen have both been a big part of that brand and their transitions into higher education leadership roles were about industry credentials and professional networks.

Karen: I was a senior journalist at the BBC for a number of years in current affairs, working predominantly on The World at 1 and The World this Weekend but I also did a lot of work in the field, for example covering the Gulf war, I was the Washington Bureau Producer for 6 months through the Clinton campaign, they were key highlights for me, so there's always been that interest in conflict reporting, foreign reporting and news, but also longer form story-telling, so all of those interests were still very much alive as I made the move into the academy and they were the things I was teaching here. I was also working with the industry councils and that blend with the academy and industry has always been really important to me and still is. We became a 'J-School' in 2015 which I think was another big career highlight for me, looking to the models in the States of J-Schools, and I did a doctorate later in life, which I got in 2013.

I ask what the doctorate was about.

I reflected on the lived experiences of practitioners moving into the academy and used the College of Journalism at the BBC as my case study. I used an autobiographical approach but did in-depth interviews with a number of different people to talk to them about their experiences and how they mapped their industry experience on to credible and useful learning experiences for students, which is another big thing for me.

Stephen: I studied languages at University and wanted to be a foreign correspondent but didn't know how to go about it so I ended up by accident joining a local newspaper group called Westminster Press and I went to work on the Brighton and Hove Gazette and Herald in the Argus stable in Brighton, there I did 2 and a half years, did my NCTJ indentures and one of my colleagues there went to work for Reuters and one day he said 'why don't you come and have an interview?' And so I did. Got a job and then was very quickly posted to Frankfurt because I had studied German and then spent 20 years with Reuters all over the world but mainly in the Middle East, Eastern Europe and America and at the end I was the Head of News. I ran the news operations based partly in Washington, partly in London and I left in 2004/2005 after the second Gulf War. I came here, became Dean, that was my first job, I don't think that today Bournemouth University would have employed me because I knew nothing about the academic world at all really so they employed me as a professional journalist, but I didn't want to become one of these hacks who go into academia and tell 'war stories' you know, I wanted to do the academic stuff and I found that very difficult to begin with as Dean because I was just essentially doing the business and tied up with meetings every day and only as time went on did I sort of understand that and carve out time to, I suppose, learn about the academic world and then also learn more about my subject and that's why I made the transition in the first place, to try to reflect on what I did, because working for Reuters, you're basically on a hamster wheel of churning out stories one after another, fantastic stories but even so, we never had time to step back and think and that's what I wanted to do here, so part of that was then doing my PhD as well and so I am now Professor of Journalism. Of course, one of the problems I found is that practice has changed so much since I left in 2005, I mean think about it, there was no Twitter, social media wasn't really an issue and I think in the 20 odd years I worked for Reuters, I think I only ever once got a letter from somebody who had read a story and that was trying to sue me! So, you know, today is a completely different environment.

I'm interested in how they feel about their identities—like art educators, I hear journalism academics talk about themselves and each other in terms of their craft first, teaching and research second. How does it work?

> *Karen*: I feel my identity is still as a journalist if I'm totally honest, the way I write, the way I research, the way I see the world. I think it has some advantages. I worked for the BBC all my life and although impartiality is a whole new other debate we can have, I think there are things that do become part of your DNA, so there have been roles that I've been given within the academy on the basis of being impartial and certainly within a leadership role that was useful too at times, but I think storytelling, seeing the world in terms of stories, human interactions, the way that we live in society together and connect, much more so than anything that's institutionalised and you know, I didn't really feel that the BBC, even though I was working for a massive corporation that the institution was a thing, it was the story, the programme, the identity of us as journalists within that, so I think if I were being really honest, I see myself as a journalist within an academic environment, yes.

Stephen: I caught myself the other day in the meeting outside the University saying I was an academic, introducing myself as an academic but I spent a lot of time as a journalist so I felt obliged to say it and my reaction is very similar, the actual underlying DNA is that of a journalist and I don't think you lose that, maybe it's because we both come from organisations which have a very strong culture, like the BBC culture and the Reuters culture was such a strong culture and I still see myself at heart as a journalist, although when I came into the academic world, which is now 14 years ago, I very much wanted to be an academic, and I do the academic stuff and I love doing that, I think research is fantastic, but probably my basic approach is still informed by journalism. I think it's not a coincidence that my research methodology quite often is interview, it's an experiential type of approach to journalism practice, I look at it through an experiential lens, something that is psycho-social and cultural and sometimes I overlay arcane theories around affect, which I think are really interesting but my primary approach is that of what a journalist does day in, day out, which is interviewing, and then when I do something like a content analysis I don't really feel very comfortable doing that and I don't get much satisfaction out of doing it either to be frank.

Moving on, I pose Natalie Fenton's argument to them, about the complicity of professional journalists in creating the crisis of trust we are facing today. Fenton supervised Jukes' PhD, so he has heard this before, but I paraphrase her view that media educators and academics must never lose sight of the fact that you guys, your profession, got us to the point where we are now.

Stephen: Natalie and I agree entirely on that, but we disagree entirely on Leveson (the inquiry into the need for new forms of regulation of the press, in the wake of the phone hacking scandal and the closure of the News of the World). But here's an example I was involved in. This was 2003 when the American troops went into Baghdad to topple Saddam Hussein and he'd already gone into hiding at that stage and do you remember how a statue of Saddam was pulled down in Firdos Square? Well I was in London, I was Head of News, I wasn't in the field then but we had live pictures coming in, we had amazing pictures and in a sense, I think the American administration wanted their Berlin Wall moment, they wanted something which symbolised victory and the fall of Saddam and the statue toppling gave them that. But when you looked at the coverage that was coming out of CNN and Fox, it was very jingoistic, it was reminiscent of 9/11, it was America's revenge and what have you and when we started to look at the pictures more carefully, it was quite clear that there wasn't a huge crowd, 3 million people lived in Baghdad, there were, like, 150 around this square and actually, when it came to it most of those people were either journalists or American military personnel or Kurds who had been bussed in by the Americans. Reuters had a wide angle shot of the square from the air in which you could see a small group of people around the statue and nobody else which is now reminiscent of the debate about how many thousands of people were at Trump's inauguration and so for me it was a classic case where a government, in this case the American government, can manipulate media, can stage something and actually, certainly for the first few days, media took the bait, they were completely engaged in the fall of Saddam Hussein and it was only later that people started to pull it apart and say, well this was actually staged, it was manipulation, you know, The great quote in Phillip Knightley's book, *The First Casualty,* is 'the first casualty when war comes is truth' (from Senator Hiram Johnson) and it's true and this was pure disinformation, so it tells me that fake news is not something new, that there are different shades of it but it's also about Government disinformation, it's about how media can be complicit, how they frame stories. Reuters had the foresight to not only have the obvious pictures, like the soldier putting the flag over the statue, but they also had the foresight to do that big wide angle shot which told you how it really was. So I take my students through that.

Karen: I agree that mainstream media is a problem and I think Natalie has a point, but I think at the moment things are different to drinking in the last chance saloon which is where we were with Leveson, it's not a self-inflicted wound and so it's about looking for ways of re-imagining journalism and I think the difficulty at the moment is that mainstream media doesn't see it as a solution at all, I don't think it's presenting itself as that, I think it's reeling from this and the febrile atmosphere after the inauguration is something which I thought was incredibly striking. I was in Washington and you had seasoned journalists from The Guardian and The BBC not knowing whether they should be chasing the next tweet or digging in the files to try and get him impeached. That felt like a very different moment in journalism to anything I had ever seen and this was because of a man who was accusing the media of being the opposition, anything that didn't suit his own narrative was fake and so I think we're in really different territory and the example that springs to mind was the migrant caravan. At the moment, a huge amount of energy is being used by the BBC to deconstruct the lies that are being constructed by the President of the United States around this story and that means they are being diverted from perhaps doing the stuff they should be doing, the normative values are not really necessarily being pursued daily because we are doing these sort of explanation pieces so that people understand that you know, it's not a bunch of ISIS terrorists who are walking over the bridge, it's Honduran men looking for a better life and proving that as a fact. So he's setting up lies which we then have to try to find a route through, and there are a number of these explainers now out there, and verification units. So I just have this sense of a mainstream media that is absolutely not seeing itself as a solution because they know that nobody's really listening, for me it's a very different space that we're now in, but as a result of something that has been around since the beginning of time.

Stephen: It's so image driven, the image of the 'caravan' migrants going across that bridge, there's that long white bridge and you just see the bridge totally packed, and that's the picture that probably Trump wants us to see because it is the threat, the mass of people, but actually how many people are there and when they were on a long road and some are being trucked and some are walking, I mean it's dribs and drabs, so images are so important.

Karen: yes, he's saying they're all democrats or they're ISIS terrorists or it's George Soros, this liberal philanthropist just paying it all, so he's using all sorts of whipping boys to create a climate of fear, which we as the media are residing in as well as everybody who's consuming media, so that to me is different to the self-inflicted wounds of hacking phones for which we absolutely deserve to be held to account.

Stephen: And going back to my example from Reuters, it just shows that fake news is not always Macedonian teenagers trying to do click bait, equally it's governments and in this case, I agree with Natalie that media is complicit, they just so wanted to have that 'democracy triumphs over the Arab world' story.

I delve deeper into the disconnect with Fenton's calls for media reforms, most notably the Leveson enquiry, on which both of these ex-journalists declare themselves to be 'in a different room'. Why is that?

> *Stephen*: It's freedom of the press, yeah it was a terrible thing (the phone hacking revelations), we're not trying to pretend it wasn't but really Draconian press regulation is not the answer to that, I mean there are editorial codes, there are guidelines and there are many, many, many journalists who would just not do that stuff, so it's like legislating for the bad apple, if you like, and that's not to trivialise what happened, because clearly it caused great upset and it did bring the profession into disrepute but there are laws, phone hacking is a criminal offence, people went to jail, you don't need to impose press regulation and it's a slippery slope.
>
> *Karen*: I agree, so you won't find me in the same room as any of the Hacked Off brigade, besides which they're defending celebrities who can afford to defend themselves, you know, I'm not going to shed a tear for Hugh Grant.

These are views 'from the field', but what about from the classroom?

> *Karen*: Transformative pedagogy is key, really, everyone is a citizen, that's what we're thinking about here isn't it, good civics and people being involved in debate, so improving journalism is one route but with media students, I get them to interrogate mainstream media and all of the normative values that they hold so dear and say - are they still fit for purpose? Should we really be getting hung up on impartiality? Does it do what we need it to do these days or should we be thinking about other things? Obviously, we're thinking about voice, bringing more people into the debate but not in a top down way, how we're engaging with others, particularly those who don't have a voice. So going through the key aspects of journalism, interrogating them, then turning them on their head, reading them against the grain, thinking about ways they are then situated in this as future journalists and building confidence in them and a sense of self in them so that if an editor tells them they've got to hack a phone they absolutely know that's not what you do, at the extreme end, but also so that whenever they go out and whatever story they're on in the early stages of their career, they are

always thinking about how they are presenting themselves to the world and the stories of others, what they're doing with those stories in terms of being responsible. So I think there's a lot that media education needs to do in terms of thinking about emotional literacy. We need different hierarchies around values to emphasise things which we didn't always think were at such a premium for journalists.

Stephen: So when I talk about fake news in seminars, I tend to have a section which looks at remedies and over the past couple of years we sort of segmented those with the students into four, so there's journalism, there's regulation - the governments and other bodies - there's the platforms and then there's media literacy and I would say that all of those four are in one way or another flawed. We need some form of reconceptualization, so leave journalism for the time being but if you take regulation, if you look at what's happening in Germany, they have laws against hate speech as we do here but they are actually fining Google or Facebook if they don't take material down within a certain timeframe. If you look at the platforms themselves, I mean to do Facebook some justice, they have partnered in 17 countries with fact-checking organisations who are trying to flag fake news and Google are doing the same. Okay, so at least they're trying to do something. If you look at media literacy, it needs reconceptualising and then when we get to the journalism bit - I think students are always very conservative about this, they know all the objectivity stuff, but then we talk about what's become known now as false balance, so you know when you put a climate change sceptic up against a climate change scientist you know, why would we give them equal airtime? That's maybe my prejudice but I also think the BBC got it wrong during the EU Referendum in 2016. So nobody is saying the core mission of journalism has changed, it's still truth and holding power to account, but you know in this age of post-truth, fake news, distrust, populism, maybe some of the practices need to be rethought.

Journalism vs Information Pollution?

This sub-heading is taken from the promotional material for the UNESCO Handbook we covered earlier—'*Developments in the last few years have placed journalism under fire*'.

I have added the question mark, to position this as another false binary. Isn't journalism ever a pollutant, in itself? Clearly yes, and Media Studies addresses this. But it is reasonable to emphasise recent years as something different to this ongoing tussle over truth and mediation.

The reason you are reading this book is because the game has changed. This is Donald Trump at a 2019 rally in El Paso: "*You know, some of the most dishonest people in media are the so-called fact-checkers. We have suffered a totally dishonest media and we've won and it's driving them crazy. The New York Times reporting is false. They are a true enemy of the people.*" But in the United Kingdom, a party leader at the other end of the political spectrum, Jeremy Corbyn, has launched a similar, if differently articulated, attack on the alleged political bias of 'mainstream media'. This extends from reporting of UK politics to the representation of events in Venezuela by the 'Western media'.

> There can be no scrutiny. Criticism is illegitimate by definition. Journalists are enemies of the people. If a journalist accuses Trump of lying, it's because of their liberal agenda. If a journalist wants to talk about anti-Semitism in the Labour Party, it can only be because they love austerity and hope hospital waiting lists increase. By attacking the media, Corbyn and Trump know exactly what they are doing. Any journalist's defence of the profession can be dismissed as special pleading: you would say that, wouldn't you? It's a cheap trick that works because everyone hates journalists already. Anyone who is aware of the threat to democratic norms posed by Trump must see the parallel with Corbyn's thoughtless media-bashing. Who would have the right to tell Prime Minister Corbyn he was wrong? Oh well. I suppose I'd better get used to being an enemy of the people. (Lewis 2019: paras 3–4)

Local News for Local People

A sub-plot of the dominant discourse articulated by journalists about the need to renew trust in professional journalism is the importance of local news in a democracy. This links back to Dave Harte's research on the hyperlocal. The Local Democracy Foundation, a charity funded by the BBC, internet companies and donations was launching as this book was nearing completion. The rationale is described here by the BBC's Director General, Tony Hall:

> The flow of information we all need to participate in democracy where we live has been drying up. My goal is to mobilise a powerful coalition behind the creation of a Local Democracy Foundation and, together, to do all we can reverse the damage that has been done to local democracy in recent years and bring about a sea change in local public interest journalism. (in Waterson 2019: 2)

Media students will observe these developments with interest and there are two critical questions to ask: (1) will this new charity impact at all on the increasingly concentrated ownership of local newspapers, itself an arguably undemocratic progression if we are to see local news as an aspect of a plural media?; (2) should we understand 'the public interest' as a neutral, fixed category? Richard Hoggart, fifteen years ago, critiquing the role of mass media in a 'mass society' warned of confusing the public interest with 'what interests the public' (2004: 114). Will it be possible to re-boot local public interest journalism in the era of clickbait, without a change to the business model for news production? Here's Natalie Fenton again, commenting on the challenges for implementing the 2018 Cairncross Review:

> Repairing the democratic deficits caused by an inadequate media environment requires not just rebuilding trust but also the creation of a healthy communications environment – one that is not just economically robust but innovative, diverse, independent of vested interests and sensitive to the changing political geography of the nation. (Fenton 2018: 7)

TOOLKIT#6 Media vs Planet

Returning to the way that consent is manufactured, Media Lens accuses the mainstream media of complicity in the climate crisis – "*the major news media are an intrinsic component of this system run for the benefit of elites. The media are, in effect, the public relations wing of a* planetary-wide network of exploitation, abuse and destruction. The climate crisis is the gravest symptom of this dysfunctional global apparatus" (Edwards and Cromwell 2018: 208).

Media educator Antonio Lopez is a pioneering campaigner for Eco-Media Studies (2020). His work, which weaves together multiple strands, provides a compelling vision of a more situated, sustainable and resistant Media Studies pedagogy for environmental sustainability and social justice. At the 2018 Media Education Summit in Hong Kong, he offered a rigorous analytical framework for mainstream media gaslighting of climate change. Using Herman and Chomsky's five filters for manufacturing consent (concentrated ownership; advertising revenue; selective sourcing; 'flak'; and defining enemies of the system), Lopez observes Big Media and Big Carbon gaslighting mediated publics through a 'shared ideological landscape of climate denial and rightwing media' (Fig. 5.1).

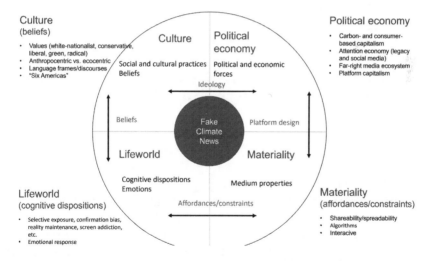

Fig. 5.1 Lopez on fake climate news—shows the complexity and depth of a Media Studies approach to this aspect of 'disinformation' (*Source* Antonio Lopez)

We are deliberately oscillating in this chapter, like a plane in turbulence, to show the working of the false binary. Critical media literacy, delivered through Media Studies, is not about a respect of mainstream media and resilience to fake news. Instead, it's about fostering critical literacy for democratic citizen engagement. This means understanding Herman and Chomsky, Media Lens and Lopez as people with a serious argument to make about media representation, but in dialogue with the journalists' perspectives from the field and the good intentions of UNESCO and others to protect the public from the clear and present dangers of fake news.

It's complicated.

Sandra Laville is a Senior Correspondent at *The Guardian*, with a current environment brief and a previous role in crime reporting at the same paper and war reporting for *The Telegraph* (*"human tyranny of war rather than the gun stuff"*).

Her sense of the fake news 'crisis' is entirely consistent with all of my participants:

> The accuracy of news has been questioned for decades, but what's different here is the scale, the sheer baselessness, the speed and believability at face value of what people are calling fake news. That's the difference, I think.

From her lived experience, are things changing within the profession as a result, or in response?

> Since social media, it's more important to really drill down further to the source. Shaking down a bit, down the line, the survivors from all this will be the ones who can carry trust. It's coming back down to credibility, and that is built up over many years. Accuracy, responsibility and trust are part of the brand (for The Guardian) and that is what it will come down to.

Her ideas about the educational response are fascinating and take us in a different direction to other journalists' ideas:

It's so prevalent that the educational remit has to be about how to question. It's part of a broader digital learning, I think, but the critical questioning is fundamental, I don't know how much of that goes on in schools now, and that's a problem. But the media have a role to play as well. I wonder if the answer might be some kind of flagging system, equivalent to how food packaging flags ingredients as red, amber and green, could news stories provide a similar kind of flagging to show to the audience how their ingredients, such as source, verification, factual basis are not fake news?

Scousers Never Buy the Sun

(Bragg 2011a)
Of his reasons for writing that song, Billy Bragg wrote:

Ninety-six people were crushed to death at a football match at Hillsborough in Sheffield on 15 April 1989. The Sun ran a front page story that accused Liverpool supporters of variously robbing and urinating on the dead bodies of the victims as they were laid along the touchline. The reports were totally unfounded. Since then, many people in Liverpool have refused to buy the Sun on principle. As I listened to the unfolding reports of the phone-hacking story last week, it occurred to me that the scousers had been right about News International all along. (Bragg 2011b: 1)

Such a total breakdown in trust is, clearly, one of the factors in the 'open door' for fake news, along with austerity, the failure of neoliberal politics and the unregulated 'outlaw space' of the web. It's not a historical case study, either, as the work of Media Lens reminds us. But it's nevertheless helpful to go back further than the phone hacking scandal and Bragg's musical comment, to the work of the Glasgow Media Group in the 1980s, which we started out with in this chapter, research which has been seminal to Media Studies.

The television representation of the 'Battle of Orgreave' was followed in the same political period as *The Sun's* reporting of the Hillsborough disaster and these are often taken together as a dual case study of what the Glasgow Media Group labelled 'Bad News'. The phone hacking scandal, leading to the closure of the News of the World, has been taken up as a broader concern about a systemically 'out of control' tabloid press, rather than a politically driven attack on a particular social group—the working class, during Thatcherism. But the current attention to bias against Jeremy Corbyn across the mainstream media may signal a return to the 'old school Bad News'; which, at the time of writing, has yet to play out. In *The Enemy Within*, Seamus Milne offers this summary of the media reporting of the Miner's Strike in the 1980s:

> Little of what was really at stake was reflected at the time in the mainstream media, which mostly portrayed the strike as an anti-democratic insurrection that defined economic logic – while the full coercive power and resources of the state were mobilized to crush miners' defence of jobs and communities. (Milne 2014: xii)

On Orgreave, specifically:

> Footage broadcast on television was reversed to show the mounted police charge as a response to missile-throwing from pickets. The real, diametrically-opposed sequence of events was only later demonstrated when the police's own video was produced at the insistence of the defence in the subsequent riot trial. (Milne 2014: 365–366)

David Peace's novel and the subsequent TV adaptation dramatized the 'deep state' media campaign on the miners as a pivotal element of the Thatcher Government's political strategy.

> Everything blurred. Everything merged. Distorted and faded – In the shadows at the back where the truths and the lies, the promises and the threats, the voices and the silences, the prayers and the curses, became one. From there everything whispered. Everything echoed. Everything moaned – These voices from the shadows, these silences and spaces, these truths and lies, their promises and threats. …. Echoes from the dark days. The Prime Minister and her Cabinet have launched a television offensive – TV Eye, Weekend

World, This Week, Next Week, A Week in Politics. The message is loud. The message is clear – No fudge. No forgiveness. No fudge. No forgiveness. Unmistakeable. Unambiguous. Unequivocal. (Peace 2004: 416–417)

The Glasgow Media Group's close readings of television broadcasts during the strike found, again and again, a process of negative agency being attributed to the miner's union President, the decision-making processes of the union and the actions of pickets. This was a systematic cultivation of negative ideas about how the miners were being led to behave, with the police's agency being deferred to that of self-defensive response to 'intimidation', a word repeatedly used in reports of legal strike action, prefaced by stories opening with 'there was more trouble today…'.

Hart conducted research into the use of metaphor and intertextuality in reporting of Orgreave, finding that war metaphors were most commonly used by journalists, depicting an 'army' of police as defenders of the state and pickets as an invading enemy. Once this framing metaphor is in place, Hart suggests, then terms such as 'battle', 'surrender', 'front line', and 'defeat' are deployed within stories, for example, "*The police were at first overwhelmed by the pickets but then re-grouped to advance under a hail of stones, bottles and bricks until the demonstrators retreated behind a barricade of burning cars, lamp posts and stones from a wall they had demolished*" (*The Times*, 19 June 1984, cited in Hart 2017: 12). The cultivation affect of the metaphorical repetition of these signifiers in the media coverage across television and newspaper reports, over the duration of the dispute, is a clear example of bias and, according to this analysis, this was a crucial aspect in the eventual 'defeat' of the miners:

> Framing the strike as a war results in particular metaphorical entailments which serve to delegitimize the NUM (National Union of Miners) and the striking miners while legitimizing the Government and the police. For example, the general WAR frame entails an opposition between two sides, one of whom is seen as 'the enemy'. As Wolf and Polzenhagen (2003) point out, there is therefore an inherent ideological dimension within the WAR frame as to which role a given participant is assigned. With the exception of the *Morning Star*, it is the striking miners who are cast in the role of the enemy. From this perspective within the

frame, references to World War I in particular serve to legitimize the Government's resolve to 'defeat' the NUM, where among the British population it is generally accepted that 'our' involvement in World War I, while devastating, was a necessary endeavour. Metaphor is therefore revealed as one semiotic resource through which an anti-trade union agenda was realised in media reports of the miners' strike. Regardless of perspective, this metaphorical framing serves to reduce a complex situation to a simple scenario with a restricted set of goals and outcomes. In so doing, the metaphor precludes the possibility of compromise and resolution. Had the media employed a different metaphor, it might have been possible to imagine the strike taking a different course and, ultimately, having a different outcome. (Hart 2017: 28)

If believed, and there is irrefutable evidence cited in Milne's book, including accounts of meetings between newspaper editors, broadcasters and MI5, then this bias was at the level of a close relationship between intelligence services and mainstream media. When the Hillsborough cover up was revealed, decades later, we could see a similar alliance between journalists, police and politicians.

Murdoch *Now*

One of the most serious problems with our false binary is that it presents the 'fake news' that Rupert Murdoch's ownership and control of mainstream media and the ideological impact of that on our media culture and our popular discourse is somehow and 'old school' example of Big Media, and that somehow this was rendered to history by the advent of social media and post-truth. This is, clearly and evidentially, fake. Martin and Yurukoglu's recent research (2017) found two important things about the Murdoch-owned Fox News network that are significant for Media Studies. Firstly, there was a 0.5% influence of Fox News on Republican voting in 2000, rising to 6% in 2008. Secondly, and more significantly, perhaps, the editorial agenda of Fox is now more right wing, politically, than its audience's existing position, suggesting a clear intention to take its audience to the right, rather than merely maintain market share by feeding viewers what the broadcaster assumes it wants to hear. In the United Kingdom, the influence of *The Sun* on political allegiance, election by election, has been a longstanding case study for media students. Now, however, it is argued that the position taken by the Murdoch media on immigration has underpinned the right-of-centre discourse leading up to, and since, the vote to Brexit and that the position of the BBC has shifted to the right accordingly, as neutral impartiality reflects assumptions about the prevailing mindset. This argument is accepted less readily in the United Kingdom than in the United States, however:

> UK journalists tend not to talk about the partisan press as a key political player, perhaps in part because they would be talking about colleagues who work for that press. The myth that the media just reflects and does not influence is too convenient for many, so the media remains the elephant in the room in discussions about politics and political extremism in the UK. (Wren-Lewis 2019: 2)

The danger of, for want of a more sophisticated description, Media Studies just 'forgetting about' Murdoch, or jettisoning him as an old case study in favour of getting to grips with 'fake news', is serious. If anything, recent analyses suggest he is upping his game in terms of naked agenda-setting. Along with Fox as a vehicle for shifting the centre ground to the right in the United States; in Australia, where News Corp enjoys a 70% circulation share, journalists are reported (by other journalists) to have reached a tipping point. Here's David McKnight from the University of New South Wales on the political pressure on editorial practices at the *Sydney Daily Telegraph*:

> I've never seen it quite so bad. In some ways, it was not a bad paper, it still had a big journalistic staff. But in the last sixth months, there's not a lot to read that isn't biased in such a way that you just scratch your head and say: 'Is this really true?' (in Alcorn 2019: 31)

Glasgow vs Birmingham

One of the biggest problems with fake news is rarely discussed. I am referring to the way that the rich but complex legacies of Media and Cultural Studies are either lumped together or brushed aside in favour of media literacy 'competences' or fact-checking tools. Therefore it is important to wrestle back a little space here to remind ourselves of 'where we've been'.

The Glasgow Media Group's approach (discussed earlier) was a departure from the work of the Birmingham School for Contemporary Cultural Studies, set up by Richard Hoggart and later led by Stuart Hall:

> We wanted to explore the 'common sense' that provided a basis for moral and social as well as literary and visual judgements …. We were attempting to make up, on almost a week to week basis, something that today has become widely known as 'cultural studies'. (Hall 2014: 3, foreword to CCCS: 50 Years On. Birmingham: UoB/Midland Arts Centre).

The Birmingham Centre's analysis of mass media representations was set in the context of class and race hegemony, theorized by attention to reception and meaning making. The methods employed embraced new approaches to the dialogue between the self, culture, knowledge and education: "*As a main object of study we must take the systems of culturally mediated social relations between classes and their internal cultural resources and repertoires*" (Johnson, in Hall et al. 1980: 48).

In *Cultural Studies Goes to School* (1994) Buckingham and Sefton-Green accounted for ways in which young people in schools were able to explore the politics of identity through various pedagogic strategies aimed at making sense of the media. In the analogue, pre-internet context, their study included students in a London comprehensive school engaging, through media production work, with theories of stereotyping set against the creation of positive images of minority groups. However, the students' refusal to engage in 'serious' academic discussion of their own highly parodic work (Slutmo) in relation to theories of gender representation by disclaiming it as 'having a laugh' (1994: 190) is a central discussion point in the account. The female student (Zerrin) who constructs, and accounts for in a highly personal evaluation, 'Slutmopolitan', is too complicated for the academic insulations that frame her work to articulate:

> If Zerrin cannot disentangle the levels of parody and power explicitly in her own writing, what can one claim for the educational value of the activity? Of course, this question raises a secondary one: the educational value for *whom*? (Buckingham and Sefton-Green 1994: 198–9)

This enduring problem was also captured in Judith Williamson's comparison (1981) of her struggles with teaching her student Astrid about gender representation to Sissy Jupe's silence as 'Girl 20' in Dickens' *Hard Times*.

It seems clear that ideas, from the Cultural Studies inventory, of textuality, encoding and decoding and media representation and the compulsion to account for creative, playful and highly parodic activity in relation to this rather narrow idea (that 'the media' represents people and things in particular ways and that students can choose to 'reinforce or challenge' this through their own) is problematic.

Cultural Studies emphasizes both difference in cultural activity and reflexivity in our understanding of ourselves as culturally mediated. Culture is dynamic and contingent, a process, and extends to everyone and all aspects of lived experience in and as culture.

Looking back at the findings of the Glasgow Media Group, Philo (2001a), however, accused the Birmingham School (namely, Hall and Morley) of overstating the extent to which audiences decode media messages through negotiation. Citing their work on viewers' readings of the coverage of the miners' strike discussed earlier, Philo offers numerous examples of audiences adopting the 'preferred reading' whilst being aware of alternative positions and contested the idea of the meaning being made each time in the decoding, arguing instead that viewers' react according to other ideological frameworks:

> The main problem which I have with the encoding/decoding model is the impact which it had on the subsequent development of media and cultural studies. The view which many took from it was that audiences

could resist messages, safe in the conceptual boxes of their class and culture, and renegotiating an endlessly pliable language. This led eventually to the serious neglect of issues of media power. It happened to such a degree that contemporary text books on audience research can simply miss out a large body of work which points to the strength of media influence. (Philo, in Miller and Philo 2001b: 15)

This disagreement plays an important role here. We need to remember that our false binary is further eroded by the complexity of the discipline of Media Studies itself. We must not throw the baby out with the bathwater.

David Hesmondhalgh's *The Cultural Industries* (2019) is a set text for Media Studies. It's value to the field has been significant in its focus on the working practices of media professionals and how, within these industries, cultural production is complicated. Media students may consider the difference between Adorno's influential work on *The Culture Industry* (as part of the Frankfurt School of Critical Theory) and Hesmondhalgh's contemporary, plural reading. If so, they might conclude that Adorno was concerned with the standardisation of culture through mass media genres, and in this way, the political economy of popular culture locates it as distinct to art. Hesmondhalgh, instead, offers a socio-cultural account of structure and agency within these industries, comparing media workers' levels of autonomy, on a *"contested ground upon which different kinds of cultural texts are produced"* (Laughey 2007: 126).

Taken together, the introductions to each edition of *The Cultural Industries* offer another interesting 'history of the present'. In the fourth edition, the author confesses to feeling overwhelmed by the sheer scale of 'cultural abundance' (2019: xxiii). Unsurprisingly, he reflects on the dampening of the enthusiasm of the new technology 'cheerleaders' but also argues against inverting the equation to replace optimism with despair in the wake of algorithms and big data. His series of books have always maintained the importance of a focus on change and continuity, in tandem. But what of journalists, specifically, their degrees of professional autonomy and freedom to challenge power? Aside from the threat of fake news, Hesmondhalgh observes a paradigm shift in self-perception as a result of the Hacked Off campaign in the early part of this decade, when "the media themselves finally began to acknowledge what critical journalism researchers had been writing for many years: that the ethical practices of many UK newspapers were simply abysmal" (2019: 442). His analysis does, however, assert the importance of this all being the outcome, itself, of investigative journalism, an aspect of events often overlooked in the narrative. That stated, his is another voice of antidote to our false binary, it is not as simple as fake news vs 'proper media':

> While it is surely right that social media platforms such as Facebook should have to take responsibility for the content they host and ensure its accuracy and reliability, 'fake news' is only part of the wider problem of the failure of news in modern societies. The IT industries are increasingly capturing the advertising income that might previously have sustained investigative and other socially valuable forms of journalism, but the problem goes deeper than that, to the embrace of marketization, the erosion of public service media, and the failure to design regulation that would protect the public interest in the age of social media. (2019: 443)

It's important at this juncture, also, to think back to the chapter on democracy and Owen Jones' breakdown of the unrepresentative demographic of professional journalists, to safeguard against considering *their* professional autonomy in terms of some kind of David and Goliath battle between the virtuous fourth estate and the evil power-brokers. The network of privilege runs through and across, as he asserted on Twitter in 2018:

> The main thing I've learned from working in the British media is that much of it is a cult. Afflicted by a suffocating groupthink, intolerant of critics, hounds internal dissenters, full of people who made it because of connections and/or personal background rather than merit.

In *Respectable* (2016), Lynsey Hanley returns to Richard Hoggart's *The Uses of Literacy* as a framing for her personal account of the lived experience of social class and mobility in the English Midlands:

Our culture contains many silent symbols more powerful than money. It contains keys that can't be bought, which gain access to rooms whose existence you can barely imagine, unless you get to enter them. Social and cultural capital works on a compound-interest model, the more you have, the more you get. The more knowledge and influence you accrue, the more you get to know other people with knowledge and influence, and the more knowledge and influence you acquire to share among people who have it already. Mainstream media, including social media, function both as an expression and as a propagator of this model, to emphasize and intensify the existing imbalances of power, in terms of who gets to have a voice and who can be persuaded to listen to it. (2016: xii–xiii)

Unfortunately, this can't just be reduced to personal accounts from people with 'an axe to grind', put down to 'how it used to be' when Hanley was living through this in the 1980s and 1990s or as the confirmation bias of a 'leftie' author of the same age and from the same part of the world. A large-scale 2018 research project (*The Class Ceiling*) by Friedman and Laurison concluded that, on the basis of substantial empirical data:

In contemporary Britain it quite literally pays to be privileged. Even when individuals from working-class backgrounds are successful in entering the country's elite occupations they go on to earn, on average, 16% less than colleagues from more privileged backgrounds. More significantly this class pay gap is not explained away by conventional indicators of 'merit'. A substantial gap remains even when we take into account a person's educational credentials, the hours they work and their level of training and experience. In fact, more powerful than 'merit' are drivers rooted in the misrecognition of classed self-presentation as 'talent', work cultures historically shaped by the privileged, the affordances of the 'Bank of Mum and Dad', and sponsored mobility premised on class-cultural similarity and familiarity. (2019: 209)

Journalism is included in 'elite occupations'.

But looking at journalism through an *intersectional* lens, rather than through a version of class that privileges either class or gender, or both, over race, poses an awkward question for this book, written by a white, male author, looking at 'the media' as unrepresentative, but drawing on a convenience sample of interviewees who speak in and to a 'white space'.

Eddo-Lodge (2017) is clear on why this is a problem:

> Complicating the idea that race and class are distinctly separate rather than intertwined will be hard work. It involves piercing a million thought bubbles currently dominating conversations about class in this country. Although some deal with class prejudice, others deal with racialized class prejudice. It's that complexity that needs to be navigated successfully if we ever want an accurate understanding of what it means to be working class in Britain today. (2017: 210–211)

These things are all *really* important to Media Studies, because this subject must not be reduced to a vocational training for an industry which works in this way. Where is the critical thinking in that? If there is a good aspect to fake news, then it might just be in the way we are forced to think again about the media, or even after the media (see Bennett et al. 2011), to reflect on how mainstream media need to change, if we are to find a way out of the crisis of 'information disorder' and if Media Studies is going to play a significant part in that.

Tamsyn Dent's research (2017) investigates, in particular but not exclusively, the lived experience of female working parents in the media. Her work demonstrates how pluralist media representation, in a democracy, is curtailed by the industries' reinforcing of inequalities, rendering the means of production of media as largely open to white, male, middle class professionals. The media's 'axes of exclusion' *allow for concepts of 'choice' and 'preference' to mask deeply complicated processes of oppression and exclusion and expose a paradox between celebratory concepts of creative practice and the lived realities of the creative workforce.* (Dent 2017: 3).

This quote was in my mind when I interviewed Jackie Long. She has five children, so scheduling a time to talk took some back-and-forth emails. I'm determined not to make a big deal of it in the interview or the write-up, as none of the prominent male journalists mentioned their domestic 'lifeworlds', apart from Fergal Keane's nostalgia for Hong Kong, from which his fusing of the personal and the professional was cited as part of his approach to journalism, as opposed to the everyday demands of juggling a top job at Channel 4 with being a mother.

Maybe for this reason, Long is very helpful and tolerant of my pestering for an interview. I realise, as she confirms, the obvious truth that journalists are more accepting of this (than academics, in my experience) as they do it themselves for a living. It's a phone call, and we're tight for time, so I am looking more for examples of the lived experience of providing 'real news' than the broader debates around 'fake', albeit that this reinforces the false binary I'm supposed to be debunking.

Firstly, she reflects on the changes she has observed during her journey from local media to the BBC (a 20-year stay, including The World at One, PM and Newsnight) and to her current role as social affairs editor and presenter for Channel 4 News. Some of this is to do with experiential learning of the trade (*if you sat in someone's chair for long enough, you would end up doing their job*) but we soon move on to the 24/7 news cycle and the difficulties of working within ethical guidelines in the era of social media. On this subject, she talks openly about her reporting of three very challenging stories and how the contexts have changed so quickly between them.

When we arrived at the scene of Lee Rigby's murder, there were already competing versions of what had happened out there on social media, so that was a very different case. Comparing that to reporting on a murder in my days as a local journalist, before social media, you could pretty quickly work out who was giving you an accurate eye witness account and who was speculating. Now it's entirely different. But when we got to Grenfell, we were told by the police that there were a specific number who had died. It was clearly going to be more, but that was the number confirmed at that stage, so we reported that, faithfully. But on social media, a much higher number was being reported and instantly you are part of the conspiracy, the media, the police and the state are deliberately under-stating the tragedy. So here are multiple versions of events, multiple opposing "truths" and ours becomes one of them. As we filmed, people said "Where are the media?" "Where have the media been?" So we are working to the rules – find sources, establish facts, but on social media those rules don't apply and we are accused of taking the side of the state, part of a conspiracy. I would say that, in my career, something is changing that means it is just so much more difficult to operate ethically as a professional journalist.

From the other side of the tracks, Darren McGarvey's 'Poverty Safari' won the Orwell Prize in 2018. It is not cited here to challenge Jackie Long's account—far from it—they are working to the same objectives for social justice. But it does capture the crisis in trust in 'elites' that Long, Fowler-Watt and others are reflecting on in these pages:

> Countless newspaper articles, bulletins and radio programmes attempted to capture what it was like to live in a tower block. Having been ignored – and dismissed – for so long, now suddenly everyone was interested in what life in a community like this entailed. But most people, despite their noble intentions, were just passing through on a short-lived expedition. A safari of sorts, where the indigenous population is surveyed from a safe distance for a time, before the window on the community closes, and everyone gradually forgets about it. (McGarvey 2017: xix)

TOOLKIT#7 *I, Daniel Blake*

If we take another look at curricular content for Media Studies, we can argue that teaching students about *media production, distribution and circulation; the regulatory framework of contemporary media; the impact of new digital technologies on media regulation; the impact of digitally convergent media platforms on media production, distribution and circulation; the role of regulation in global production, distribution and circulation and the effect of individual producers on media industries; how media representations convey values, attitudes and beliefs about the world and how these may be systematically reinforced across a wide range of media representations; how audiences respond to and interpret media representations; the way in which representations make claims about realism; the impact of industry contexts on the choices media producers make about how to represent events, issues, individuals and social groups; the effect of historical context on representations; how representations may invoke discourses and ideologies and position audiences* and *how audience responses to and interpretations of media representations reflect social, cultural and historical circumstances* is likely to equip young people with a more sophisticated understanding of the mediation of information and the representation of people, issues and events through digital and social networks than the more reactive dismantling of 'fake news' after the event.

Here's one example, zooming in on *how representations may invoke discourses and ideologies and position audiences.*

Ken Loach's 'social realist' political films seek to explore inequality through narrative. *I, Daniel Blake* (2016), a set text in Media Studies, was researched in collaboration charities and public sector organisations to fictionalize the real experiences of people claiming benefits in the immediate aftermath of austerity reforms to the welfare system. Blake is declared unfit to work, medically, unable to claim benefits, after an assessment in the new system:

> The logic is, if we could all be Daniel Blake then we should all be angry at the system that, as represented on screen, lets him down. At a preview screening in Manchester, Loach argued that even though *I, Daniel Blake* creates a picture of a Britain that marginalises and impoverishes its weakest, he still has hope in the will of the people to change things in the face of the sort of brutality shown in his film. (Willis, 20 October 2016: *The Conversation*)

The Media Studies approach to the film requires application of theories of realism - *Who is being represented?; How are they represented?; What seem to be the intentions of the representations? and What range of readings are there?*

These culminative representations built up through the use of camera, 'non-diegetic' elements such as music, voice over; editing and, of course, the 'extra-diegetic' layer of social media. The questions Media Studies asks of this text are How does *I, Daniel Blake* represent the social issues of welfare, benefits and citizen rights and responsibilities in the current period of austerity?; Which discourses are presented by the main characters in *I, Daniel Blake*? Which do students accept, and which do they oppose, and why?; What ideologies are presented by the film and how do they relate to the dominant ideology, as students understand it and who, in the film, is marked as 'other'?

Why is the Media Studies analysis of this film relevant here? Because the film became the subject of a heated debate on social media, in the mainstream media and among politicians over its 'truth claims' and the extent to which its status as a 'social document' of austerity was verifiable. Most notably, the Work and Pensions Secretary at the time, Damien Green, called the film 'monstrously unfair', though he later admitted that he hadn't seen it (see Smith and Bloom 2016).

TOOLKIT#8 Cairncross vs Public Interest vs Grenfell vs New Zealand

The Cairncross review was commissioned by the UK Government to *"examine the current and future market environment facing the press and high quality journalism in the UK... [and to] make recommendations on whether industry and/or government action might be taken to ensure a financially sustainable future for high quality journalism."*

The review poses some of the key questions we've asked here—why should we care about the future of journalism and public interest news, what's the role of these in a democracy? But media academics question *"the extent to which the consultation is designed to solicit evidence to justify subsidising corporate news organisations that are failing both in serving citizens and public interest and ability to profit in a changing market."* (Thorsen 2018: 1).

The way the review and the ensuing debate balances those 'macro' societal concerns with the devil's-in-the-details of the economic context for news (the 'micro') is 'very Media Studies'.

Tracking the reception and implementation of the review will be important for media students working towards subject criteria such as how the media industries' processes of production, distribution and circulation affect media forms and platforms. But going further, the critical question is about how the kinds of ethical journalism required for our future democracy by every single 'stakeholder' in this project can be enabled in the current economic precarity. Media students might reflect on the statements made by several journalists in these pages about reporting on the Grenfell Tower atrocity, set against Darren McGarvey's accusations of journalists contributing to *Poverty Safari* (2017) and the more recent *New York Times'* reporting of right wing extremist terrorism in New Zealand: "The manipulation of technology and use of online social platforms to document the killings, publicise them and try to inspire others to imitate them posed significant ethical challenges for our journalists running the coverage." (Ingber 2019).

It's another difficult and complex task, but a critical, open discussion about how to learn from the mistakes of Grenfell and build on the reflections from New Zealand—and the capacity to take those forward within the framing of the Cairncross review—is needed. And where better than the Media Studies classroom?

Follow up: https://www.nytimes.com/2019/03/19/reader-center/new-zealand-media-coverage.html.

Summary and Links to Next Chapter

In Karen Fowler-Watt's workshop (2018) with the Salzburg Global Academy, she uses the thought leadership third space the academy facilitates to ask students to 'reimagine journalism's core values' for the post-truth era. When definitions of self are in flux, she suggests, the interrogation of subjectivity and empathy with the other are even more important values in journalism. If post-truth means anything, it must be to do with the limits of human knowledge and a negotiation of how one human (journalist) tells stories about other humans' realities with greater or lesser degrees of objectivity or empathy, and how truth claims operate in a post-truth environment. These are existential questions. In Kafka's *Investigations of a Dog* (1922), the canine narrator asks:

> Why do I not do as the others: live in harmony with my people and accept in silence whatever disturbs the harmony, ignoring it as a small error in the great account, always keeping in mind the things that bind us happily together, not those that drive us again and again, as though by sheer force, out of our social circle? (p. 4)

Putting Kafka to work here serves an important purpose as we move into a consideration of post-truth. It helps us deal with another false binary. Just as Media Studies must remain critically vigilant about *all* news, to avoid 'real vs fake' and challenge both trust as naïve faith and the hyper-cynical 'open goal' of distrust *in all* media, so it must also remain faithful to critical theory, which deconstructs truth claims without accepting the dangers of relativism and alternative facts. In this way, Media Studies itself might face an existential crisis. As Kafka's dog notes (p. 25–26), "*One begins to seek causes, to stammer together a kind of aetiology – yes, one begins, and of course will never get beyond the beginning. But it's something – a beginning. The truth may not appear – one won't get that far – but at least something of the deeply rooted nature of the lie.*"

Onward Journeys (Applications)

App 14 BBC ireporter is another interactive, experiential resource, situating the BBC as the bastion of trust and truth. The user plays the role of a BBC journalist covering a breaking news story—"*Your story will be judged on how well you balance accuracy, impact and speed*".

Follow up: https://www.bbc.co.uk/news/resources/idt-8760dd58-84f9-4c98-ade2-590562670096.

App 15 ... and here's *The Guardian's* offering: this is a news literacy project, another valuable intervention by the mainstream media, but arguably with some 'virtue signalling', from a Media Studies perspective and perhaps complicated by Google funding.

Follow up: https://www.theguardian.com/newswise.

App 16 For critical balance, applying the Glasgow Media Group's analysis techniques to the reporting of Grenfell is a valuable Media Studies activity. Can the GMG's *Media Kit* be applied to the Grenfell atrocity and how did the media representation of austerity in the years before the fire contribute to the negligence of the authorities to provide a duty of care to residents? Working back from Grenfell to previous Glasgow Media Group deconstructions of media bias (and considered with current work by Media Lens), can we use the performance art of Jeremy Deller on the 'Battle of Orgreave' to think through this link?

Follow up: http://www.glasgowmediagroup.org/media-kit and http://www.jeremydeller.org/TheBattleOfOrgreave/TheBattleOfOrgreave_Video.php.

References

Alcorn, G. (2019, May 11). Murdoch Press: Even News Corp Staff Are Asking: Is What We Print the Truth? *The Guardian*, p. 31.

Bennett, P., Kendall, A., & McDougall, J. (2011). *After the Media: Culture and Identity in the 21st Century*. London: Routledge.

Buckingham, D., & Sefton-Green, J. (1994). *Cultural Studies Goes to School: Reading and Teaching Popular Media*. London: Taylor & Francis.

Bragg, B. (2011a). *Scousers Never Buy the Sun*. Self-released CD.

Bragg, B. (2011b, July 13). Liverpool Was Right About News International All Along. *The Guardian*.

Dent, T. (2017). *Feeling Devalued: The Creative Industries, Motherhood, Gender and Class Inequality*. Ph.D thesis, Bournemouth University, Bournemouth.

Dowling, T. (2018, June 24). Reporting Trump's First Year: The Fourth Estate—Heroism in These Dark Days. *The Guardian*.

Eddo-Lodge, R. (2017). *Why I'm no Longer Talking to White People About Race*. London: Bloomsbury.

Edwards, D., & Cromwell, D. (2018). *Propaganda Blitz: How the Corporate Media Distort Reality*. London: Pluto Press.

Fenton, N. (2018). *What Should the Cairncross Review Do?* 3D issue 31. http://legacy.meccsa.org.uk/news/three-d-issue-31-what-should-the-cairncross-review-do/. Accessed 2 September 2019.

Fowler-Watt, K. (2018). *From Where I Stand*. Interview with Fergal Keane. https://www.youtube.com/watch?time_continue=1562&v=tXh512ZjxOI.

Friedman, S., & Laurison, D. (2019). *The Glass Ceiling: Why It Pays to Be Privileged*. Bristol: Bristol University Press.

Hall, S. (2014). Foreword. In K. Connell & M. Hilton (Eds.), *50 Years On: The Centre for Contemporary Cultural Studies*. Birmingham: University of Birmingham.

Hall, S., Hobson, D., Lowe, A., & Willis, P. (Eds.). (1980). *Culture, Media, Language: Working Papers in Cultural Studies*. London: Routledge.

Hanley, L. (2016). *Respectable: The Experience of Class*. London: Penguin.

Hart, C. (2017). Metaphor and Intertextuality in Media Framings of the (1984–1985) British Miner's Strike: A Multimodal Analysis. *Discourse and Communication, 11*(1), 3–30.

Herman, E., & Chomsky, N. (1988). *Manufacturing Consent: The Political Economy of the Mass Media*. New York: Pantheon.

Hesmondhalgh, D. (2019). *The Cultural Industries* (4th ed.). London: Sage.

Hoggart, R. (2004). *Mass Media in a Mass Society: Myth and Reality*. London: Continuum.

Ingber, H. (2019, March 19). The New Zealand Attack Posed New Challenges for Journalists. Here Are the Decisions The Times Made. *The New York Times*.

Kafka, F. (1922). *Investigations of a Dog*. London: Penguin.

Laughey, D. (2007). *Key Themes in Media Theory*. Maidenhead: Open University Press.

Lewis, H. (2019, March 1–7). Enemies of the People. *New Statesman*.

Lopez, A. (forthcoming, 2020). *Teaching Ecomedia: Educating for Sustainable Media Ecosystems*. London: Routledge.

Martin, G., & Yurukoglu, A. (2017). Bias in Cable News: Persuasion and Polarization. *American Economic Review, 107*(9), 2565–2599.

McGarvey, D. (2017). *Poverty Safari: Understanding the Anger of Britain's Underclass*. Edinburgh: Luath Press.

Miller, D., & Philo, G. (2001a). *Market Killing. What the Free Market Does and What Social Scientists Can Do About It*. London: Longman.

Miller, D., & Philo, G. (2001b). The Active Audience and Wrong Turns in Media Studies: Rescuing Media Power. *Soundscapes, 4* (2011).

Milne, S. 2014. *The Enemy Within*. London: Verso.

Peace, D. (2004). *GB84*. London: Faber and Faber.

Philo, G., Hewitt, J., Beharrell, P., & Davis, H. (1992). *Really Bad News*. London: Writers and Readers Cooperative Society.

Smith, M., & Bloom. D. (2016, November 1). Damian Green Has Never Seen I, Daniel Blake—But Branded It 'Monstrously Unfair' Anyway. *The Mirror*. https://www.mirror.co.uk/news/uk-news/damian-green-never-seen-i-9166462.

Tanz, J. (2017). Journalism Fights for Survival in the Post-truth Era. *Wired*. https://www.wired.com/2017/02/journalism-fights-survival-post-truth-era/.

Thorsen, E. (2018). *3D 31: Quality Journalism, Internet and Politics*. http://www.meccsa.org.uk/nl/three-d-issue-31-quality-journalism-internet-and-politics/.

Waterson, J. (2019, March 19). BBC Plans Charity to Fund Local News Reporting in Britain. *The Guardian*.

Williamson, J. (1981). How Does Girl No. 20 Understand Ideology? *Screen Education, 40*, 80–87.

6

Post-truth

Hypernormalisation, the film by Adam Curtis, observes the strange, fake and corrupt nature of our reality and traces how we got to this point:

> Over the past forty years, politicians, financiers and technological utopians, rather than face up to the real complexities of the world, retreated. Instead, they constructed a simpler version of the world, in order to hang on to power. And as this fake world grew, all of us went along with it, because the simplicity was reassuring. (Curtis, BBC, 2016)

The film strikes a nerve with much of what we're dealing with in this book, and I often point students to it with regard to the claim that we're living in an era of post-truth, not least because it takes its title from a book about a mindset of acceptance of falsehood in the late Soviet Union (Yurchak 2006). On our line of enquiry, he laments:

> Journalism - that used to tell a grand, unfurling narrative - now also just relays disjointed and often wildly contradictory fragments of information. Events come and go like waves of a fever. We - and the journalists - live in a state of continual delirium, constantly waiting for the next news event

© The Author(s) 2019
J. McDougall, *Fake News vs Media Studies*,
https://doi.org/10.1007/978-3-030-27220-3_6

to loom out of the fog - and then disappear again, unexplained. And the formats - in news and documentaries - have become so rigid and repetitive that the audiences never really look at them. (ibid.)

Curtis declined to be interviewed for this book, saying: "*I think that the whole post truth thing has become something rather weird. It's become a sort of comfort blanket for people who don't want to face up to what the Trump election and the Brexit vote really meant. And I think that's wrong.*" I come back with more detail and reassurance that what he says might be kind of the point. But he's busy, and I don't hear from him again.

Watching Curtis's films puts a particular filter on the arrest of Julian Assange (on my final day writing this book). In 2010–2011, *Wikileaks*, in collaboration with mainstream media, including *The Guardian*, disseminated US Government documents, previously kept under strict secrecy. Shirky (2011) argued that WikiLeaks had 'created a new media landscape' and Assange forecast that society would come to distinguish between state power in pre- and post-WikiLeaks terms—this, at least, has happened but some of the bolder claims for the historical paradigm shift are now in check:

Assange clearly regards what WikiLeaks did 10 years ago as the vanguard of a new era of democratic awareness. He held that what governments did in our name should be public. Likewise, early social media was promoted as the welfare state of the information age. It would enable ordinary people to participate in a global village free of charge. We would all be laptop legislators of mankind. This was fanciful then and dangerous now. (Jenkins 2019: 2)

The implications of Assange's arrest are far reaching, with journalists and academics expressing outrage that the charges against the WikiLeaks founder were in contravention of the protection of free journalism by the first amendment of the US Constitution. According to The Center for Constitutional Rights, "*This is a worrying step on the slippery slope to punishing any journalist the Trump administration chooses to deride as 'fake news'*" (Pilkington 2019: 2). However, it must be clearly stated at this point that these concerns over Assange's legal rights as a journalist are irrelevant to the separate allegations of sexual assault against him.

Like fake news; post-truth is a signifier, to which vested interests can be attached. The cynical disengagement of the public from politics, academia and other elite arenas, during austerity, can be harnessed by representatives of those groups to suit their agendas—Trump on climate change, Michael Gove on how we've 'enough of experts'. As discussed in the chapter setting out the contexts for this topic, the notion of post-truth is also utilized to attack the left-wing of critical theory and postmodernism in particular, from which academics encouraged us to view truth-claims as subjective and relative; the argument now being along the lines of 'careful what you wish for'.

This chapter will explore the relationship between post-truth, fake news and Media Studies, the ground for which has already been prepared in the preceding chapters and in Contexts. Importantly, the conditions of possibility for post-truth are, likely, aspects of the same spreadable media affordances that our field has celebrated. For Jenkins, Ford, and Green *Spreadable Media* (2013) is a dissemination mode, for mainstream media distribution, which also provides a catalyst for new forms of mediated civic engagement, *By Any Media Necessary* (2016), the "*media strategies, creative vision, organizational activities and informal learning practices through which American youth are conducting politics in the early 21st century*" (Jenkins et al. 2016: 56). Mihailidis and Viotty explore the double edge of this, linking Jenkins' concept back to Guy Debord, to link *spreadable to spectacle*:

> Citizen expression online initiated, sustained, and expanded the media spectacle that pervaded the 2016 U.S. presidential election. Spreadability offers an intriguing backdrop for revisiting Debord's work on spectacle. It allows us to explore the ideological construction of spectacle that separates the consumer from reality through the conscious actions that citizens make to spread spectacle outside the framework of mainstream media and unhindered by the "lie" of reality. (Mihailidis and Viotty 2019: 442–443)

Back to Bias

As Buckingham reminds us (2017) and the preceding chapter sought to hammer home, *"the focus on fake news rather leaves aside the question of 'non-fake' news – the news reporting provided by professional journalists."*

One thing seems clear, and it's at the very least an inconvenient truth about truth. That is the fundamental point that Media Studies has always worked on: the assumption, that if we can teach students that representation is always subjective, representational and in that sense biased, then that would be an impactful revelation, and people would care. But if we are really in a post-truth environment where people are happy with alternative facts if they agree with the argument, then the foundations of Media Studies are at risk. On the other hand, we've seen—with examples from Russian research and provocations by the likes of dannah boyd—that we are now *too* media literate, both observing a state of hypercynicism where engagement with seeing through bias gives way to a total distrust of information, playing more and more into the hands of the 'mass misinformers', to paraphrase Hoggart. Here's Buckingham's view:

> I believe we can and should still teach about media bias. The changing political and media context – the so-called 'post-truth' age – makes this more complex and problematic, but it also makes it more necessary. However, it is important to avoid simply blaming the media, or overestimating their power. Aside from anything else, this can lead to a situation where the mediation of politics comes to be seen as more important than politics itself. Ultimately, such arguments reinforce a generalized distrust and cynicism that is increasingly shared across the political spectrum. It's not something I would regard as a good outcome for media literacy education.

In their evidence to the UK Government's fake news inquiry, Lilleker et al. summarized this conundrum, thus: *In a pluralist media system fake news is contested and challenged. However research on media habits show that many people choose not to enjoy a pluralist diet of information* (2018: 1). Like the Russian academics above, this research group is presenting evidence of the confirmation bias inherent to much media engagement, combined with the failure of most citizens to resist data tracking and algorithmic interventions by the digital corporations which serve to further insulate people from alternative perspectives. Lilleker et al.'s most important contribution, though, regarded how we think about bias in a democracy, asserting that there are degrees of bias and degrees of untruth and that *confirmation bias can only be relied upon where facts, and the sources of facts, are contested and so lack credibility. In other words, citizens will rely on their beliefs when they are unable to believe alternative accounts* (2018: 2).

Moscow, February 2019. I've been invited to the National Research University Higher School of Economics to give a talk and run a workshop on this book's topic at a conference on 'Digital Media for the Future'. The event brings together academics and media literacy educators from all over Russia, and I am struck by the richness of the critical dialogue. Vasily Klucharev shares neurolinguistic research on conformism and Evgeny Osin asks if happiness in the information age is 'an ideal or a trap'? Aleksey Neznanov reflects on 'Digitisation 4.0', a zeitgeist of 'post-truth A-I' (or '*keep calm the matrix has you*'). In this world, the old media of AI (with us since 1956) is put to use for 'deep fakes' and General Adversarial Networks (GADs)—again, this is about *the uses* (of AI, in this case). All speakers shared empirical findings about confirmation and positivity bias, the power of the algorithm that understands what we like better than we do and low coping resources among Russian citizens for uncertainty and feeling at odds with dominant discourse—or, darker, 'correcting norm violations':

> Why is it easier to agree with the majority? Why do fake news spread faster than truth and cause polarization of opinion? Why is it hard to reach consensus about the truth? What does one need to know about connections between algorithms and misbelieves? How does artificial intelligence influence views on ethics and the situation of post-truth? How do we learn to live in the world of uncertainty, accept something that is 'different' and 'unknown' and to keep balance of emotions? Is there a connection between the digital world, the concept 'I am media' and happiness? (Klucharev et al. 2019: 5)

Media, Post-*studies*

Hong Kong, November 2018. We're running our annual conference here and it's an apt setting on many levels. Hong Kong is a city in transition, reflecting the various threats journalism is under, and the complex relationship between politics, economics and technology, to say the least. Iain Williamson is Head of Film, Media and Digital Literacy at South Island School and our partner for the Youth Summit, a project that brings local media students into the conference to produce media (which we screen as the conclusion to the event) and engage with the academics who spend their time otherwise talking about and on behalf of young people! We are talking in the media department and I am dripping with sweat after an ill-judged brisk walk up the hill to the school. An ex-pat media teacher is an interesting animal, I suggest:

> I was educated originally at Warwick University so I studied there under the likes of Richard Dyer and my background was very much in film theory and so the practical elements of media education came a little bit later for me. I was very lucky that once I'd finished my first teaching post I went overseas with VSO (Voluntary Services Overseas) and I was lucky enough to be given a commissioned project where I was able to make short documentary films for returning volunteers, so those volunteers when they went back to their original donor country, whether that was Canada, Holland or the UK were able to take their films with them and show a little bit about the advocacy work that we did, and from that I managed to get a couple of projects with Nepal TV so that gave me confidence in film making as well so by time I arrived in South Island I'd been able to personally supplement the theory with the practical skills that I'd never really developed when I was at Warwick. And then over the last ten or fifteen years I've been lucky enough to be able to make a film every year here at the school with a professional film crew where I've been able to write the script and direct on set, shadowed by students. So I get the chance to get back into the field and upgrade the skills that I teach in my classes from one day to the next, so I think I've been quite lucky to bring together those two skill-sets in my role.

His course is unique, a hybrid of UK-legacy Media Studies and a localized curriculum designed by his team and accredited by Agence France Presse (AFP), titled simply 'Media' for two reasons—to distance his bespoke, accredited curriculum from the GCSE subject and because of a distaste in the region (among parents) for courses with 'Studies' in the title.

The issue for me was that speaking to some of the colleagues I have in the ESF who continue to teach GCSE media courses, there was a general feeling that some of the topic areas were a little bit banal. I felt that our students were asking questions about the big issues that related to media at that time and as much as film posters is an interesting topic, it's probably not the most pressing issue in the world in terms of media literacy at the moment! Then I met Eric Wishart from AFP who was in Discovery Bay, the same place I live in Hong Kong, and we started talking about some of the frustrations I had with current media teaching and he made the suggestion that perhaps there could be some kind of a partnership through the AFP and the school, where we could design a course really from the base up. That excited me because as a team we were able to start having conversations about stripping the course right down to the essentials, what do we think is important, what would we teach students if all things were equal, what would we like to teach students, what's important for their futures? The AFP accredit us now and they are particularly interested in one of our flagship units which is all about combating fake news and the issues which students face in trying to be critically astute in understanding and wading through all the noise that's out there, combined with our coding academy because we also felt, in this day and age, increasingly that coding languages are so important and media education should be shouldering some of the burden for that in terms of giving that kind of exposure to our students. So we felt it was time for a rebranding and there's not a parent in this school who doesn't think, in the conversations that I've had since I've been here, that media is important since the Web 2.0 digital revolution. So we're in a place now where parents are the ones pushing their kids towards doing Media courses, saying you've got to do this, this is essential for your future, as much as the kids wanting to opt for it themselves, so that's been quite a nice little paradigm shift that we've noticed in recent years.

I can only imagine, and envy! And since he mentions fake news directly, I pursue this line.

> I think that our subject is really vanguard in dealing with fake news at the moment. The critical analysis skills which schools are crying out for are embedded in what we do. I think what's also happened in recent years is that there are so many digital tools that most people are unaware of to assess the kind of news that they are consuming, so some of the ones that we teach in school, tools like reverse image searches that enable students to discover when an image was first posted on the internet, so they can see, for instance, with stories where images are taken out of context, quite often images from wars that were fought ten years ago are presented via all kinds of stuff, different news feeds, Twitter quite often, I will use this technique myself to see that somebody is trying to make an inflammatory or emotive point about a situation in Israel or Palestine or wherever it might be. There are search tools to provide students with an opportunity to find the original source of information or the original posting of information on the internet with the web-based article so it provides you with the kind of matrix of how an article draws upon previous articles, perhaps deliberately only selecting particular features from the original post which then of course leads to exposure of bias, some provide a trust rating for students. I think these kinds of algorithmic approaches to news we wouldn't have had access to ten years ago in media education and now we do, so these tools really need to start to come into the classroom environment alongside the traditional media theory concepts that we've taught very effectively over a number of years.

I ask about the dynamic relationship between teaching this subject in Hong Kong, considering the employment and skills focus and Iain's political perspective on media and power?

> I think I'm afforded a certain level of freedom here that perhaps might surprise people. I think that's because I work in an international school, so we still have GCSE qualifications and also there hasn't yet been a crackdown from China on freedom of speech that's had an impact on schools in the international field. That may well change and I think it's already starting to change in Hong Kong and if we have this conversation

in ten years' time, then I think my answer will be very different. On my own political views, I've always sought to try and be as objective as I can in the classroom, I mean I teach theory of knowledge in school, which is essentially an analysis of epistemology and when we look at the great debates of our time that have engaged philosophers down through the centuries so even though I'm not a big fan, for instance of self-interest theory, I teach that to students, I explain what it is, I try to give it a sense of parity in my teaching to perhaps to some of the more left-wing views that are closer to my own. I think in terms of media practice, hand on heart the research that I've done has shown that news has moved more and more to the right and I don't think there's any great surprise that politically we're seeing a wave of different countries moving to a right-wing political system because I think the media is essentially feeding that process. The right-wing has for a long time fought battles where if they can't win an argument then they'll muddy the waters enough to draw on and skew particular issues and I think that was the case with the Brexit vote in the UK, certainly with the election of Trump, so I guess I've moved beyond any sense that there is a conspiracy to think that the world media is essentially run by billionaires and the media therefore serves the interests of a minority, an elite who want to continue to enjoy the kind of status quo that they've enjoyed up until now. So the freedom that's afforded by the rise of the internet and social media has been in danger of challenging some of that. What I think we're seeing is more of an attempt to control those channels of and the right have garnered control and manipulated those social media forms.

As a media teacher I still try to remain objective and I try to divorce as much as possible my own political views but I do think the work that's going on with the likes of Media Lens shows us that we've got to move beyond traditional liberal sources of news where we might have expected to get closer to the truth like The Guardian or the BBC because these seem to be just as guilty of avoiding drawing our attention to the terrible crimes which have been committed in Yemen over recent years, deliberate attempts to demonise the likes of Julian Assange, the importance of climate change which continues to be reduced in scope in these kinds of liberal newspapers and organisations. I'm used to being able to demonstrate political bias and let's be honest, fake news is nothing new, The Sun made its name on fake news over a forty year period as have many other media outlets, but what's new is the that we have to increasingly get beyond mainstream media if we want to get to the heart of what's really going on in some of the big issues worldwide. For us as practitioners to give that kind of information to our students, to give them the tools with which to see that themselves, without simply telling them but to allow them to come to those conclusions themselves by simply presenting them with the facts and critical analysis skills has increasingly been a significant part of my job. We've always created free thinkers, Media Studies always promoted textual analysis, but I think those critical thinking skills are more necessary than ever and more complex in terms of getting to the truth of particular issues.

Team Human vs *Post* Human

In *Blade Runner* and the *2049* sequel, the existential question of whether the protagonist is human or a designed, artificially intelligent 'replicant' extends to a filmic thinking through of what it means to be human anyway. Various baselining tests are used in the two films to provoke emotions and empathy, aspects of having a soul that are held as distinctive of humanity. In Rushkoff's *Team Human*, his central thesis—which this project looks like it shares—is that the digital oligopoly's economic model is anti-human, to the point of it being surprising that a public so well versed, by now, in the generic narratives of horror and science fiction, haven't noticed:

> Think about algorithms. We progamme these little things to understand our weaknesses, to figure out our exploits and then leverage them in order to get us to do things against our own best interests, automatically. That's like a definition of a demon! And we created them. (Rushkoff, in Brand, 2019: 1:03:10)

If that is a definition of a demon, then Media Studies teachers are exorcists.

As part of his campaign for *Team Human*, Rushkoff puts a spiritual dimension to work, looking for the essence of humanity in the embracing of ambiguity, play, social bonds and the higher ideal of Reason, with which we can, as team human, re-capture Renaissance thinking to move past the current crisis, address climate change and 'find the others' and, crucially, this is not to do with 'screen time' or tuning out from networked digital media, as such a response would conform to 'the binary logic of the thing we are resisting' (2019: 171).

In the conversation with Russell Brand cited above, he uses a medical analogy. Rather than see the 'disease' as digital, and thus go analogue or offline as a response:

> *Rushkoff:* What about looking at the vitality of the patient instead? So rather than coming up with a new algorithm to filter dangerous, weaponized memes from my teen's Instagram account what about if I just make my teen, and our culture, more resilient to this? So I'm trying to promote our humanity so we're less vulnerable to the insanity rather than looking at the insanity as the problem to be fixed.
> *Brand:* Yeah, you might be right about that.

This would make the Media Studies teacher either a yoga teacher, nutritionist or lifestyle coach, as opposed to a doctor or surgeon. And the logic works, in the sense that critical media literacy, this project argues, will go some way to enabling such 'resilience' through a healthy skepticism—a kind of vitality—towards mediated information of all kinds and, if we get this right through enough attention to the underpinning and overarching questions of civics, democracy and living together in the world for good (in Rushkoff's words, 'being human is a team sport'), then education can be 'the answer' in the ways Biesta is suggesting, and we discussed those ideas in the chapter on democracy. So, this would be critical media literacy as an exorcism of anti-human demons already at work and a preventative vitamin infusion to guard against them in the future.

Paul Mason has come to a similar conclusion, also optimistic on the whole, in *Clear Bright Future* (2019). Like Rushkoff, he traces the 'redesign' of humans for the purpose of coercion, control and obligated competition and in the failure of the neoliberal project to secure 'the end of history' (Fukuyama 1992), he also sees the open, fertile ground for a 'return to humanity'. Neither Rushkoff nor Mason are religious, though the former attaches a sense of 'spiritual essence' to his proposal, while Mason is overtly materialist and rooted in socialist politics:

> Technology could free us from work, ignorance, and much of our ill health. But only if it remains under our control. The key to reasserting control, Mason argues, is micro-level resistance: refusal to "perform" as the routines of market capitalism demand. As we do so, he says, we have begun to find each other and act, just as the pioneers of the labour movement did in the 19th century. (2019, Penguin: 1)

Sounds convincing, right?

However:

> There is an important sense in which practices of knowing cannot be fully claimed as human practices, not simply because we use nonhuman elements in our practices but because knowing is a matter of part of the world making itself intelligible to another part. Practices of knowing and being are not isolatable, but rather they are mutually implicated. We do not obtain knowledge by standing outside of the world; we know because "we" are of the world. We are part of the world in its differential becoming. The separation of epistemology from ontology is a reverberation of a metaphysics that assumes an inherent difference between human and nonhuman, subject and object, mind and body, matter and discourse. Onto-epistem-ology—the study of practices of knowing in being— is probably a better way to think about the kind of understandings that are needed to come to terms with how specific intra-actions matter. (Barad 2006: 829)

This view links back to the earlier discussion of non–media-centric Media Studies (Moores 2017). Or Media Studies *After the Media* (Bennett et al. 2011). In the same way as the notion of common values for democracy goes along with the marginalisation of the victims of colonialism, in order to deal with more important things first, the post-human argument is about the problem of just adding extra bits to the humanist project, to make the category of human more inclusive, instead of recognising that the construction of 'human' itself is loaded towards particular dominant ways of 'being human' (Bayley 2018).

This argument is similar to Judith Butler's work on the performance of gender and the playful act of 'troubling' it. The post-human project is about performing human agency, as a state of *dynamic* flux and fluidity, rather than as a stable category. This embraces the way in which the representational categories of, and boundaries between, human and non-human are always a version of events or 'practices of knowing' (Barad 2006: 829). Another false binary?

I *think* that, for this project and Media Studies in general, it's OK at this juncture to put Rushkoff's ideas about the vitality of the patient and Mason's 'clear, bright future' to work for critical media literacy, *in dialogue with* new thinking about non–media-centric and post-human analyses of the material-discursive relations of mediation. I *think* it's OK. But I concede that as a white male writing this book as part of my day job, that might be easy for me to say. As Benjamin Zephaniah puts it: "*there's nothing wrong with being white, male, middle class and heterosexual. It's just that we've already been listening to you for hundreds of years*" (BBC Radio 4 interview, 1 May 2018).

Riga to RIBA (or Team Human to Posthuman to *In*human)

The Great School Libraries campaign states:

> School libraries aren't statutory, and in the UK no one knows how many there are, or if they are staffed or funded. The Great School Libraries campaign is a three-year campaign which aims to change this – collecting data about school libraries as well as working towards securing school library funding; producing a national framework for school libraries and recognition of school libraries within Ofsted. (https://greatschoollibraries. edublogs.org/)

UNESCO's policy steering on the link between media literacy and libraries area is framed as MIL, to include information literacy as well as media. In 2016, days after the referendum result, it was uncomfortable to be contributing to the Riga declaration on MIL, as the drafting event was hosted by the National Library of Latvia, proudly symbolic of the country's status as the newest member of the European Union. The declaration obliges policymakers to "*address knowledge gaps between MIL mediators such as library and information specialists, teachers, parents, journalists by providing relevant resources, funding and training as a part of professional development and lifelong learning.*"

> It can be challenging for primary and secondary school pupils to ana-lyse how accurate information is – and understand what 'Fake news' is. Critical Literacy is one approach that can help identify it. The theme of Critical Literacy is a whole-school, cross-curricular approach towards the teaching of literacy that has the library at the centre and encourages read-ers to be active participants in the reading process as opposed to passive absorbers of information. The School Library Association has been to the forefront of creating awareness about the term 'Fake news' and promot-ing resources that school librarians can use to inform and educate pupils, teachers, governors, and parents. (Coyle 2019: 2)

Three years later, with Brexit unresolved, I am meeting Alison Tarrant, who heads up the campaign, at another 'flagship' library, in Birmingham. But this one is not such a source of shared civic pride. It's a spectacular design, to the tune of nearly £200 million and is the larg-est public library in the United Kingdom and, apparently, the largest public cultural space in Europe. But the project came to culmination during the first wave of austerity cuts and is now only open from 11 a.m. due to the axing of staffing budgets. The design is divisive, win-ning a Royal Institute of British Architects (RIBA) award but described by one social media commentator among many as *one of the most dis-gusting and inhuman buildings I've ever seen.* A more nuanced perspec-tive is offered by Rowan Moore, architecture critic: "The Library of Birmingham is a good building. It is a sketch, or a pixelation, of a great one" (2013: 3).

We're joined by Mel Crawford from Peters, a supplier of books for schools and libraries, who are partnering on the campaign.

The link between media literacy and libraries in the UK context has hitherto been somewhat tangential, in terms of implementing the

UNESCO declaration. This changed with this recent inclusion in the GSL campaign's list of key library functions: *Deliver and teach essential Information/critical literacy skills to combat fake news and engender independent learning.* The Library and Information Association (2018) offers its own definition of 'information literacy', which includes digital and media literacies and aligned knowledge and understanding. This definition is articulated in five contexts: everyday life; citizenship; education; the workplace; and health, and it also signposts inter-professional collaboration, between information professionals and teachers, academic advisers and educational technologists. I am struck by the alignment of the definition with the specification objectives of Media Studies:

Information literacy can be seen as the critical capacity to read between the lines. It enables learners to engage in deep learning – perceiving relationships between important ideas, asking novel questions and pursuing innovative lines of thought. This active and critical way of learning encourages students to quickly master factual and descriptive elements of content ('What' and 'How') and then move on to investigate higher-level aspects such as source, degree of authority, possibility of bias, and what it means in the wider context. It is in line, for example, with the English National Curriculum aim to equip students, "to ask perceptive questions, think critically, weigh evidence, sift arguments and develop perspective and judgement." (CILIP 2018: 5)

At this point it looks pretty clear that there's a healthy situation already set out in UK schools. We have Media Studies, which does critical capacity, with an explicit focus on mediated information. We have information professionals working on the same project, which maps well to the English National Curriculum. So, if we made Media Studies mandatory and brought in school librarians to support the underpinning information literacy, we'd be in a good place to tackle fake news. But that is not happening. The opposite is the case. Media Studies is taken by a small minority of students, seen as a 'lightweight' subject by politicians and the top universities and often ridiculed by the media it is aiming to both critique and supply with a workforce.

My conversation with Alison and Mel gives me a more detailed understanding of the threats to school libraries, and the misconceptions among parents and the wider public about their role.

> *Alison*: During my Masters we did a module on the digital world and society. I have always wanted to have a positive impact on the world around me, and I realised that actually I didn't have to change the world, but I could change someone's world. School libraries improve the quality of life for young people, not just their education.

As well as talking to me for this book, Mel and Alison are helping me recruit library professionals for the workshop I am running in London for the US Embassy-funded project on the same topic. Because not all of the participants in this category will be librarians, strictly speaking, I use the term 'information professionals' to describe them in the workshop materials. This plays well, and opens a can of worms around advocacy and identity and the role of 'fake news' itself in the work of libraries (see also Barclay 2017):

> *Alison*: People still don't see school librarians as professionals – as with children's literature – is the lesser regarded. I got asked by a colleague 'when I was going to become a teacher' – the concept that this would be a *profession*, that I had *chosen*, had never occurred to him. When adequately funded and properly staffed, school libraries deliver enhanced and independent learning as well as reading and curriculum support. Librarians have a huge and well documented positive impact on the education and mental health and wellbeing of young people, but still people don't grasp what we do.

Then we move onto the issue at hand:

> *Mel*: School libraries are a space for critical thinking, when the subject curriculum is so compressed. Libraries help children with critical thinking skills like having an awareness of the source, the messages behind information, looking at opposing views and having to pick your way through them. The role of teachers and parents in society is very important but their job is even harder without school libraries, I don't think people realise this.

Alison: The way we look at information literacy, it's about embedding, co-designing and co-teaching, so it's librarians and teachers working together. So rather than a separate subject or teachers trying to do this within their subjects, the library support allows for that integration, it's in everyone's interests and more so now than ever with young people bombarded with so much information and the problem of fake news, so it's in the campaign as reducing funding for libraries is going to make that problem worse.

Mel: Things like evaluating websites, how to spot misinformation and fake news, how to reference sources, teachers may not find time for this kind of information literacy, but school librarians offer it. So if there's really so much concern about fake news and the idea that we need to do something in schools, it really needs to be joined up.

History of the Present

Nick Crowson is Professor of Contemporary History at Birmingham University. In his office, a stone's throw from the old CCCS, we discuss Brexit and the (inevitable) link between his work and this book. In reading a feature he published in *The Observer* (Crowson 2018) on the enduring 'Europe question' in British Conservative Party politics, it struck me that it would be unwise for media educators using the referendum campaign as a case study in this debate to neglect this historical perspective. As with everything, you need to know *what* is being mediated in the first place. I ask him, from the historian's viewpoint, if all this is just 'old wine, new bottles'?

Speaking historically, it's always been there. Has it got worse? Probably not, but the difference is, I suspect that it's open potentially for a much greater scale. But what we essentially see as historians is that every generation has to exploit new media, new forms of subverting messages and different publics receiving and absorbing this information have responded and sometimes these (fake) stories have taken hold within both public and political memory.

On the question of whether hard times are a breeding ground for misinformation:

There are always points historically where populations have been discontented or economic hardships have been exacerbated. So you think of the early 80s and Thatcherism and take something like the right to buy council houses as an example. The Government were selling it politically through manifestos, through political speeches, the usual kind of forums where a speech by minister is reported by The Times or whatever. But then the other side of it is that they're using things like the official information films of the era. If you look at those via the national archives now, they present a vision of what council houses are, which doesn't bear any relation to the reality of the majority of council housing stock, exceptionally white, a family, two kids, sitting down for tea, in a semi-detached property. Go back to the 60s, that era of kind of social awakening, there's discontent, you've got a new educated young middle class, an aspiring working class coming through who benefitted from educational reforms in the late 40s, they're now educated, they're aspiring to university, they're in political campaigns involving anti-apartheid, anti-war, Vietnam movements, yet these were all open to forms of exploitation and manipulation. Go back to Suez, Anthony Eden is using various film outlets to sell a very particular vision of how he's going to respond, go back to the 30s and you've got a Conservative party and there's a journal called Truth, basically financed by Conservative party funds. The leadership don't know about this. That journal is used as an outlet through a former intelligence officer confidante of Neville Chamberlain and he is using the editor to write various pieces that essentially politically kneecap opponents of Chamberlain's foreign defence policies. None of it is founded on any truth but the gossip in and around Westminster leads to resignations. The editor puts out a story that when Anthony Eden resigns in February of 1938 as Foreign Secretary, Anthony is a bit unwell, mentally. That's why after his resignation speech he needs to go off to the South of France to recover his wits and his health. The flip, the reverse of that is Eden can't wait to get away because he's realised he's made a monumental mistake actually resigning. He's allowed the hotheads around him to persuade him to resign and then he's realised actually he shouldn't have done and he spends the rest of the time trying to persuade Neville Chamberlain that he should come back into office. But that story about his mental health takes hold and so in 1956, in the height of the Suez crisis, we hear individuals saying 'well of course we know Anthony isn't very stable', so there's an old example of how a fake story has taken hold with serious political consequences.

Since he cites the 1930s, does he see a parallel with our current austerity context and the use of fake news by the alt-right, in particular?

Well everything works at a different pace, obviously. We know that ordinary people acquired their understanding of news from in the 1930s from cinema newsreels first and foremost. Then it's newspapers and that might not be The Times, the dailies, it might be the evening local papers that they are acquiring on their way home from work. And then it's the wireless, as television's in its infancy at this point. So those talkies, those newsreels, they are run by corporations such as Pathe news, amongst others. A number of those are in with the government of the day in terms of how they should present things and what they should and shouldn't say about particular aspects of foreign policy. So there's a constant element of misinformation operating within this. The British are very concerned at this point that in terms of their external propaganda, they're struggling to counter in Germany the propaganda machine of the Third Reich so how the hell to you get your messages into Germany? So they co-opt Radio Luxembourg, who were broadcasting by short wave radio into Germany and they have these recordings of Neville Chamberlain and other ministers' speeches about the sincerity of the British people and the British government securing peace. So they are pressing gramophone recordings and flying them over at high speeds to Radio Luxembourg and these speeches are being broadcast and this reveals the extraordinary lengths of soft propaganda, which is the term historians would use rather than 'fake news' as a way of explaining what's going on there.

TOOLKIT#9 *The War of the Worlds* vs The Media

The radio broadcast of H. G. Wells' science fiction novel is currently a set text in Media Studies. It's a very old text, but it is often cited in debates over 'media effects'—the same trajectory that manifests itself in the moral panic we are addressing here, over fake news. In *The War of the Worlds*, aliens invade and the story is told through the narrator's diary account. The radio play, directed and narrated by Orson Welles in the late 1930s, adapted the narrative to locate the story in the United States.

The conventions of news reports were adopted for dramatic realism, so for the audience to suspend disbelief and engage in the plot as though it was subject to radio journalism. This hybrid approach, postmodern, before the term was in use, was innovative and unfamiliar to radio listeners. Welles is known for his critique 'from within' of media power (see *Citizen Kane*) and clearly this was an example of such a satirical intent— *'We wanted people to understand that they shouldn't take any opinion predigested, and they shouldn't swallow everything that came through the tap whether it was radio or not'* (Welles, in Chilton, 2016). CBS broadcast a disclaimer prior to the narrative starting, stating clearly that this would be fiction, but a significant section of the audience switched channels too late and 'the rest is history'—a classic 'moral panic' ensued, fueled by the mainstream media in the form of headlines in newspapers about 'terror', 'hysteria', and 'mass panic'. As the Media Studies analysis of moral panics has proven (see Cohen 1972), the mediation of the panic amplified and reactivated a much-exaggerated version of the real issue, with claims about evacuations, heart attacks and suicide attempts. Fake news? Or the anticipated circulation of a satire on propaganda?

Orson Welles benefitted from the overblown coverage of the play. Not only did it provide him with useful personal publicity, it also reinforced his hypothesis of the dangerous power of the media. Welles was a committed anti-fascist who wanted to alert the American public to the potentially manipulative uses of the mass media as demonstrated by Nazi propaganda. The context of the time should also be taken into account. The news – the real news – in October 1938 was dominated by events in Europe, which in less than a year's time exploded into World War Two. An explanation for the tenacious grip of the War of the Worlds' 'panic' myth is that the public then and now have a deep-rooted anxiety about the power of the media. We are not particularly frightened by Martians but powerful media institutions which can change the way we think really do scare us. For this reason, we need stories based in fact or fiction which confirm these prejudices. (Bennett et al. 2019)

Propaganda vs 'The Media'

Igor Kanižaj is Associate Professor at the University of Zagreb, in the Faculty of Political Science, Department of Journalism and Media Production. He is an important researcher in the European fields of media education and media literacy and we've met often at conferences and network events. He is an academic with impact; his project *Djeca medija* reached 12,000 participants in Croatia and won the Evens Foundation Special Jury Prize for media education in 2017. His current work, with Renee Hobbs, concerns media literacy and propaganda (*Mind over Media*, funded by the European Commission). We talk over pizza in Zagreb. I'm there for another EC event, in between the Brussels seminar on common values and a symposium in Tbilisi. This meeting is at the Croatian Ministry for Education, a site for dialogue on media literacy, history and identity between representatives from the host nation, Bosnia and Herzegovina, Serbia and Turkey, members of the European Parliament and European Commission stakeholders from Brussels and Amsterdam. I am there to deliver a keynote address, 'Uses and Abuses of Media', and, being from the United Kingdom, suffering from self-inflicted outsider status at this juncture.

Igor is busy, and tired. He's on his way home from work. On top of all the above, he's now on the Croatian National Council for Children.

> I'm a former journalist, I started to work as journalist in the high school, back in the 90s. I enrolled for Journalism studies, finished an MA, a PhD and since then I've been working on the study of Journalism. And then afterwards I started to research the field of media and children, media and violence and it all came together through models of media education that became practical through our Association for Communication and Media Culture, which is one of the biggest NGOs in Croatia for media education at the moment. So I'm trying to combine practical work along with several research projects.

I am interested in the degree to which his approach to media education was informed by his experience as a journalist.

> I think it gave some added value to it, because I understand the sociology and the production of the news because I was working as a news editor, I had a big political show for 2 years on one radio station so I know the procedures, I know the problems of the journalist's world, I know how to work with the sources and that became one of the biggest advantages in the research afterwards and helped me also to get some new perspective. Even when I'm doing research afterwards and collaborating with journalists on different projects I think this was very useful.

And onto 'fake news':

I would like to go back at least one hundred years in history. At the beginning of the 20th century, the biggest news rooms at that time initiated and established their fact checking departments. So I would say that this was the first origin of the fight against fake news but from a totally different perspective, because their idea was to fight with credibility. I do like to call it fake news even now. Although it has a negative connotations because of the presidential election in the USA, I would not like to run away from fake news, because it has become a term that is accepted in the general public. Although the European high expert group had the position that it's not good to use the term, I still use it because of the historical context and because it points to the possible solution of the whole problem we have, together with journalism as a profession. Yes, we have information disorder, we have misinformation, we have disinformation, we have mal-information. Yes, we have totally different approaches brought by social networks. Yes, we have people who would like to do harm as their main purpose and use the credibility of the media in order to send false information and produce some harmful things. But I think that all these aspects, all these practices have fake news somewhere in together. And it's not fair to claim that when you have some mistake produced by journalists in the media companies to proclaim this as fake news. So you have to be very careful, especially because most of the research that has been done is not including a cultural framework, so you have totally different perceptions of fake news in Asia and also in Croatia. Coming from the journalists' perspective, 10 years ago we've done the first research in Croatia on news credibility. This was a comprehensive content analysis of the main media outlets. And even then we were trying to build partnerships with all kinds of organisations because we had findings that were pointing to the totally new approach that will later on happen as fake news, a decade since.

So how does 'fake news' relate to propaganda, the focus of his current work?

So, the 'Mind over Media' project (Fig. 6.1) is happening right now in Croatia, I've run a workshop with librarians and when I asked them to give the first association on propaganda, two words appeared. The first one was 'racism' and the second one was 'Hitler'. And then in 90 minutes time

Fig. 6.1 Mind over Media: crowd-sourcing resilience (*Source* Igor Kanižaj)

when we go on with the workshop we end by recognising propaganda in all other areas of our lives, in all other aspects. Because it is a crowd-sourcing project, the idea is that we are trying to upload examples of propaganda all over the world. We are not proclaiming that something is propaganda and other things are not, we are trying to point out that, depending on our previous experience in the cultural framework we live in, our ideas of propaganda are changing so we are building this new tool that for a totally new approach to propaganda research.

I offer him the hypothesis that young people have media literacy but lack media morality.

I like this concept of emphasizing morality but I don't agree actually because I would say that youngsters have higher levels of information skills, of digital skills, but they are not media literate always, the problem is students come with the approach 'we know everything about fake news, disinformation, viral campaigns, propaganda'. But when I start to show the examples that I know they were not exposed to, at the end they really become aware of low level of critical thinking in their consuming of media content, especially for social networks. So the first level is the scale, then we come to the competencies, then we have the critical awareness and then you can include morality in that concept.

And on the future of media literacy, how optimistic is he for positive change?

I think it's coming home. (*this is a Croatian football supporter talking to an English author!*)

One of the good things that happened with fake news is that it revealed the problems we have in our information systems. Even the most credible media have examples of mal-information, disinformation, misinformation and fake news in general and propaganda as well. But still they manage to survive I think about huge media outlets such as New York Times or Wall Street Journal or even yours as well, like The Guardian and BBC, so in almost every country you can find the media that has been recognised as credible and has an established connection with the public and in these cases, the public is able and ready and willing to pay for the content. So now is the time that we have to recognise that quality media costs, that credible information definitely costs. For us as the scientists, as the researchers, as the workers in the field, information is a public good still. But in order for us to have the opportunity to consume credible information, it costs more than it did ever before in history. And this is the problem for those who are not able to pay for it. By saying 'pay' I also mean intellectual skills, about being able to study and not just about being able to buy or produce. So for me this is the biggest challenge. That's why I think that the high quality media will prevail, because they will find their public. But the overall public will have problems and we see this with this fake news situation we have. I don't think that the social networks will be the solution, I don't think that the algorithms will be solutions. I don't think that the coding will be a solution. But it's not the same everywhere, in all markets. In Asia newspapers are living for their next future I would say. In the old continent, in Europe, the newspaper industry is facing the biggest problems ever. So these are different worlds but we all are fighting for credible information.

TOOLKIT#10 Stuart Hall vs Michael Gove

In an argument for teaching 'objectivity' in the post-truth era, Blackburn (2019) offers a compelling call to arms, but, once again, ignores the remedy in front of him – Media Studies. He says: "*The only remedy for bad ideas and bad mental habits is the cultivation of better ones. We need leaders to set better examples and we need to raise people good at distinguishing what is trustworthy from what is not. Clearly, this is not going to be achieved by a Gove- instilling of facts, or formulae, or grammar, which merely trains children in the bovine receptivity that is the very opposite of any active, intelligent, and critical response to the world"* (here he refers to the recent Minister for Education, Michael Gove, widely seen as responsible for a profoundly uncritical turn in the UK school curriculum). *What we need is an education system that encourages cautious scepticism and an imaginative open-mindedness, allied with the sensible assessments of probabilities. We also need to develop dispositions towards decency and civil debate. In a "post-truth" world characterised by cascades of misinformation and politicians with no shame, we ought to bring the practices of philosophy into our classrooms. What a subversive thought! But then as the saying goes, if you think knowledge is expensive, try ignorance.*

Once again, if only there was a subject doing this already?!

In this example, we go back to where we set out, to the overarching framework. Toolkit #1 described the key concepts. The *application* of those concepts to popular culture, including media, is largely inherited from Stuart Hall. In an engaging video about Hall's approach from Al Jazeera, the theorist's outsider status is linked to his political 'doing theory' on the mass media and he is paraphrased thus: *He saw pockets of resistance that undermine dominant media narratives. If you want to understand society, then maybe avoid the news, those formalised spaces that house official discourse. Find different stories, different perspectives, different realities.*

This is the essence of Media Studies. Understanding society. Linking Hall to Blackburn, this is about the cultivation of critical habits of mind, an active, intelligent, critical response to the world.

Follow up: https://www.youtube.com/watch?v=FWP_N_FoW-I.

Truth vs Trust

Whilst the dystopian claims that we're in a post-truth era are contentious and reports of the demise of truth are exaggerated, a Media Studies analysis of post-truth needs to deconstruct the conditions of possibility for media audiences to believe media representations. Alternatively, media students might come to a more Foucaultian or postmodern acknowledgement of the relativity of all truth-claims. But at this point in the research for this book, it seems like all of this is hinging more on the relationship between ontological *truth* and epistemological *trust* (the value of knowledge). Journalists come back, over and over, to trust. Here's Jon Snow, in conversation with Karen Fowler-Watt and students at my institution, again citing Grenfell as an awakening of sorts for the profession:

> You think about community and you think about society and you think about a country and you think about its people and then you discover that there's incredible disconnection from the roots upwards and that was brought home to me by Grenfell in a big way. You are there in fact to represent the people who the state has failed. That sounds like a political statement, it's not, it is our job. Our job is actually to give voice to people who have no voice.

Specifically on the topic we are dealing with:

> Fake news is not new – and there are many PR agencies whose stock in trade has always been a dash of fake news, just to disturb the system. But, the problem is we have to try and use the same media to combat it, to find really credible alternatives.

(see Snow 2019, for the development of these perspectives).

Summary and Links to Next Chapter

So far, our journey in the false binary has taken us through multiple, inter-related contexts: political, economic, philosophical, technological and educational. Assumptions about democracy have been assessed against citizens' entitlement to a plural media, and the threats to both by fake news and misinformation. The specific role of the internet in, well, everything, and the nature of the Media Studies response has been considered. The dubious notion of a post-truth era has been taken seriously and (partly) debunked, but without dispensing with important critical projects towards a decentered and diverse thinking through of what it is to be human and what we are thinking about when we talk about truth. At every turn, we have heard from media educators and journalists and illustrated the travelogue with examples of Media

Studies in action and onward connections to resources and materials in the public domain.

So, to put it all together. It's time for the final round.

Onward Journeys (Applications)

App 17 *Mind over Media* is a project and educational resource which, perhaps controversially (to journalists, at least) doesn't differentiate between propaganda and the persuasive, conventional practices of mainstream media. In this sense, it is much more in synch with the Cultural Studies legacy of Stuart Hall than the current plethora of fact-checking resources. For example, a *Time* magazine cover features prominently in a section on 'propaganda techniques: activate strong emotions'. The online resource is interactive, inviting users to rate media material on a scale from 'beneficial' to 'harmful' and to upload material for others to assess. For the Media Studies topics in question here, these activities and lesson plans provided by *Mind over Media* could be put to work with an overarching, critical theme—is *all* media propaganda?

Follow up: https://propaganda.mediaeducationlab.com/node/1.

App 18 In the interview with Iain Williamson, we discussed the way that, in Media Studies, "*We've always created free thinkers.*" This video essay, by South Island Student Yan Phu, investigates news sources revolving around the media representation of the case in Hong Kong of Ken Tsang, otherwise known as the 七警 incident. In 2014, pro-democratic activist Ken Tsang was beaten by Hong Kong police officers after being arrested during the Umbrella protests. Phu uses the kinds of image-reverse searches learned on the SIS Media course and referred to in the interview. In this way, the critical thinking required for resilience to misinformation is applied to the production context of the video format and distributed, open access.

Follow up: https://vimeo.com/219175314.

App 19 *Malware for Humans* is not a resource, rather an argument. Watching it together with Adam Curtis' *Hypernormalisation, Blade Runner 2049,* Rushkoff's *Team Human* and Paul Mason's *Clear, Bright Future* will be challenging but it will cover a range of concerns, expressed through fiction, polemic and documentary. Then, to consider the research-informed perspective from our field—media and journalism education—take a look at Sarah Jones' keynote at the Media Education Summit, for a critical triangulation.

Follow up:
Malware for Humans https://www.byline.com/column/67/article/2412.
Team Human https://teamhuman.fm/.
Clear, Bright Future https://www.paulmason.org/clear-bright-future-a-radical-defence-of-the-human-being/#more-145.
Sarah Jones at MES https://www.youtube.com/watch?time_continue=4&v=R36DujXd7Pg.

References

Barad, K. (2006). Posthumanist Performativity: Toward an Understanding of How Matter Comes to Matter. In D. Orr (Ed.), *Belief, Bodies, and Being: Feminist Reflections on Embodiment*. Lanham, MD: Rowman & Littlefield.

Barclay, D. (2017). The Challenge Facing Libraries in an Era of Fake News. *The Conversation, 5*(1), 17.

Bayley, A. (2018). *Posthuman Pedagogies in Practice: Arts Based Approaches for Developing Participatory Futures*. Basingstoke: Palgrave Macmillan.

Bennett, P., Benyahiya, S., & Slater, J. (2019). *A Level Media Studies: The Essential Introduction*. London: Routledge.

Bennett, P., Kendall, A., & McDougall, J. (2011). *After the Media: Culture and Identity in the 21st Century*. London: Routledge.

Blackburn, S. (2019, February 18). How Can We Teach Objectivity in a Post-Truth Era? *New Statesman*.

Buckingham, D. (2017). *The Strangulation of Media Studies*. https://david-buckingham.net/2017/07/16/the-strangulation-of-media-studies/.

CILIP. (2018). *Definition of Information Literacy 2018*. https://cdn.ymaws.com/www.cilip.org.uk/resource/resmgr/cilip/information_professional_and_news/press_releases/2018_03_information_lit_definition/cilip_definition_doc_final_f.pdf.

Cohen, S. (1972). *Folk Devils and Moral Panics*. Oxford: Martin Robertson.

Coyle, C. (2019). *Identifying Fake News: Critical Literacy and the School Library*. Swindon: School Library Association.

Crowson, N. (2018, December 9). 'How Europe Became the Tories' Eternal Battleground. *The Observer*.

Curtis, A. (2016). *Hypernormalisation*. London: BBC.

Fukuyama, F. (1992). *The End of History*. London: Penguin.

Jenkins, S. (2019, April 11). Julian Assange's Cyber-Sins Seem Quaint in Comparison to Those of Big Tech. *The Guardian*.

Jenkins, H., Ford, S., & Green, J. (2013). *Spreadable Media: Creating Value and Meaning in a Networked Culture*. New York: New York University Press.

Jenkins, H., Shreshova, S., Gamber-Thompson, L., & Zimmerman, A. (2016). *By Any Media Necessary: The New Youth Activism*. New York: New York University Press.

Klucharev, V., Neznanov, A., & Osin, E. (2019). *Media Education, Media Ecology, Media Literacy: Digital Media for the Future*. Moscow: National Research University Higher School of Economics.

Lilleker, D., Alexander, J., ElSheikh, D., McQueen, D., Richards, B., & Thorsen, E. (2018). *Evidence to the Culture, Media and Sport Committee 'Fake News' Inquiry Presented by Members of the Centre for Politics & Media Research*, Bournemouth University, UK.

Mason, P. (2019). *Clear, Bright Future*. London: Penguin.

Mihailidis, P., & Viotty, S. (2019). Spreadable Spectacle in Digital Culture: Civic Expression, Fake News, and the Role of Media Literacies in "Post-Fact" Society. *American Behavioural Scientist, 61*(4), 441–454.

Moore, R. (2013, September 1). Library of Birmingham Review. *The Guardian*.

Moores, S. (2017). *Digital Orientations: Non-media-centric Media Studies and Non-representational Theories of Practice*. New York: Peter Lang.

Pilkington, E. (2019, April 12). Julian Assange's Charges Are a Direct Assault on Press Freedom, Experts Warn. *The Guardian*.

Rushkoff, D. (2019). *Team Human*. New York: W.W. Norton.

Shirky, C. (2011, February 5). The whistleblowing Site Has Created a New Media Landscape. *The Guardian: After Wikileaks*, p. 2.

Snow, J. (2019). Connected or Disconnected. In K. Fowler-Watt & S. Jukes (Eds.), *New Journalisms: Rethinking Practice, Theory and Pedagogy*. London: Routledge.

Yurchak, A. (2006). *Everything Was Forever, Until It Was no More: The Last Soviet Generation*. Princeton, NJ: Princeton University Press.

7

Fake News vs Media Studies

Richard Hoggart wrote *The Uses of Literacy* in 1957, observing the societal implications of 'mass literacy' and half a century later, he reflected on the shifts to a 'mass media society'. His key criterion for a democracy endures: "As many as possible of the citizens of a democracy must be not only literate but critically literate if they are to behave as full citizens" (Hoggart 2004: 189).

Over the course of the year of *this* project, the paradoxical situation it addresses became a parody of itself. At the end of March, just as I was switching off my radar to any new interventions on the topic, David Robson was promoting *The Intelligence Trap; Why Smart People Do Stupid Things*. His argument in the book is interesting enough—that psychological studies show how misinformation is designed to bypass our critical faculties and mainline to our biases, but that this depends on our cognitive preferences (thinking styles). And this:

> Given the sheer prevalence of misinformation around us, I believe that ways of identifying misinformation, combined with critical thinking, should now be taught in every school. (Robson 2019: 37)

© The Author(s) 2019
J. McDougall, *Fake News vs Media Studies*,
https://doi.org/10.1007/978-3-030-27220-3_7

What, no Media Studies?

Déjà vu. The same elephant as was in the room at the Oxford Reuters panel. During workshops on this topic overseas (in Brussels, Moscow, Zagreb and Hong Kong, specifically), there was general disbelief that Media Studies is ignored in such discussions in the United Kingdom. When we brought journalists, media teachers, library professionals and students together in London for our US Embassy project event, the media teachers encountered the same conundrum when talking to journalists.

> While the core concepts and questions of media literacy may be seen as tools for inquiry and reflexive (thoughtful and strategic) media practice, they are also 'practices of the self', ways in which we act upon ourselves, to monitor, test, improve and transform. Media education acts as an intervention in power relations by asserting knowledge, skills and habits of mind to protect from media effects and influences, to emancipate from oppressive ideologies or to facilitate participation in digital culture. (Robbgrieco 2016: 103)

Marcus Learning, Professor of Digital Media Education at the University of Winchester, describes all this as 'a weird place to be'. Media Studies, he observes, is an educational subject sector with momentum (numbers of media students are increasing, in higher education), fuelling the UK's Creative Industries. But at the same time, its presence in schools is subject to the ongoing populist 'Mickey Mouse' attack we've rehearsed, at precisely the same time as the anxious desire for renewed criticality in the face of fake news. So this is a field being challenged by contrasting opinions of what it should be and in this space we can discern conflict between the overt industry and employment agenda of media production and the more critical, challenging British Media Studies with its ancestry in the Centre for Contemporary Cultural Studies (Leaning 2018).

I concur.

Forgive the 'broken record', but the argument this book makes is twofold.

1. Learning a critical media literacy as a practice of being in the world is what we need, as opposed to either training to work in 'the media' without wanting to change it (a lot) or fact-checking tools, alternative algorithms or a faithful return to 'real news'.
2. Media Studies can do this, but it's in the margins. It needs to be in the centre of the school curriculum.

This idea of a critical understanding of media as pivotal, now, to the practice of being in the world with others is also about democracy. The chapter on democracy concluded that it isn't a natural state and that education has a role to play in fostering the conditions for it. Thus, Media Studies can become far-reaching and vitally civic. We can go as far as to say that Media Studies is an essential pillar of freedom.

Bragg (2019) offers three dimensions of freedom—liberty, equality and accountability:

> Now authoritarians and algorithms threaten democracy, while we argue over who has the right to speak. To protect ourselves from encroaching tyranny, we must look beyond a one-dimensional notion of what it means to be free and, by reconnecting liberty to equality and accountability, restore the individual agency engendered by the three dimensions of freedom. (2019: 102)

All of the people I have met on my travels in the false binary have agreed with these sentiments. Anxieties about what happens to democracy in the short-term future, a desire to both restore trust in media and increase its accountability have been part of every conversation. The community of practice, at the intersection of media education and journalism, agrees that the role of media education is to offer an agentive 'safe space' (or a 'third space', I will call it) for a dynamic, critical and *theorised* navigation of new media reception, engagement and production. My journey ends with the group workshops, where all these strands, and the stakeholders with skin in the game came together, bookended here by two interviews with media teacher-trainers who are, more than anyone else, at the vanguard of Media Studies as a pillar of freedom.

On Cohering a Bit Better

> We tried to use the power of media education to make society – or at least the little section of it that we worked with – cohere a bit better. We can see media education here as a kind of glue, sticking people and things together through analysis, collaboration and production. These activities allow (students) to both question and represent themselves in the world they inhabit, to be included in it. In an age when society is increasingly fragmented through social and economic circumstance, this inclusivity is why we need media education more than ever. (Connolly 2013: 53)

This informed argument was made pre-Brexit, pre-Trump, before the moral panic over misinformation and the renewed concerns about bias of the mainstream media.

Steve Connolly is a Visiting Fellow at Bournemouth, and we talk during one such visit. Like me, he now works in a University (of Bedfordshire), working with teachers and trainees, researching and writing about teaching media, degrees of separation from 'the chalkface'. The chapter quoted above, on media education for social inclusion (2013) is, I think, one of the most moving accounts of the subject as a project and very much 'mission central' to the argument being made in this book. His previous experience is especially important to capture:

> My degree is in America studies, I certainly wasn't expecting to teach Media Studies when I first qualified to be a teacher and then I found that no one else would do it, then I got into it the Masters at the Institute of Education which is where I met people like David Buckingham and Andrew Burn and then, through doing some work there and being a Head of a Media Studies department in a school I developed some really clear ideas about what I wanted to do as a media educator. I knew that I really wanted to have lots and lots of kids do media education, I didn't ever see it as something specialist that was just for a small particular group of kids because I'd seen the effect that it had on lots of kids that I'd taught and the way that it allowed them to access educational opportunities more generally. I ended up becoming Director of Specialism in a visual and media arts school in a very deprived bit of South London where we were able to apply some principles of media education across

the curriculum. It wasn't totally successful but we managed to do some things that were beneficial. When that came to an end I freelanced for various people and then I ended up at Bedfordshire doing teacher education where I teach a lot of stuff about new literacy. My research now is around creativity and media education more generally, philosophies of media education, questions of knowledge.

Examples of implementing Media Studies as a mandatory subject and the link he makes between media education and broader opportunities are detailed in the chapter cited above. In that broader, epistemological context, then, is fake news a thing?

There's always been people in history who will use alternative facts, as the Americans would say, to tell their own story, it's there throughout history isn't it? But the thing that problematizes it for educators now is the way it shifts where you would find the truth to somewhere else, so historically in education you think about sources of knowledge and how you establish what knowledge or truth is, there were some fairly reliable places where you would get truth, the university as an example. But in the age of social media, that centre doesn't hold, so where you find your information and how you value that information has moved for all sorts of reasons but primarily for me, the technology allows people to challenge the origins of information so in some respects knowledge is always moving and so how does that affect what teachers do? There are lots of people selling an answer to that but I think for media education, particularly, it's complex and you can't boil it down to a single formula or recipe, it's a problem that's multiplied because of our relationships with technology and social media.

Predictably, I pick up on his experience of teaching Media Studies at scale, across a school. If my hypothesis were accepted and it became a mandatory subject, what would it offer in this complex space, right now?

My view of media education is quite conventional, I mean it seems odd to say it's old-fashioned when it's only 30 years we've had Media Studies but I think it's worthwhile kind of revisiting the sort of the models that we used at the start to see what's still valid in them, that stuff about the connection between the institutional and textual. If you want to ask questions about news, you have to think about who makes news and how they make it, and how particularly modern technology and social media challenge our ideas of what news is. Now if you think about media education, it's starting from conventions and using that to ask some bigger questions about where stuff comes from and that's still a valid and important thing, even though the nature of institutions has changed beyond belief in the time that I've been teaching media. Asking what are these people doing, who are these organisations, who are the people who are not part of an organisation but can still influence the news, the Minecraft guy, Dan TDM, the YouTuber. He's an unemployed bloke from Northampton who last year made 12 million quid. There's an institutional thing there about a guy who is on one level outside an institution but of course requires an institution to do the thing that he needs to do. And I think in media education, actually in lots of ways you can't understand anything else unless you understand the industrial backdrop to what's going on.

I had an argument with my son last night about that YouTuber. He said, 'well he's not unemployed, he earns loads of money', and I said 'well, is it employment?' Actually, it's probably more like the Renaissance idea of patronage, that he is given lots of money to do product placement so that he can talk for two hours about Fortnite which is what he really wants to do. English teachers say people need English in order to deal with all this and with the greatest will in the world, English is never going to do that, because it is never going to ask those questions about the institutional and the industrial, that are really important to understanding why a text is the way it is and who the people are making the text and why they're making it.

So where to strike the balance between the textual and the industrial? In the era of 'surveillance capitalism' and the algorithm, where the business model depends on the proliferation of click baits and then the harnessing of data, which then leads to behavioural change, can any of the conventional Media Studies concepts or models help you get into that or should we really just be teaching people about power and capitalism and economics?

I always think that media education encourages that propensity for enquiry, the Tony Benn questions, who's power is it? But also as a philosophical and epistemological enquiry, what is this thing that I am looking at, what does it tell me about the world? Actually, media education can encourage lots of the kinds of enquiry that you need in science but we don't really make that connection. It's really important to talk about power and capitalism but the way that media education works is to start with the thing that kids are close to, to ask – OK, that thing that you're doing every day, that video, Dan TDM or whatever you're watching, what is that really about? It's that kind of enquiry for me that's at the heart of it, so Media Studies will always have a really important function in that sense.

On the Cusp

In the special issue of *Cultura y Educación* on 'digital literacy', fake news and education (for which David Buckingham offered the framing editorial cited earlier), which went into production at the same time as this book, we curated a range of examples from international contexts. That project began with the findings of a European report on digital literacy (Brites 2017). The report drew conclusions about the importance of digital literacy education just as the moral panic over fake news was emerging, so we put out a call for examples of research on that specific dimension. In the resulting publication (McDougall et al. 2019), the international authors shared research into the progressive dimensions of digital literacy—*aprender* (learn); *ser capaz* (be able); *hacer/crear* (create) and *actuar* (act). They also stressed the importance of using focussed resilience on YouTube, clickbait and 'I like' actions; offered a more optimistic approach to questions of trust and online news and compared media competencies of university professors and students in Spain, Portugal, Brazil and Venezuela. They defined these competencies as the ability to act critically in the digital world and a "need to develop transversal actions for instructing both university professors and students in media competences to face an ecosystem dominated by fake news and disinformation, as well as public policies directed at improving these skills among citizens at large." They also outlined a typology for 'trustworthiness judgments' for Italian students to read information on vaccination, specifically; pointed to Spanish students' difficulties in establishing truthfulness of news sources and mapped out a strategy for diagnostics to orient teachers, professors and education policymakers in the digital media environment.

Three workshops were convened for this project—the first at Hong Kong Baptist University, which hosted the 2018 Media Education Summit; the second in Moscow at an event on Media Education, Media Ecology and Media Literacy at the National Research University Higher School of Economics in February 2019; and the third at Loughborough University's London campus at Olympic Park a month later. The stakeholder groups for these workshops included journalists, teachers, students and library professionals.

These are reflections on the London workshop from Jane Secker, Chair of the CILIP Information Literacy Group, cited earlier with regard to the role of library professionals.

> My group had a lively mix of people and the students had some really interesting perspectives on how they developed an understanding of who to trust online, how to find 'real' news and how to behave on social media.

> In our first discussion we looked at the phenomenon of fake news or disinformation, which pretty much everyone concluded was a dreadful term, but one that had captured the public's attention. We considered why it mattered and what we could do about it and what role schools and education played. The journalists in our group were clearly concerned that claims of fake news undermine quality journalism and make their work far harder.

> In our second discussion we talked about trust and news and how we know who to trust and what we wanted our media to commit to so we knew it was trustworthy. We talked about things like transparency, the need to make facts and opinions very differentiated and a commitment to trying to get to the truth, which meant that journalists needed to build relationships with individuals who are close to the story. They also needed to be clear about their sources.

In our final workshop we looked at existing media literacy resources that are designed to help highlight the issues associated with fake news. My group concluded we needed any new resource to be reliable, engaging and succinct. The journalists were surprised that librarians had such an important role, they hadn't realised that. The students said that anyone clicking on fake news and sharing links readers are part of the problem here. But they felt it was a big responsibility to have to check every website they looked at to make sure it wasn't 'fake'.

What struck me during the day was that uncertainty and starting to question if anything was true was not a helpful situation to be in and also something that could be quite unsettling for students and young people, getting to grips with the world. Fake news and dis or mis-information is a real challenge, and certainly not one that librarians can solve alone, however it was great to find some like-minded and new people to collaborate with on tackling this.

(Secker 2019: https://infolit.org.uk/media-literacy-versus-fake-news-a-bournemouth-university-workshop/)

In London, the workshops were preceded by a public event, featuring keynotes and a panel with David Buckingham, Monica Bulger, Paul Mihailidis, Karen Fowler-Watt and Roman Gerodimos (see CEMP 2019). All of the workshops were designed to generate dialogue on four issues:

1. Clarifying the problem (the apparent 'information disorder') from lived experience of the stakeholders, as opposed to what they had read about it or been exposed to through networks or 'echo chambers'. This was a form of audience / reception study, as we were interested in collective framing by stakeholder category;
2. Identifying any competing or partly integrated discourses around the concept of trust in media and information, and from this, exploring participants' relationships with 'real' journalism now and in the future—put bluntly, why do we need it?
3. Evaluating a range of educational resources already in the world—we called this 'testing the wheel', so that we could come away with

a brief on what might be needed to avoid reinvention. Again, we were investigating stakeholder perceptions; for example, were some resources appealing to teachers but not to students, how would journalists feel about a resource that situates all media as 'propaganda'?

4. Agreeing on what media education can realistically do, and accepting what is just too big, too external to the social practices of teaching and learning, for us to address. The intention here was to move beyond 'solutionism' (Buckingham 2019a) towards a more viable, modest proposal for Fake News vs Media Studies. Where *do*/*can* we have agency?

In the plenary and data analysis stages, our line of enquiry shifted from inter-related, competing or tangential discourses, and whether these were framed by role, so that we could move towards extrapolation of the common ground. These multi-stakeholder experiences of 'fake news' shared some common ground, such as the desire for trust and truth and how does/can media literacy create resilience? This common ground is of interest for this book, summarized as follows:

Diagnosis

Fake news is a continuum. Multiple people interpret it in different ways.

Studying poetry at 19, I discovered there is no such thing as truth … it's a slippery beast.

There was agreement that the problem is not only about an information disorder and new modes of propoganda (see Pomerantsev 2019) but also the failure of education to create resilient, critical thinkers—"*we need a conversation about the purpose of education. Why is it necessary to be educated? Different modes of education mean different paradigms and worldviews for students*" and "*What is a school education that is fit for the future? Media literacy is peripheral instead of central, that needs to change.*" Also, the lack of a civil, debating culture in state education was identified as part of the problem.

On questions of trust, participants agreed that the blind trust in social media was a problem, that genuinely trustworthy media would have "no hidden agenda" but that, in the post-truth era, there might be a generational distinction between a broad skepticism ("there's always an agenda") and a more trusting engagement—"*You can piece together your own trust, from different perspectives on twitter*". The dialogue 'zoomed in' in two themes—objectivity is an illusion ("*Get the extreme views from both sides and the truth is somewhere in the middle*") but "*if you don't trust anybody or anything, then you're kind of lost*"—and an agreement that there is a new danger here, in the shape of 'the dark art of the algorithm' and thus, media literacy is about something new, something else, these days—"*The browser that you choose is not a neutral choice.*"

On trust, journalists articulated a different discourse in every group at every workshop, both asserting an insider position and defending the profession:

My relationship is with my sources, refugees in camps in Libya – anything inaccurate can have real world affects. If I get something wrong, then my sources are going to be in a very bad situation. And if one thing is wrong, somebody can use that to discredit the entire report.

With breaking news, it's hard to verify things, especially from social media. There is an expectation that the BBC should be first – so the pressure comes from social media.

The difference between articles taking months to verify information compared to those that have taken minutes – there's a difference and we need to be able to distinguish between the two. And that gets confused on social media.

There was also a much clearer sense of definition of terms from journalists than the other groups. Journalists could 'tell the difference' and saw fake news as 'more of a thing'. The closest other group were library professionals, described more in terms of information literacy as checking sources. Students and teachers were generally either more sceptical about the term 'fake news' or less inclined to see a distinction between fake and real.

Treatment

Clearly, participants volunteering to attend workshops on media education and disinformation are likely to agree that education is part of the solution. But whilst several of the online resources and fact-checking tools already in the public domain were evaluated positively, there was widespread agreement on the greater need for critical thinking 'before the event'—"*like driving a car, you may not need to know everything that's under the bonnet but it would help if you broke down, and you definitely need to know how to steer*". Extending the metaphor, "*the internet warrior behind a screen is a bit like road rage, so how do we equip people to de-escalate?*"

Two less predictable findings emerged. Across the stakeholder groups, participants tended to agree that (1) The fine balance between media education/literacy for critical resilience and the tipping point into distrust of all information was where we should be applying our energies; and that (2) If the critical thinking fostered in Media Studies were integrated throughout all the curriculum, we wouldn't need Media Studies. Currently, however, young people are at more risk without Media Studies as it's the only place in education where questions of trust in information are located. This is a deeply ironic situation in the United Kingdom, where it is derided for its lack of 'substance'.

> Critical not cynical. Blind faith and unthinking trust is also a problem.

> You don't have to assess the problem negatively. Can be a conversational thing and can be a positive thing, while still building a critical mindset and creating skills.

> It's moral ownership of what we put out and its broader citizenship, not just a question of media literacy. But studying media is a good place to start, and then broaden out to those issues.

And on resisting the pitfalls of moral surveillance in the classroom:

> Some of this has to be trial and error. As with sex and drugs, there is a danger that teachers being overbearing and just talking down to students might not help. The same is true with media literacy.

The economic modality of education was also enacted. Whilst not a common perspective, this is an important angle, since it moves us beyond a purely oppositional position in terms of the current, 'neoliberal' framing of education:

> Economic status for young people is predicated on them being knowledgeable. Knowing what's true and what's not is part of that and provides credibility, as information is currency.

There was less consensus on the value of trust, per se. This seemed a loaded premise, with each group attaching its own emphasis to, perhaps, validate their own agency: trust in journalism; students lacking trust as a rationale for disengagement with the public sphere, teachers as agents in discerning trust; library professionals as custodians of trustworthy information. Buckingham's critique here was reflected in the dialogue:

> There seems to be a fundamental contradiction here. On the one hand, a healthy democracy depends upon trust: we need to trust our elected representatives, and we have to rely on trusted sources of information. Yet on the other hand, we don't want people to place blind faith in authority: we want people to be sceptical. Too much trust is a bad thing, but so is too little. So how much trust do we need – and especially for those of us concerned with education, how much trust do we want to cultivate? Are people who are more 'media literate' more or less likely to trust the media? Ultimately, I don't think there is an easy answer here. Too little trust is dysfunctional, but too much can also be dangerous. As educators, we need students to be critical, rather than merely cynical. We want them to analyse and question media, but we don't want them to distrust or reject everything. So how much trust in media do we actually want or need? (Buckingham 2019a: 3)

Prescription

The suggested resources and strategies cited as 'apps' at the end of each chapter of this book are those which got the green light in each of the mixed-group workshops, so there is triangulation in that they are (a) generated by, or recommended by, the network sample I interviewed; (b) verified as valuable for Media Studies in this particular context by me; and (c) considered to have utility by all of the four groups we were working with at the workshop.

In the recorded conversations, the participants agreed on a way forward for both journalism and education, in an ideal world, making suggestions that resonated with many of the interviews from preceding chapters:

> Upfront transparency – we are funded by so and so. Political bias is so and so, open and upfront. Fact and opinion, clearly labelled and signposted.

> Journalism that is close to the community and as close as possible to the source.

> We need the transparency and the critical education in tandem. It's a matter of balance and dual responsibility.

On the other hand, journalists—as in the interviews—were much keener to prescribe for students an 'appreciation' of their work, and this problematic fault-line has run through this project, echoing Crilley and Gillespie: *In the context of declining trust in the news media and in an age where individual subjectivity and even narcissistic self-promotion on social media is prized over measured evidence-based opinion, it is now more important than ever for journalists to stay committed to accurate, fair and independent reporting* (2019: 175).

> Make students understand good journalism is expensive, and valuing it leads to more of it being done. Don't just criticise. Knowledge surrounding journalism architecture and values is missing.

On extracting the viable agency for resilience, there was agreement that, in the UK context, where Media Studies exists, my proposal was a good one, and that in other countries, adopting the same model would also be beneficial. But in all contexts, there was consensus that more inter-agency work is crucial in the short term, and that this might be a longer-term project than I am claiming, but that we should be optimistic:

Everybody's looking for a quick answer, but what we're talking about here is going to take twenty to forty years. We need a new literacy for the twenty-first century and it's not going to happen tomorrow and nobody around education wants to hear that. And the corporations are not going to change, their business model is to keep people on their platforms.

There are alliances we should be wary of. Recently we were approached by Russia Today for a partnership, involving our students. Is that an alliance we want? If Google funds a project, what's lying behind that?

The most important alliances in the short term are across the curriculum, media educators working with teachers in Science, Maths, raising media awareness in all subjects, for example there's plenty of fake news about science.

There's that old line – in a democracy, you get the politicians you deserve. Well, in the twenty-first century, we get the information we deserve. If we build resilience in our students, make them critical consumers of media and information, not just cynicism but inculcating critical thinking, then the environment will change. Ultimately, if we teach our students to demand better media, it will happen.

Giving a Fish

In addition to the plethora of online tools and resources for fact-checking, verification and knowing fake news when you see it, the best of which (according to the stakeholders at our London workshop) are featured in this book as 'onward journeys', there are also an abundance of broader initiatives working hard to resurrect trust in the mainstream media. Here are some examples that also met with approval at our US Embassy project event and have not already been cited in this book:

PBS NewsHour Student Reporting Labs is a project-based learning program that supports teachers and young people to report on important issues in their community, creating impactful video reports for local media outlets and the national PBS NewsHour.
Follow up: https://studentreportinglabs.org/.

Be Media Smart offers an effective motto: 'Stop, Think, Check'. It puts the onus on young people to think about the choices they make with information.
Follow up: https://www.bemediasmart.ie/.

The Trust Project is a group of global news companies that offers a set of 'Trust Indicators' to tackle fake news.
Follow up: https://thetrustproject.org/.

NewsGuard provides a Green-Red signal, to indicate if a website is *"trying to get it right or instead has a hidden agenda or knowingly publishes falsehoods or propaganda"*.
Follow up: https://www.newsguardtech.com/.

DeepNews.AI uses machine learning to link quality journalism to economic value, using a metric which will *"interface with ad servers to assess the value of a story and price and serve ads accordingly. The higher a story's quality score, the pricier the ad space adjacent to it can be. This adjustment will substantially raise the revenue per page."*
Follow up: https://www.deepnews.ai/.

IJNet's *9 Media Literacy Guides and What They Have in Common* is a set of quick and easy shortcuts that guide users through the step-by-step process of information verification.
Follow up: https://ijnet.org/en/story/9-media-literacy-guides-and-what-they-have-common.

The National Literacy Trust's *Fake News and Critical Literacy* resources are *"designed to help primary and secondary teachers, parents and school librarians equip children with the critical literacy skills they need to survive and thrive in today's digital world."*
Follow up: https://literacytrust.org.uk/resources/fake-news-and-critical-literacy-resources/.

Media Lens has been cited in this book but the website has not featured until now as part of the 'toolkit'. Here's its statement of intent: *We check the media's version of events against credible facts and opinion provided by journalists, academics and specialist researchers. We then publish both versions, together with our commentary, in free Media Alerts and invite readers to deliver their verdict both to us and to mainstream journalists through the email addresses provided in our 'Suggested Action' at the end of each alert.* Follow up: http://www.medialens.org/.

Common Sense.Org guides educators through the use of Google's own reverse image verification tools to 'turn students into fact-finding web detectives'. This involves three elements—access to fact-checking resources; literacy skills for reading the web differently than print; and developing a framework for 'showing your search', analogous to 'showing the working' in Mathematics. Follow up: https://www.commonsense.org/education/teaching-strategies/turn-students-into-fact-finding-web-detectives.

Teaching *About* Fishing

In countries with media literacy education initiatives, but no formal, assessed subject in schools (so, everywhere except the United Kingdom, currently), we can find a huge range of evidence of 'what works', with varying degrees of scale. Furthermore, in comparison to Media Studies, it is often seen that the successful implementation and outcomes of these pedagogic interventions approach the more holistic, critical media education being advocated here. For example, Hodgkin and Kahne's account of civic media literacy education in response to fake news found that, in the United States, focus on 'what teachers can do' resulted in defining three elements: developing nuanced skills and strategies for assessing truth claims, reflectively thinking about students' own biases and assumptions; and then 'Practice, Practice, Practice' to foster an experiential learning process to cultivate new habits of mind. Here's a discrete example of this at work:

> Ms. Blake, a high school humanities teacher in Dallas, Texas, integrated regular opportunities for her students to practice judging the credibility of online information via a weekly activity at the start of class. Students responded to a current event via Twitter using a common hashtag and briefly shared their perspectives on the issue. Ms. Blake drew on content

developed by KQED—a public media station in northern California—through a program called "Do Now" in which students across the country responded to and engaged in an online discussion centered around a weekly question about a timely and relevant current event. In their responses, Ms. Blake asked students to include at least one link to a credible source they found that backed up their opinions, which meant students had to conduct some initial research, determine the credibility and reliability of a variety of sources, and weigh what they had learned against their ideas in order to succinctly state their opinions. (Hodgkin and Khane 2018: 211)

This is good work, and typical of an abundance of such responsive activity across the world (see De Abreu et al. 2017; McDougall et al. 2018, 2019). It is *in between* the provision of open access resources by the mainstream media, independent third parties, NGOs or the likes of Google and Facebook themselves and a fully formed media education. In this sense, these interventions are more than *giving a fish* but less than *teaching to fish*.

Teaching *to* Fish

Chapter 1, in setting out our key contexts, opened with a statement from the Data and Society Research Institute's 2018 report, that *Media literacy has become a center of gravity for countering "fake news"* (Bulger and Davison 2018: 3). The report concluded with a set of open questions (2018: 21). Here, they are followed by my responses at the end of this journey:

1. Can media literacy even be successful in preparing citizens to deal with fake news and information? *Media Studies prepares citizens to take a critical, but not a cynical, approach to engagement with all media, including professional journalism, 'mainstream media' more broadly, and social media. So yes.*
2. Which groups should be targeted for media literacy interventions? *If our current problems are the work of 'baby boomers', then the civic engagement of young people in schools now is our priority so that, in the*

future, 'the media' is produced more ethically and consumed more critically. If every young person takes Media Studies in school, that seems like the starting point.

3. How can media literacy programs effectively address overconfidence in skills? This can manifest preemptively (individuals who feel they need no media literacy training) and reactively (individuals who overestimate the effectiveness of their media literacy training).
Media Studies has a track record in working in the 'third space', fostering a porous exchange of critical, theoretical thinking (from teachers) and media engagement (from students).

4. Are traditional media literacy practices (e.g., verification and fact-checking) impractical in everyday media consumption? How can media literacy initiatives respond to the powerful systems of media i-literacy (e.g., clickbait, feed algorithms), which already condition individuals' media behaviors? *Yes, instead of offering verification tools, we should think of critical media literacy, via Media Studies, as the best 'toolkit'.*

5. How are groups committed to disinformation and propaganda able to harness the language of literacy and critical analysis to sow new distrust of media and establish adversarial political spaces? *We need a focus on the 'Uses of Media Literacy' rather than a set of apparently neutral competences for citizens. Media Studies doesn't necessarily do this, but it is closer to it than media literacy alone, as it has a critical, societal dimension.*

6. How will the overlapping efforts of media literacy stakeholders interact? Will new signals for trustworthiness aimed at limiting "fake news" backfire, producing new uncertainty around media messages? *This field ethnography, the set of interviews and the findings from the workshops culminate in a strong, multi-stakeholder consensus that Media Studies should be mandatory in schools. If every young person learns the key concepts of Media Studies—genre, narrative, representation, audience, ideology, and applies 'classic' deconstructive approaches to contemporary media texts, news content and technological developments in mediation, we will avoid both the false binary of 'real vs fake' and the danger of hyper-cynical distrust of all media. Media Studies puts media literacy to work in an academic context, connecting the study of media to questions of history, politics and ethics.*

On Carving Out Space

The last word goes to Claire Pollard, with justification. Right now, she works at an intersection that probably makes her the most important media teacher to talk to about this subject. She's a classroom teacher, runs one of the few Media Studies teacher training courses in the country and edits *Media Magazine* (Fig 7.1) at the English and Media Centre. The PGCE course is accredited by Goldsmiths, where I started out in a discussion with Natalie Fenton, so this closes a loop. She's also a masters' graduate of CEMP, which I run at Bournemouth, and recently when I was invited to update a textbook for media students, I persuaded Claire to co-author, as I knew she'd have the mainline to the current curricula and the students' perspective.

We're in a seminar room at the English and Media Centre, where I've been to meetings, ran workshops, attended other people's workshops 'man and boy' for decades. I love the English and Media Centre. Anyway, for this visit, I am working with Claire's trainee teachers. As always, we start with her journey.

I'm a media education consultant now but how far back do you want to go? I started out training as an English teacher because what I wanted to do was work in the media, ironically, as a writer and a filmmaker, and I was doing stand-up and I thought if I trained to be a teacher then I could use it to fund that. Then I fell in love with English teaching, and was then asked to set up media studies in a school that had previously not had media studies. I don't know if that experience is common to a lot of media teachers, but I've been head of media now for about 13 years and in all of that time I've been mainly working alone or with trainees. So I've got imposter syndrome, because I've never really had any sort of official validation. But I was good at it and I liked it, and it was much more democratic and more interesting than teaching English, I had a lot more freedom, it was a lot more engaging than teaching English. Then I sort of felt quite bad being head of media for 10 years and having no official media qualification, my degree was English and Creative Studies, so I did a masters at Bournemouth in CEMP and gave myself a little bit for validation I guess. In terms of how I got here, I don't know I just say yes to everything, even if I know I can't do it, and that's how I got here.

Fig. 7.1 *Media Magazine*: The zeitgeist (*Source* Claire Pollard/English and Media Centre)

And where she got to is important. Training the next generation of media teachers and editing the 'go to' resource for school and college students (who are also regularly published in the magazine):

> I edit 'MediaMagazine' which is for Film and Media students, it's looking at things out there which are relevant to exam specifications. It's quite difficult because it's a quarterly magazine so trying to keep up with trends and things that students are interested in, a lot of which I don't know about and I have to find that out through people like you guys (refers to the PGCE students in the room) who are slightly more in touch with the younger generation than I am.

> This PGCE is actually really important because there's a time in Media Studies, where teachers have just been sort of trotting through content and not really thinking about the bigger picture. And it is my great privilege to be able to try and send you guys off with a little bit of that bigger picture into a job, into a school where you're probably going to be forced into quite a narrow focus; on exam results and set texts and set theories. I know that's frustrating for you at the moment – on a day to day basis – because you just need to get through the next week but hopefully 4 years, 5 years, 6 years down the line, these experiences will shape the kind of teachers that you are. And you know this centre, the English and Media Centre and this PGCE course, it has a good reputation for all those reasons. And so I do sometimes think who am I? Why do I belong here? But then, in 16 years of teaching, I've been so steadfast in my beliefs about what teaching and learning should be that actually, I am very confident in that. Cocky almost.

So, from this vantage point, what's new about fake news?

> The conversation around it is new. If I can specifically link it to the classroom: I've taught mostly in inner city London schools and issues around bias and misinformation have always been issues with teenagers I've taught in these contexts because they don't necessarily have the understanding of a newspaper being part of a bigger institution with political bias. So, I think the problems are not new, although obviously with the technology that we have now, and the kind of rhetoric that we have now, and the President of the United States that we have now mean that it is a

bigger deal at the moment. And what's interesting, I suppose, is that that were getting to a stage where people in education want to teach about it. Bias has become less of the conversation in English, so therefore it needs to be more of the conversation in Media Studies. Yes, possibly this is the sort of thing that should be done through PSHE and citizenship but in the five schools I've worked at it never really has been, that part of the curriculum has always been really under-used.

So, to the endgame. As previously stated, the proposal this book is making is that the subject, Media Studies, if made mandatory in schools, would be the best starting point for a societal response to the crisis of fake news.

There's no space. There's no space for it because, we've got nine set media forms to get through in 2 years and it's something people are really struggling with. I think we touch more on these sorts of issues now when teaching about industry and regulation, but you would have to really carve out some space for it. So yes, Media Studies teachers are the best equipped to teach it but there is no space in the curriculum. They are currently just getting across what needs to be put across and then trotting on to the next thing as quickly as possible.

But the subject and the prescribed curriculum are not the same thing.

The Manifesto

Before it takes centre-stage as a compulsory subject in all UK schools, there's some work to do. This research has found agreement in the intersection between media education and journalism that Media Studies should be mandatory in schools as a first response to the information disorder and the threats it poses to freedom and democracy or even to humanity.

Before it can be effective as a front-line response, Media Studies needs a 'reboot', to foster a critical resilience through advanced academic deconstruction, and theorised production, of media. The research suggests that this is a more effective and sustainable approach than 'giving a fish' through fact-checking tools or surface level media /information literacy competences. We need a 'new manifesto for Media Studies (see Buckingham 2019b), with three key policy pledges:

1. Rather than producing competence frameworks for media literacy, as though it is a neutral set of skills for citizens, media education needs to enable students to apply the *critical* legacies of both Media Studies and literacy education on the contemporary media ecosystem. For Media Studies, that means the 'old school' work of the Birmingham Centre for Contemporary Cultural Studies and the Glasgow Media Group and the decentering critical lenses offered by feminism, poststructuralism, radical, de-colonial pedagogy and post-humanism;

2. Media Studies must adopt *a dynamic* approach to media literacy and increase the experiential, reflexive aspects of media *practice* in the curriculum, with reciprocal transfer between the critical rhetorics above and creative media practice in order to respond, academically, to media as primarily a question of representation. In other words, resilience *to* representation is enhanced by expertise *in* representing.

3. We need to add the critical exploration of social media, algorithms and big data to the Media Studies curriculum, accompanied by applied practical learning in the *uses* of them for social justice, as opposed to training the next generation in the use of these for even further commercial and political exploitation of one another.

Its' clear to me that Media Studies is already in a good place to be easily adapted and developed for objectives (1) and (2) but as a community of practice we will need a watching brief on (3) in the longer term.

So, is this a viable hypothesis—that this kind of reboot of the Media Studies we already have should be the go-to for a response to all the problems wrapped up in the moral panic over fake news and that we can do this by refreshing the subject to *"design and deliver more inclusive teaching based on the principles of a social justice education that prepares students to become active agents of change"* (Gabriel 2017: 19)?

If so, this work seems as far away from a 'Mickey Mouse subject' as we could imagine right now. For Claire Pollard, then, someone right at the heart of the zeitgeist for the subject, is she buying it?

I agree with your proposal. There're still loads of people that really don't understand what media studies is like. I was talking to a 'TV personality' in the green room yesterday (before the big student conference that she convenes) and they asked whether it was unfair to have so many people studying Media Studies when there aren't that many jobs in the media. Whenever I interview people from the industry for conferences, they always think that what we are doing is training people to work in the media industry, that's what people think we're doing. They don't understand the 'understanding the media' and 'critical reading of media' aspects of it, that media students understand this landscape of multiple voices coming from multiple places, with different types of restrictions, and because they understand that, they'll make more informed decisions about what they believe, rather than just either believing the news or believing the rhetoric and conspiracy. Media Studies is THE conversation for that.

Absolutely.
The conversation.
Fake News vs Media Studies.
Game on.

Onward Journeys (Application)

App 20 Throughout this book, the aligned project on the same topic, funded by the US Embassy in London, has been referred to. The outcomes of that project culminated in an open access resource for media literacy, critical thinking and resilience. This consists of a field review; the film of the public event held in London; a curated set of resources that our stakeholder groups all rated highly as fit for purpose in fostering critical media literacy whilst resisting the false binary; and new materials produced to fill the gaps those groups identified.

Follow up: http://mlfn.cemp.ac.uk/.

References

Bragg, B. (2019). *The Three Dimensions of Freedom*. London: Faber and Faber.

Brites, M. J. (Ed.). (2017). Digital Literacy and Education, National Reports (Portugal, UK, Ireland, Spain, Serbia and Italy). *ELN: European Literacy Network, Digital Literacy Team*. https://www.is1401eln.eu/en/gca/index.php?id=149.

Buckingham, D. (2019a). Teaching Media in a 'Post-Truth' Age: Fake News, Media Bias and the Challenge for Media/Digital Literacy Education. *Cultura y Educación, 31*(2), 213–231.

Buckingham, D. (2019b). *The Media Education Manifesto*. London: Polity.

Bulger, M., & Davison, P. (2018). *The Promises, Challenges and Futures of Media Literacy*. New York: Data and Society Research Institute.

CEMP. (2019). *Media Literacy Versus Fake News: Critical Thinking, Resilience and Civic Engagement*. http://mlfn.cemp.ac.uk/. Accessed 4 September 2019.

Connolly, S. (2013). Media Education: A Tool for Social Inclusion. In J. Wardle (Ed.), *Current Perspectives in Media Education: Beyond the Manifesto*. Basingstoke: Palgrave Macmillan.

Crilley, R., & Gillespie, M. (2019). What to Do About Social Media? Politics, Populism and Journalism. *Journalism, 20*(1), 173–176.

De Abreu, B. S., Mihailidis, P., Lee, A. Y. L., Melki, J., & McDougall, J. (Eds.). (2017). *The Routledge International Handbook of Media Literacy Education*. New York: Routledge.

Gabriel, D. (2017). Pedagogies of Social Justice and Cultural Democracy in Media Higher Education. *Media Education Research Journal* (8.1).

Hodgkin, E., & Khane, J. (2018). Misinformation in the Information Age: What Teachers Can Do to Support Students. *Social Education, 82*(4), 208–211, 214.

Hoggart, R. (2004). *Mass Media in a Mass Society: Myth and Reality*. London: Continuum.

Leaning, M. (2018, November 1–2). *Different Destinations: The Divergence of Goals in Higher Education Media Education in the UK*. Media Education Summit, Hong Kong Baptist University.

McDougall, J., José Brites, M., Couto, M., & Lucas, C. (Eds.). (2019). Digital Literacy, Fake News and Education. *Cultura y Educación, 31*, 203–212.

McDougall, J., Zezulková, M., van Driel, B., & Sternadel, D. (2018). *Teaching Media Literacy in Europe: Evidence of Effective School Practices in Primary and Secondary Education* (NESET II Report). Luxembourg: Publications Office of the European Union.

Pomerantsev, P. (2019). *This Is Not Propaganda: Adventures in the War Against Reality*. New York: Public Affairs.

Robbgrieco, M. (2016). Micheal RobbGrieco on Michel Foucault. In R. Hobbs (Ed.), *Exploring the Roots of Digital and Media Literacy Through Personal Narrative* (pp. 94–106). Philadelphia: Temple University Press.

Robson, D. (2019, March 30). Would You Believe It? *The Guardian*, pp. 36–37.

Secker, J. (2019). *Media Literacy vs Fake News: A Bournemouth University Workshop*. https://infolit.org.uk/media-literacy-versus-fake-news-a-bournemouth-university-workshop/.

References

Adi, A., Gerodimos, R., & Lilleker, D. G. (2018). "Yes We Vote": Civic Mobilisation and Impulsive Engagement on Instagram. *Javnost, 25*(3), 315–332.

Ahmed, S. (2004). *The Cultural Politics of Emotion.* Edinburgh: Edinburgh University Press.

Alcorn, G. (2019, May 11). Murdoch Press: Even News Corp Staff Are Asking: Is What We Print the Truth? *The Guardian*, p. 31.

Aneez, Z., Neyazi, T., Kalogeropoulos, A., & Nielsen, R. (2019). *India Digital News Report.* Oxford: Reuters Institute for the Study of Journalism.

Arendt, H. (1951). *The Origins of Totalitarianism.* Berlin: Schocken Books.

Audi, R. (2010). *Epistemology: A Contemporary Introduction to the Theory of Knowledge.* London: Routledge.

Bakir, V., & McStay, A. (2017). Fake News and the Economy of Emotions: Problems, Causes, Solutions. *Digital Journalism, 6*(2), 154–175.

Baldwin, J. (2018). *Ctrl, Alt, Delete: How Politics and Media Crashed Our Democracy.* London: Hurst.

Barad, K. (2006). Posthumanist Performativity: Toward an Understanding of How Matter Comes to Matter. In D. Orr (Ed.), *Belief, Bodies, and Being: Feminist Reflections on Embodiment.* Lanham: Rowman & Littlefield.

Barclay, D. (2017, January 5). The Challenge Facing Libraries in an Era of Fake News. *The Conversation.*

© The Editor(s) (if applicable) and The Author(s) 2019
J. McDougall, *Fake News vs Media Studies,*
https://doi.org/10.1007/978-3-030-27220-3

Barlow, D., & Mills, B. (2015). *Reading Media Theory: Thinkers, Approaches and Contexts*. Harlow: Pearson.

Bayley, A. (2018). *Posthuman Pedagogies in Practice: Arts Based Approaches for Developing Participatory Futures*. Basingstoke: Palgrave Macmillan.

Beckett, A. (2018, November 10). Mystic Mogg. *The Guardian*.

Bennett, P., Benyahiya, S., & Slater, J. (2019). *A Level Media Studies: The Essential Introduction*. London: Routledge.

Bennett, P., Kendall, A., & McDougall, J. (2011). *After the Media: Culture and Identity in the 21st Century*. London: Routledge.

Berners-Lee, T. (2019, March 11). The World Wide Web Turns 30: Where Does It Go from Here? *Wired*. https://www.wired.com/story/tim-berners-lee-world-wide-web-anniversary/.

Bernstein, B. (1996). *Pedagogy, Symbolic Control and Identity: Theory, Research, Critique*. London: Taylor & Francis.

Biesta, G. (2017). Touching the Soul? Exploring an Alternative Outlook for Philosophical Work with Children and Young People. *Childhood and Philosophy, 13*(28).

Biesta, G. (2018). *Teaching Uncommon Values: Education, Democracy and the Future of Europe*. Neset II and EENEE Conference, Brussels, 22 November 2018.

Biesta, G. (2019). *Obstinate Education: Reconnecting School and Society*. Leiden: Brill Sense.

Blackburn, S. (2019, February 18). How Can We Teach Objectivity in a Post-Truth Era? *New Statesman*.

Bliss, J., Monk, M., & Ogborn, J. (1983). *Qualitative Data Analysis for Educational Research*. London: Croom Helm.

Bordac, S. (2014). Introduction to Media Literacy History. *Journal of Media Literacy Education, 6*(2), 1–2.

Bourdieu, P. (2013). *Outline of a Theory of Practice*. Cambridge: Cambridge University Press.

boyd, d. (2017). Did Media Literacy Backfire? *Data and Society: Points*. https://points.datasociety.net/did-media-literacy-backfire-7418c084d88d.

Bradshaw, P. (2018). Journalism's 3 Conflicts: And the Promise It Almost Forgot. In S. Hill & P. Bradshaw (Eds.), *Mobile First Journalism*. London: Routledge.

Bragg, B. (2011a). *Scousers Never Buy the Sun*. Self-released CD.

Bragg, B. (2011b, July 13). Liverpool Was Right About News International All Along. *The Guardian*.

Bragg, B. (2019). *The Three Dimensions of Freedom*. London: Faber and Faber.

Briant, E. (2018, April 17). Cambridge Analytica and SCL: How I Peered Inside the Propaganda Machine. *The Conversation*.

Bridle, J. (2018). *New Dark Age: Technology and the End of the Future*. London: Verso.

Brites, M. J. (Ed.). (2017). Digital Literacy and Education, National Reports (Portugal, UK, Ireland, Spain, Serbia and Italy). *ELN: European Literacy Network, Digital Literacy Team*. https://www.is1401eln.eu/en/gca/index.php?id=149.

Buckingham, D. (2017a). *The Strangulation of Media Studies*. https://david-buckingham.net/2017/07/16/the-strangulation-of-media-studies/.

Buckingham, D. (2017b). *Can We Still Teach About Media Bias in the Post-Truth Age?* https://davidbuckingham.net/2017/02/01/can-we-still-teach-about-media-bias-in-the-post-truth-age/. Accessed 29 September 2019.

Buckingham, D. (2019a). Teaching Media in a 'Post-Truth' Age: Fake News, Media Bias and the Challenge for Media/Digital Literacy Education. *Cultura y Educación, 31*(2), 213–231.

Buckingham, D. (2019b). *Beyond Fake News*. https://davidbuckingham.net/2019/02/27/beyond-fake-news-disinformation-and-digital-literacy/.

Buckingham, D. (2019c). *How Much Trust in Media Do We Need?* https://davidbuckingham.net/2019/03/12/how-much-trust-in-media-do-we-need/.

Buckingham, D. (2019d). *The Media Education Manifesto*. London: Polity.

Buckingham, D., & Sefton-Green, J. (1994). *Cultural Studies Goes to School: Reading and Teaching Popular Media*. London: Taylor & Francis.

Bucy, E., & Newhagen, J. (2018). Fake News Finds an Audience. In J. E. Katz (Ed.), *Social Media and Journalism's Search for Truth*. Oxford: Oxford University Press.

Bulger, M., & Davison, P. (2018). *The Promises, Challenges and Futures of Media Literacy*. New York: Data and Society Research Institute.

Butler, J. (2011). *Gender Trouble*. London: Routledge. Buzzfeed: *Fake News Quiz*. https://www.buzzfeed.com/tag/fake-news-quiz.

Cable, J., & Mottershead, G. (2018). Can I Click It? Yes, You Can: Sport Journalism, Twitter, and Clickbait. *Ethical Space: The International Journal of Communication Ethics, 15*(1/2), 69–80.

Cadwalladr, C. (2019, March 17). The Cambridge Analytica Files. *The Observer*.

CEMP. (2019). *Media Literacy Versus Fake News: Critical Thinking, Resilience and Civic Engagement*. http://mlfn.cemp.ac.uk/. Accessed 4 September 2019.

Centre for Excellence in Media Practice. (2011). *Manifesto for Media Education*. Bournemouth: Centre for Excellence in Media Practice. http://www.manifestoformediaeducation.co.uk/.

Chakrabarti, S. (2018, November 12). *Nationalism a Driving Force Behind Fake News in India, Research Shows*. BBC. https://www.bbc.co.uk/news/world-46146877.

CILIP. (2018). *Definition of Information Literacy 2018*. https://cdn.ymaws.com/www.cilip.org.uk/resource/resmgr/cilip/information_professional_and_news/press_releases/2018_03_information_lit_definition/cilip_definition_doc_final_f.pdf.

Commission on Social Mobility and Child Poverty Commission. (2014). *Elitist Britain*. London: Gov.UK.

Connolly, S. (2013). Media Education: A Tool for Social Inclusion. In J. Wardle (Ed.), *Current Perspectives in Media Education: Beyond the Manifesto*. Basingstoke: Palgrave Macmillan.

Cramp, A., & McDougall, J. (2018). *Doing Theory on Education: Using Popular Culture to Explore Key Debates*. London: Routledge.

Crilley, R., & Gillespie, M. (2019). What to Do About Social Media? Politics, Populism and Journalism. *Journalism, 20*(1), 173–176.

Coe, J. (2018). *Middle England*. London: Viking.

Cohen, S. (1972). *Folk Devils and Moral Panics*. Oxford: Martin Robertson.

Council of Europe. (2019). *Democracy at Risk: Threats and Attacks Against Media Freedom in Europe*. Strasbourg: Council of Europe.

Coyle, C. (2019). *Identifying Fake News: Critical Literacy and the School Library*. Swindon: School Library Association.

Crowson, N. (2018, December 9). How Europe Became the Tories Eternal Battleground. *The Observer*.

Curran, J., & Seaton, J. (2018). *Power Without Responsibility: Press, Broadcasting and the Internet in Britain*. London: Routledge.

Curtis, A. (2016). *Hypernormalisation*. London: BBC.

Dix, A. (2018). *Time Travelling to the Civil Rights Era*. https://blog.lboro.ac.uk/news/art/time-travelling-to-the-civil-rights-era/. Accessed 31 August 2019.

Daniels, H. (Ed.). (2005). *An Introduction to Vygotsky* (2nd ed.). London: Routledge.

Davies, N. (2009). *Flat Earth News*. London: Vintage.

De Abreu, B. S., Mihailidis, P., Lee, A. Y. L., Melki, J., & McDougall, J. (Eds.). (2017). *The Routledge International Handbook of Media Literacy Education*. New York: Routledge.

Dent, T. (2017). *Feeling Devalued: The Creative Industries, Motherhood, Gender and Class Inequality*. Ph.D thesis, Bournemouth University, Bournemouth.

Department for Education. (2016). *Subject Criteria for Media Studies*. London: Department for Education (DfE).

Derakhshan, H. (2019, May 9). Disinfo Wars: A Taxonomy of Information Warfare. *Medium.* https://medium.com/@h0d3r/disinfo-wars-7f1cf2685e13. Accessed 9 May 2019.

Dowling, T. (2018, June 24). Reporting Trump's First Year: The Fourth Estate—Heroism in These Dark Days. *The Guardian.*

Eddo-Lodge, R. (2017). *Why I'm No Longer Talking to White People About Race.* London: Bloomsbury.

Eduqas. (2017). *Online Media Revision Activity: DesiMag and Pointless Blog.* https://resource.download.wjec.co.uk.s3.amazonaws.com/vtc/2017-18/17-18_3-22/_eng/unit04/revision-activity-applying-theories-to-desimag-and-pointlessblog.html. Accessed 30 August 2019.

Edwards, D., & Cromwell, D. (2018). *Propaganda Blitz: How the Corporate Media Distort Reality.* London: Pluto Press.

European Commission. (2018). *A Multi-Dimensional Approach to Disinformation: Report of the Independent High Level Group on Fake News and Online Disinformation.* Luxembourg: Publications Office of the European Union.

Feigenbaum, A., & McCurdy, P. (2018). Activist Reflexivity and Mediated Violence: Putting the Policing of Nuit Debout in Context. *International Journal of Communication, 12,* 1887–1907.

Fenton, N. (2016). *Digital, Political, Radical.* London: Polity.

Fenton, N. (2018). *What Should the Cairncross Review Do?* 3D issue 31. http://legacy.meccsa.org.uk/news/three-d-issue-31-what-should-the-cairncross-review-do/. Accessed 2 September 2019.

Field, J. (2018). *Is Capitalism Working?* London: Thames & Hudson.

Firmstone, J. (2018). Saving the Local News Media: What Matt Hancock's Review Needs to Know. *LSE Politics and Policy Blog.* http://eprints.lse.ac.uk/88780/1/politicsandpolicy-saving-the-local-news-media-what-matt-hancocks.pdf. Accessed 31 August 2019.

Foucault, M. (1980). *Power/Knowledge: Selected Interviews and Other Writings 1972–1977* (C. Gordon, Ed.). London: Harvester.

Fowler-Watt, K. (2018). *From Where I Stand.* Interview with Fergal Keane. https://www.youtube.com/watch?time_continue=1562&v=tXh512ZjxOI.

Fowler-Watt, K., & Jukes, S. (2019). *New Journalisms: Rethinking Practice, Theory and Pedagogy.* London: Routledge Research in Media Literacy and Education.

Frau-Meigs, D. (2017). Developing a Critical Mind Against Fake News. *The UNESCO Courier—The Media: Operation Decontamination,* 12–15.

Freedman, D. (2014). *The Contradictions of Media Power.* London: Bloomsbury.

Freedman, D. (2015). Laughey's Canon: Review of Manufacturing Consent, by Edward S. Herman & Noam Chomsky (1988). *Media Education Research Journal, 6*(1), 92–93.

Freedman, D. (2016). Laughey's Canon: Manufacturing Consent. *Media Education Research Journal, 6*(1), 92–93.

Friedman, S., & Laurison, D. (2019). *The Glass Ceiling: Why It Pays to Be Privileged.* Bristol: Bristol University Press.

Fuchs, C. (2016). Henryk Grossmann 2.0: A Critique of Paul Mason's Book "PostCapitalism: A Guide to Our Future". *tripleC, 14*(1), 232–243. http://www.triple-c, at CC-BY-NC-ND: Creative Commons License.

Fukuyama, F. (1992). *The End of History.* London: Penguin.

Gabriel, D. (2017). Pedagogies of Social Justice and Cultural Democracy in Media Higher Education. *Media Education Research Journal* (8.1).

Galtung, J., & Ruge, M. (1965). The Structure of Foreign News: The Presentation of the Congo, Cuba and Cyprus Crises in Four Norwegian Newspapers. *Journal of International Peace Research, 2*, 64–90.

Gardiner, S. (2018). Media Studies: Why the Bad Press? *Media Magazine, 65*, 6–7.

Gauntlett, D. (2015). *Making Media Studies.* London: Polity.

Geertz, C. (1973). Thick Description: Toward an Interpretive Theory of Culture. In C. Geertz (Ed.), *The Interpretation of Cultures: Selected Essays.* New York: Basic Books.

Gerodimos, R. (2017, February 16). Russia Is Attacking Western Liberal Democracies. *Medium.* https://medium.com/@romangerodimos/russia-is-attacking-western-liberal-democracies-4371ff38b407.

Gessen, K. (2017, February 22). Killer, Kleptocrat, Genius, Spy: The Many Myths of Vladimir Putin. *The Guardian.*

Gottfried, J., & Grieco, E. (2018). *Younger Americans Are Better Than Older Americans at Telling Factual News Statements from Opinions.* Washington, DC: Pew Research Center. https://www.pewresearch.org/fact-tank/2018/10/23/younger-americans-are-better-than-older-americans-at-telling-factual-news-statements-from-opinions/.

Habermas, J. (1992). Further Reflections on the Public Sphere. In C. Calhoun (Ed.) & T. Burger (Trans.), *Habermas and the Public Sphere.* Cambridge, MA: MIT Press.

Hall, S. (2014). Foreword. In K. Connell & M. Hilton (Eds.), *50 Years On: The Centre for Contemporary Cultural Studies.* Birmingham: University of Birmingham.

Hall, S., Hobson, D., Lowe, A., & Willis, P. (Eds.). (1980). *Culture, Media, Language: Working Papers in Cultural Studies.* London: Routledge.

Hanley, L. (2016). *Respectable: The Experience of Class.* London: Penguin.

Hart, C. (2017). Metaphor and Intertextuality in Media Framings of the (1984–1985) British Miner's Strike: A Multimodal Analysis. *Discourse and Communication, 11*(1), 3–30.

Harte, D. (2018). 'Imagine Doing a Journalism Degree and Then Being Asked to Write Trash Like This'—Considerations in Meeting the Challenges of Banal Journalism. http://ajeuk.org/wp-content/uploads/2018/10/HARTE-AJE-banal-journalism-2018.pdf.

Herman, E., & Chomsky, N. (1988). *Manufacturing Consent: The Political Economy of the Mass Media.* New York: Pantheon.

Hesmondhalgh, D. (2019). *The Cultural Industries* (4th ed.). London: Sage.

Hewitt, B. (2017, December 8). How to Spot Fake News—An Expert's Guide for Young People. *The Conversation.* https://theconversation.com/how-to-spot-fake-news-an-experts-guide-for-young-people-88887.

Hobbs, R. (Ed.). (2016). *Exploring the Roots of Digital and Media Literacy Through Personal Narrative.* Philadelphia: Temple University Press.

Hodgkin, E., & Khane, J. (2018). Misinformation in the Information Age: What Teachers Can Do to Support Students. *Social Education, 82*(4), 208–211, 214.

Hoggart, R. (1957). *The Uses of Literacy.* London: Pelican.

Hoggart, R. (2004). *Mass Media in a Mass Society: Myth and Reality.* London: Continuum.

Horeck, T., Jenner, M., & Kendall, T. (2018). On Binge-Watching: Nine Critical Propositions. *Critical Studies in Television, 13*(4), 499–504.

Ingber, H. (2019, March 19). The New Zealand Attack Posed New Challenges for Journalists. Here Are the Decisions The Times Made. *The New York Times.*

Ireton, C., & Posetti, J. (Eds.). (2018). *Journalism, Fake News and Disinformation: Handbook for Journalism Education and Training.* Paris: UNESCO.

Jenkins, S. (2019, April 11). Julian Assange's Cyber-Sins Seem Quaint in Comparison to Those of Big Tech. *The Guardian.*

Jenkins, H., Ford, S., & Green, J. (2013). *Spreadable Media: Creating Value and Meaning in a Networked Culture.* New York: New York University Press.

Jenkins, H., Shreshova, S., Gamber-Thompson, L., & Zimmerman, A. (2016). *By Any Media Necessary: The New Youth Activism.* New York: New York University Press.

Jones, O. (2014). *The Establishment: And How They Get Away with It.* London: Allen Lane.

Jones, O. (2018, April 22). The British Media Is a Closed Shop. These Are the Facts. *Medium*.

Jukes, P. (2014). *Beyond Contempt: The Inside Story of the Phone Hacking Trial*. London: Canbury Press.

Kachkayeva, A., Shomova, S., & Kolchina, A. (2017). Education and Media Literacy in Russia: Genesis and Current Trends. In *Multidisciplinary Approaches to Media Literacy: Research and Practices* 媒介素养的跨学科研究与实践 (Ch. 31, pp. 401–408). Hong Kong: Communication University of China (CUC) Press.

Kafka, F. (1922). *Investigations of a Dog*. London: Penguin.

Kakutani, M. (2018, July 14). Truth Decay. *The Guardian*.

Karlsson, K., & Clerwall, C. (2018). Cornerstones in Journalism. *Journalism Studies*. https://doi.org/10.1080/1461670x.2018.1499436.

Keen, A. (2007). *The Cult of the Amateur*. London: Hodder.

Kirkby, P. (2016). *Leading People 2016: The Educational Backgrounds of the UK Professional Elite*. Sutton Trust. https://www.suttontrust.com/wp-content/uploads/2016/02/Leading-People_Feb16-1.pdf.

Klucharev, V., Neznanov, A., & Osin, E. (2019). *Media Education, Media Ecology, Media Literacy: Digital Media for the Future*. Moscow: National Research University Higher School of Economics.

Lanchester, J. (2018). *The Wall*. New York: W. W. Norton.

Laughey, D. (2007). *Key Themes in Media Theory*. Maidenhead: Open University Press.

Leaning, M. (2018, November 1–2). *Different Destinations: The Divergence of Goals in Higher Education Media Education in the UK*. Media Education Summit, Hong Kong Baptist University.

Leetaru, K. (2019). *Combatting Fake News Requires Provenance and Information Literacy*. Forbes. https://www.forbes.com/sites/kalevleetaru/2019/03/16/combatting-fake-news-requires-provenance-and-information-literacy/#52ce8101debb. Accessed 10 April 2019.

Lewis, H. (2019, March 1–7). Enemies of the People. *New Statesman*.

Lilleker, D., Alexander, J., ElSheikh, D., McQueen, D., Richards, B., & Thorsen, E. (2018). Evidence to the Culture, Media and Sport Committee 'Fake News' Inquiry Presented by Members of the Centre for Politics & Media Research. Bournemouth University, UK.

Lindgren, S. (2017). *Digital Media and Society*. London: Sage.

Livingstone, S., & Sefton-Green, J. (2016). *The Class: Living and Learning in a Digital Age*. New York: New York University Press.

London School of Economics. (2019). *Trust, Truth and Technology*. London: LSE Publications.

Lopez, A. (2016). Review of Exploring the Roots of Digital and Media Literacy Through Personal Narrative. In R. Hobbs (Ed.), *Media Education Research Journal*, *7*(2), 142–144.

Lopez, A. (forthcoming, 2020). *Teaching Ecomedia: Educating for Sustainable Media Ecosystems*. London: Routledge.

Lupton, D. (2019). *Data Selves: More-than-Human Perspectives*. London: Polity.

MacPherson, C. (1966). *The Real World of Democracy*. Oxford: Oxford University Press.

Madrigal, A. (2014). How Netflix Reverse Engineered Hollywood. *The Atlantic*. https://www.theatlantic.com/technology/archive/2014/01/how-netflix-reverse-engineered-hollywood/282679/.

Mantzarlis, A. (2018). Fact-Checking 101. In C. Ireton & J. Posetti (Eds.), *Journalism, 'Fake News' and Disinformation*. Paris: UNESCO.

Martin, G., & Yurukoglu, A. (2017). Bias in Cable News: Persuasion and Polarization. *American Economic Review*, *107*(9), 2565–2599.

Mason, P. (2015). *Post-capitalism: A Guide to Our Future*. London: Allen-Lane.

Mason, P. (2019). *Clear, Bright Future*. London: Penguin.

Mason, L., Krutka, D., & Stoddard, J. (2018). Media Literacy, Democracy, and the Challenge of Fake News. *Journal of Media Literacy Education*, *10*(2), 1–10.

McDougall, J., José Brites, M., Couto, M., & Lucas, C. (Eds.). (2019). Digital Literacy, Fake News and Education. *Cultura y Educación*, *31*, 203–212.

McDougall, J., Zezulková, M., van Driel, B., & Sternadel, D. (2018). *Teaching Media Literacy in Europe: Evidence of Effective School Practices in Primary and Secondary Education* (NESET II Report). Luxembourg: Publications Office of the European Union.

McGarvey, D. (2017). *Poverty Safari: Understanding the Anger of Britain's Underclass*. London: Picador.

McIntyre, L. (2018). *Post-truth*. Cambridge, MA: MIT Press.

McLuhan, M. (1964). *Understanding Media: The Extensions of Man*. Cambridge, MA: MIT.

Media Reform Coalition. (2019). *Who Owns the UK Media?* London: Goldsmiths Leverhulme Media Research Centre/Media Reform Coalition. https://www.mediareform.org.uk/wp-content/uploads/2019/03/Who_Owns_the_UK_Media_2019.pdf.

Melki, J. (2018). Towards a Media Literacy of the Oppressed. *Media Education Research Journal, 8*(1), 5–14.

Melki, J., & Maalaki, L. (2017). Manouvering Entrenched Structures of Arab Education Systems: The Agency of Arab Media Literacy Educators and Activists. *Journal of Media Literacy, 64*(1–2), 56–60.

Merrin, W. (2014). *Media Studies 2.0*. London: Routledge.

Mihailidis, P. (2018). *Civic Media Literacies: Re-imagining Human Connection in an Age of Digital Abundance*. New York: Routledge.

Mihailidis, P., & Viotty, S. (2019). Spreadable Spectacle in Digital Culture: Civic Expression, Fake News, and the Role of Media Literacies in "Post-Fact" Society. *American Behavioural Scientist, 61*(4), 441–454.

Miller, D., & Philo, G. (2001a). *Market Killing. What the Free Market Does and What Social Scientists Can Do About It*. London: Longman.

Miller, D., & Philo, G. (2001b). The Active Audience and Wrong Turns in Media Studies: Rescuing Media Power. *Soundscapes, 4* (2011).

Milne, S. 2014. *The Enemy Within*. London: Verso.

Moore, R. (2013, September 1). Library of Birmingham Review. *The Guardian*.

Moore, M. (2018). *Democracy Hacked: Political Turmoil and Information Warfare in the Digital Age*. London: Bloomsbury.

Moores, S. (2017). *Digital Orientations: Non-media-centric Media Studies and Non-representational Theories of Practice*. New York: Peter Lang.

Morozov, E. (2017, January 8). Blaming Fake News Is Not the Answer. *The Guardian*.

Myers, F. (2019, April 9). The Era of Internet Freedom Is Over. *Wired*.

Neveu, E. (2016). On Not Going Too Fast with Slow Journalism. *Journalism Practice, 10*(4), 448–460.

Nichols, T. (2016). *The Death of Expertise: The Campaign Against Established Knowledge and Why It Matters*. Oxford: Oxford University Press.

Nielsen, R., & Graves, L. (2017). *"News You Don't Believe": Audience Perspectives on Fake News*. Oxford: Reuters Institute for the Study of Journalism.

Oates, S. (2008). *An Introduction to Media and Politics*. London: Sage.

O'Hara, K., & Hall, W. (2018). *4 Internets: The Geopolitics of Digital Governance*. Ontario: Centre for International Governance Innovation.

Oprea, M. (2019, February 25). The Spread of Fake News Has Had Deadly Consequences in Mexico. *Pacific Standard*.

Peace, D. (2004). *GB84*. London: Faber and Faber.

Peim, N. (2018). *Thinking in Education Research: Applying Philosophy and Theory*. London: Bloomsbury.

Philo, G., Hewitt, J., Beharrell, P., & Davis, H. (1992). *Really Bad News.* London: Writers and Readers Cooperative Society.

Picketty, T. (2013). *Capitalism in the Twenty-First Century.* Harvard: Harvard University Press.

Pilkington, E. (2019, April 12). Julian Assange's Charges Are a Direct Assault on Press Freedom, Experts Warn. *The Guardian.*

Poitras, L. (2014). *Citizen 4.* USA: Praxis Films.

Pomerantsev, P. (2019). *This Is Not Propaganda: Adventures in the War Against Reality.* New York: Public Affairs.

Posetti, J., & Matthews, A. (2018). *A Short Guide to the History of Fake News and Disinformation.* Washington, DC: International Center for Journalists.

Potter, J., & McDougall, J. (2017). *Digital Media, Education and Culture: Theorising Third Space Literacy.* London: Palgrave Macmillan.

Press, A., & Williams, B. (2010). *The New Media Environment: An Introduction.* Oxford: Wiley-Blackwell.

Prutsch, M. (2015). *European Historical Memory: Policies, Challenges and Perspectives.* Strasbourg: European Parliament. http://www.europarl.europa.eu/thinktank/en/document.html?reference=IPOL_STU(2015)540364.

Read, M. (2018). *How Much of the Internet Is Fake?* New York: Intelligencer. http://nymag.com/intelligencer/2018/12/how-much-of-the-internet-is-fake.html.

Resser, M. (2017). Fake News: Sound Bites on a Burning Topic. *The UNESCO Courier—The Media: Operation Decontamination*, 11.

RiResta, R., et al. (2018). *The Tactics & Tropes of the Internet Research Agency.* New Knowledge.

Robbgrieco, M. (2016). Micheal RobbGrieco on Michel Foucault. In R. Hobbs (Ed.), *Exploring the Roots of Digital and Media Literacy Through Personal Narrative* (pp. 94–106). Philadelphia: Temple University Press.

Robson, D. (2019, March 30). Would You Believe It? *The Guardian*, pp. 36–37.

Rosenberg, H., & Feldman, C. (2009). *No Time to Think: The Menace of Media Speed and the 24 Hour News Cycle.* London: Continuum.

Rosling, H., Rosling, A., & Rosling, O. (2018). *Factfulness: Ten Reasons We're Wrong About the World: And Why Things Are Better Than You Think.* London: Sceptre.

Rusbridger, A. (2018). *Breaking News: The Remaking of Journalism and Why It Matters Now.* London: Canongate.

Rushkoff, D. (2019). *Team Human.* New York: W.W. Norton.

Secker, J. (2019). *Media Literacy vs Fake News: A Bournemouth University Workshop.* https://infolit.org.uk/media-literacy-versus-fake-news-a-bournemouth-university-workshop/.

Shaker, J. (2016). The Cure for Fake News Is Worse Than the Disease. *Politico.* https://www.politico.com/magazine/story/2016/11/the-cure-for-fake-news-is-worse-than-the-disease-214477.

Shirky, C. (2011, February 5). The Whistleblowing Site Has Created a New Media Landscape. *The Guardian: After Wikilieaks*, p. 2.

Smith, M., & Bloom. D. (2016, November 1). Damian Green Has Never Seen I, Daniel Blake—But Branded It 'Monstrously Unfair' Anyway. *The Mirror.* https://www.mirror.co.uk/news/uk-news/damian-green-never-seen-i-9166462.

Snow, J. (2019). Connected or Disconnected. In K. Fowler-Watt & S. Jukes (Eds.). (2019). *New Journalisms: Rethinking Practice, Theory and Pedagogy.* London: Routledge.

Snyder, T. (2018). *The Road to Unfreedom: Russia, Europe, America.* London: Random House.

Sonwalkar, P. (2005). Banal Journalism. In S. Allan (Ed.), *Journalism: Critical Issues* (pp. 262–273). New York: Peter Lang.

Starbird, K. (2018, October 20). The Surprising Nuance Behind the Russian Toll Strategy. *Medium.* https://medium.com/s/story/the-trolls-within-how-russian-information-operations-infiltrated-online-communities-691fb969b9e4.

Stewart, H., & Hern, A. (2019, April 4). Social Media Bosses Could Be Liable for Harmful Content, Leaked UK Plan Reveals. *The Guardian.*

Subedar, A. (2018, November 27). The Godfather of Fake News. *BBC News.* https://www.bbc.co.uk/news/resources/idt-sh/the_godfather_of_fake_news.

Susskind, J. (2018). *Future Politics: Living Together in a World Transformed by Tech.* Oxford: Oxford University Press.

Tanz, J. (2017). Journalism Fights for Survival in the Post-truth Era. *Wired.* https://www.wired.com/2017/02/journalism-fights-survival-post-truth-era/.

Taplin, J. (2017). *Move Fast and Break Things: How Facebook, Google and Amazon Cornered Culture.* London: Macmillan.

Tapscott, D. (2009). *Grown Up Digital: How the Net Generation Is Changing Your World.* New York: McGraw-Hill.

Thorsen, E. (2018). *3D 31: Quality Journalism, Internet and Politics.* http://www.meccsa.org.uk/nl/three-d-issue-31-quality-journalism-internet-and-politics/.

Thurman, N. (2016). *Journalists in the UK*. Oxford: Reuters Institute for the Study of Journalism.

Tooze, A. (2018). *Crashed: How a Decade of Financial Crises Changed the World*. London: Random House.

UNESCO. (2016). *Riga Recommendations on Media and Information Literacy*. http://www.unesco.org/new/fileadmin/MULTIMEDIA/HQ/CI/CI/pdf/Events/riga_recommendations_on_media_and_information_literacy.pdf.

Varoufakis, Y. (2017). *Talking to My Daughter: A Brief History of Capitalism*. London: Vintage.

Viner, K. (2017, November 16). A Mission for Journalism in a Time of Crisis. *The Guardian*.

Wardle, C., & Derakhshan, H. (2017). *Information Disorder Toward an Interdisciplinary Framework for Research and Policymaking*. Strasbourg: Council of Europe.

Waterson, J. (2019, March 19). BBC Plans Charity to Fund Local News Reporting in Britain. *The Guardian*.

Watson, J., & Hill, A. (2003). *A Dictionary of Communication and Media Studies*. London: Edward Arnold.

Williamson, B. (2017). *Big Data in Education: The Digital Future of Learning, Policy and Practice*. London: Sage.

Williamson, J. (1981). How Does Girl No. 20 Understand Ideology? *Screen Education, 40*, 80–87.

Wren-Lewis, S. (2019, April 9). A Partisan Media Is Fuelling Far-Right Extremism: The UK Needs to Wake Up. *New Statesman*.

Yablokov, I. (2018). *Fortress Russia: Conspiracy Theories in Post-Soviet Russia*. London: Polity.

Yaloyan. M. (2017). Aftenposten Versus Facebook: Triggering a Crucial Debate. *The UNESCO Courier—The Media: Operation Decontamination*, 16–19.

Yurchak, A. (2006). *Everything Was Forever, Until It Was no More: The Last Soviet Generation*. Princeton, NJ: Princeton University Press.

Zuboff, S. (2019). *The Age of Surveillance Capitalism: The Fight for a Human Future at the New Frontier of Power*. New York: Public Affairs.

Zuckerberg, M. (2019, March 30). The Internet Needs New Rules: Let's Start in These Four Areas. *The Washington Post*.

Index

Druck:
Customized Business Services GmbH
im Auftrag der KNV-Gruppe
Ferdinand-Jühlke-Str. 7
99095 Erfurt